Learning Teaching,
Teaching Teaching . . .

Learning Teaching, Teaching Teaching...

A Study of Partnership In Teacher Education

Les Tickle

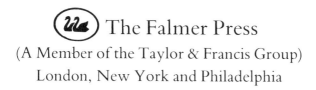 The Falmer Press

(A Member of the Taylor & Francis Group)
London, New York and Philadelphia

UK	The Falmer Press, Falmer House, Barcombe, Lewes, East Sussex, BN8 5DL
USA	The Falmer Press, Taylor & Francis Inc., 242 Cherry Street, Philadelphia, PA 19106–1906

First published 1987

Library of Congress Cataloging-in-Publication Data

Tickle, Les.
  Learning teaching, teaching teaching.

  I. Teachers—Training of—Great Britain.
2. Teaching. I. Title.
LB1725.G6T58 1987   370'.7'1   86–29301
ISBN 0–85000–157–X
ISBN 0–85000–158–8 (pbk.)

Jacket design by Caroline Archer

Typeset in 10/12 Bembo by
Imago Publishing Ltd, Thame, Oxon.

*Printed in Great Britain by
Redwood Burn Limited, Trowbridge, Wiltshire*

Contents

Acknowledgements

In 1982, when the concept of *Student Attachment to Schools* was first developed in the School of Education at the University of East Anglia, the idea was negotiated with headteachers and teachers in eight schools before it was put to sixteen second year BEd students, who were invited to participate in testing its initial practical implementation. The professionalism which the headteachers, teachers and students brought to the pilot project is sincerely acknowledged. It was characteristic of that which has since been the hallmark of many other students and teachers who have participated in the subsequent dissemination, development, evaluation and reform of *Student Attachment*. My deepest gratitude is due to Ruth Goodall who, as Schools Officer in the School of Education, was instrumental in devising and implementing those early developments with an investment of faith in the notion of professional partnership. A sense of authentic partnership in the venture has resulted from the involvement of many colleagues from the School of Education. Their commitment to the improvement of teacher education, especially through the development of ideas and practices associated with the conception of research-based initial teacher education, has been a source of intellectual inspiration and practical challenge. The *Student Attachment* venture has had special support from Professor Hugh Sockett, to whom I am grateful for his encouragement. The task of translating ideas into practical activity has also been greatly helped by John Jennings at Norwich Teachers' Centre.

When *Student Attachment* was about to be launched I was asked by a colleague 'What would constitute failure?'. I replied that it would have failed if none of the sixteen students thought the idea worth taking up. Every one of them participated — not only in the initial implementation, but also in dissemination activities and research which followed. Recognition of the success of the project is due in very large measure to the work of: Ann Alexander, Guy Beard, Kaushika Buddhdev, Deborah Cleave, Jo Frankham-Smith, Fay Gregory, Anne Haydock, Tania Marcanik, Melanie Macro, Susan Merriman, Elizabeth Miller, Jill Parr, Amanda Peirce, Toby Salt, Kathleen Staszewska and Karen Taylor.

Introduction

The major concern of this book is the search for improvements in the process of professional development for student teachers. It focusses on professional preparation during *initial* teacher education. The ideas on which it draws and the research it reports, however, are also concerned with the professional development of practising teachers and teacher educators, working in partnership with student teachers. Finding the means of achieving long-term professional self-development for all three, as a means of meeting the challenges of reform in schooling, is the main aspiration of the work it reports. A central conceptual theme is research-based teacher education; its practical implementation is examined through *Student Attachment to Schools*, an innovative element of curriculum development within teacher education programmes at the University of East Anglia.

The idea that teachers should do research and enquire into their own classrooms now has substantial foundation within the profession. As a mode of professional development among serving teachers 'applied research' is practiced in various forms throughout Britain and internationally, as some teachers seek to extend their professionalism through critical scrutiny of their practice and their pupils' curriculum experiences. Teaching which is based on an intention by teachers themselves to improve its quality is the essence of that professionalism. Where the intention to improve practice exists, it is necessary also to develop the tools of enquiry and the skills to use them for renewed practice to be firmly based upon systematic learning which relates to practical teaching situations. Yet the disposition to investigate teaching, to understand its processes, and to improve its quality is not a universal characteristic of teachers. Certainly many teachers have not had the opportunity to master research techniques and to base the quality of their learning and their teaching on classroom enquiry.

The pursuit of research-based teacher education has mostly occurred at the in-service stage. The development of professional dispositions towards research-based teaching, the learning of skills which enable systematic investigation of teaching, and the development of practical capabilities which can enhance teaching quality, ought properly to begin at the stage of initial teacher education. Pre-service classroom experience has, however, largely remained at the conceptual and practical level of *training* in general technical competences — efficient use of resources; questioning techniques; classroom control; the presentation of information; organization and balance of learning activities; and so on. The pressing necessity of the mastery of such competences at the initial teacher education stage is understandably the major concern during very short exposure to learning classroom practice. (Current requirements for practical teaching are fifteen weeks in a postgraduate certificate of education or three-year BEd course; twenty weeks in a four-year BEd course.) Classroom practice is often divorced from the study of educational research and issues of theory which have the potential to inform practice. Research studies, including those concerned directly with classroom strategies, are often confronted by professional prejudice against theory and face major problems in becoming accessible to teachers and student teachers in the bid to acquire practical competence or to change established practice. The practice-theory gap is both wide and deep.

Learning of classroom competence at the stage of initial teacher education and improving it later in a continuous process of review, research, and renewal through critical self-reflection (that is, within a conception of research-based teacher education), with the concurrent mastery of tools of enquiry and analysis, offers a professional key to the improvement of teaching quality. I will argue that it is possible to encourage the development of professional dispositions, research procedures, and improved practice which will facilitate educated participation in a flexible, innovative profession capable of im-plementing and sustaining curricular change for the benefit of pupils in schools now and in the future. That development, though, depends on effective activities being conducted through the partnership of student-teachers, teachers, and teacher-educators. Such activities, which will be discussed in detail in the report of *Student Attachment to Schools*, can incorporate enhanced mastery of classroom skills, with competent teaching developed to profession-al practice which stretches well beyond competence. That can be achieved through the promotion of commitments to continually improve the practice of teaching in all its aspects.

There is wide recognition of the problematic nature of the education of teachers. Responses to that recognition have in the past included a series of major changes in course length and structure; the move to an all-graduate intake; and the recognition that certification for teaching must accompany graduate status. Despite such changes concerns about the quality of teacher education expressed in recent policy statements from the Department of Education and Science (DES) have included:

    (i)   low entry standards in academic subject qualification, personal qualities, and professional commitments;

    (ii) too many irrelevant, over-theoretical courses;

(iii) too little recent, relevant school teaching experience among teacher-educators;

(iv) fragmentation of teacher education programmes into subject, professional and practical elements;

(v) poor induction into teaching;

(vi) inadequate provision for in-service education of teachers.

In initial teacher education fluctuations in numbers and the scale of changes in course structures have created their own pressures, leaving a need for better understanding of teacher education processes. That gap needs to be filled, in my view, by imaginative conceptions and innovative practices, recasting and redefining educative experiences for student-teachers, teachers, and teacher educators. Conventional training for routinely performed, competency-tested 'teaching skills' which are used to convey narrowly-defined curriculum content have not proved to be sufficient to meet the demands made of teachers. Asserting alternative curricular and professional processes based on innovative practice offers the opportunity to understand the best means of achieving long-term professional self-development, as well as achieving school reform for the education of coming generations of children. I will show that such alternatives would incorporate the best aspects of competent, skilled teaching but would also go well beyond essential competence to develop what I will call professional excellence.

In the expressions of concern about the quality of teacher education, which have also been reflected in the publications of professional associations and committees, the theme of disjunction recurs. Disjointed practice and theory; fragmented courses; and disparate pre-service, induction and in-service provision are common issues. The purported disjunction between ivory-towered academics, classroom teachers and students is another issue for which 'solutions' are demanded in the catchword of partnership. Like some kind of panacea, close working partnership between the various parties involved, and particularly between schools and initial teacher education institutions, has become a major part of DES strategy for improving the quality of schools through the improvement of teacher education. Partnership, as I will show in detail later, can take different forms with quite different potential consequences for those involved. The form which it takes is determined by the conceptualization of partnership and the attitudes and dispositions of the partners, upon whom its effective practice depends. Conceptualization, disposition and practice stem from the way in which the purpose of partnership is perceived. Perception of purpose affects the investment (i.e. professional commitment) by students, teachers and tutors, and also the results. In the case of teacher education results must be judged by the quality of learning and teaching, for all concerned, and professional development through improved knowledge of teaching and learning. So far little consideration has been given to the purpose, conception and realization of partnership, leaving the catchword well used but relatively unexamined.

The shift in concern from student numbers and teacher-supply planning, and course length and structures, to the content and quality of programmes is a recent feature of DES policy-making which shows 'improvement' in teacher education to be an overtly political intent as well as a professional one. There are clearly expressed views that the ways of the past have been inadequate in preparing teachers in such a way as to ensure the maintenance of standards in education (linked to economic prosperity and value-for-money schooling) (DES, 1985a). Yet the proposals emerging seem in some respects to reinforce the inadequacies of teacher education by attempting to reimpose practices which have been found wanting. At least, there are contradictions and inconsistencies which need sorting out. For example, requirements for more substantial elements of school experience and teaching practice for student teachers are matched by bare minima of time allocated for school-based teaching. Demands for substantially more subject study in many BEd/BA courses, and the establishment of thirty-six weeks as the length of PGCE courses (almost universally acknowledged to be too short for adequate preparation for teaching) reinforce the difficulties of disentangling policy. Requirements for substantial elements of school practice by teacher educators, and greater involvement of practising teachers in teacher education courses are set alongside persistent criticisms of schooling provision and teachers' per-formances. Yet in the bureaucratic mechanisms which are being strengthened in relation to teacher education, through the work of the DES and the Council for the Accreditation of Teacher Education (CATE), there is no sense of new or alternative ways of achieving improved professional development from the early stages of teacher education. Alternative approaches which might make long-term teacher *education* a reality incorporating improved classroom prac-tice which is based on understanding need to be considered. As a long term mode of professional development, within a conception of partnership based on educative criteria, such an education would be likely to have respect and commitment from students, teachers, and teacher-educators as well as from policy makers. The criteria would need to be ones which, when fulfilled, would make teacher education educative for all involved. I will argue that the principles of research-based teacher education, and its practice in partnership for initial teacher education, provide for that fulfilment.

In Part One I will outline the major themes of teacher education policy from the decade 1975–1985, providing some links with changes in the context and policy for the schools in which student teachers will work. The potential consequences of recent policy in terms of the kinds of teachers who might enter those schools to serve well into the next century will also be considered. One might expect that policy and practice of such importance to future generations of citizens would be based on extensive and thorough understand-ing of the processes of learning teaching. I have included in Part One therefore a brief account of teacher education research and some discussion of what I have called the search for educational excellence in professional preparation and practice. That account shows the inadequacies of our understanding of how to achieve excellence in learning teaching. It will also show that the professional practice of teaching incorporates many activities, and demands the requisite capabilities to perform them, which have not featured in research on learning teaching. Research has mostly been restricted to teacher-pupil instruction. Preparation for professionalism beyond the classroom, in community relationships, teacher self-appraisal, curriculum review and development, and so on, is increasingly a self-conscious part of teaching which needs to be included in learning teaching.

In Part Two I will discuss ways in which orientations to educational research in general (including research on teacher education) have changed in response to the perceived failure of research to affect practice. The development of action research, the principles on which it is based for enabling teachers to research their own practice, and its potential for improving teacher education and curriculum in schools, will be outlined. This section is based on the work of Lawrence Stenhouse in recognition of the considerable influence he had upon those currently engaged in furthering the potential of teacher research as an empowering mode of professional development. The conception of research-based teacher education, which derives from the principles of teacher research, will be elaborated and extended to consider its potential for *initial* teacher education and the issue of partnership.

Practical knowledge in teaching, I will argue in Part Three, is the heart of the professional enterprise and the key to professional credibility. Yet it is not always treated sufficiently seriously in trying to understand and improve teaching. Part Three will explore the relationship between practical knowledge and reflective understanding which is seen as the key to its improvement. The importance of that relationship is based on an appreciation of the student-teacher as autonomous, self-motivated learner who, together with teachers and teacher-educators can develop the dispositions and capabilities to research their own practices. By such means, it will be argued, practical competence can be enhanced to become professional excellence. The cultivation of excellence as the major objective of education is defined, in Bruner's terms, as facilitating the achievement of optimum development for each student. In that sense Part Three interprets 'student' in the context of long-term professional self-development by teachers and tutors as well as student-teachers.

The principles and potential of research-based teacher education, within a notion of partnership for professional excellence, are aspirations based on ideals. They offer a proactive conception of teacher education which needs to be translated into practice. Its consequences in terms of the kinds of professionals which result need to be judged. Part Four will show what the practice begins to look like, focussing on student teachers' experiences and the need to recast partnership for learning teaching. The need, too, for recasting the formal structures of teacher-education programmes, and reformulating the treatment of practical experience will be explored. The development of *Student Attachment* at the University of East Anglia and its place in the nature of practical experience in initial teacher education is outlined. The work of students and data from the evaluation of *Student Attachment* illustrate the practice of research based initial teacher education and of partnership. An optimistic view of partnership's potential of achieving professional excellence is balanced by consideration of the constraints on authentic partnership.

The research and analysis of experiences in *Student Attachment to Schools* illustrate the complexity of the issues of partnership arising from attempts to improve the practical experiences of student teachers and the quality of their practical teaching. The programme of attachments was developed within a framework of 'institutional freedom in professional matters and the value of variety and experiment in the curriculum of teacher education' (DES, 1983c, p. 3) well before the advent of Circular 3/84 (DES, 1984a) and the Council for the Accreditation of Teacher Education (CATE), which require close partnership between schools and teacher education institutions. The premise of partnership in *Student Attachment* maintains an optimistic view of particular kinds of professional development and professionalism, with implicit values of pluralism, autonomy, responsibility and participation in teacher education. This optimism seems to differ from some of the notions of teacher training and assessment of teacher performance invoked in recent interventions into teacher education by central government in Britain. As I shall show, institutional freedom has already fallen prey to coercion and standardization amid concerns for the control of minimum standards of competence in teaching and teacher education, as the arms of accountability reach in the directions of all quarters of the education service.

Challenging my optimism therefore is a different set of assumptions about the means of achieving professionalism which recent economic and political attacks upon schools and teachers have manifested. Changes in schooling policy since 1975 have shown increasing attempts to reassert conformity in content and pedagogy of the curriculum towards a more basic industrially relevant training for the majority of pupils with increasing control over the work of teachers to ensure efficiency in manpower production. Teacher education has more recently been subject to those reassertions of control in a process which, it has been argued, is part of the mechanism of legitimating more basic education and reduced expectations in the population to accompany a reduction in state educational provision. It is in full awareness of the complexity of tensions between economic and political influences for change and professional aspirations for improvements in schooling that this book is written.

Part One

Teacher Education Policy and Processes 1975–1985

Reasserting Central Control of the Education of Teachers

The recent context and the nature of state intervention in education in Britain have been the focus of a number of analyses (for example, Ahier and Flude, 1983; Lawton, 1984; Salter and Tapper, 1981; Taylor, 1984). In itself, tightening central government control of the agencies and institutions responsible for curriculum planning, provision and evaluation amounts to a reassertion of state powers which were devolved particularly in the period spanning the middle part of this century. In that sense, increased use of centralized power is a return to the past. That has also been the case in teacher education, which has formerly been subject to fluctuating central control. (Alexander, Craft and Lynch, 1984). A recent, sudden and rapid surge of intervention in the developments of policy for the curriculum of teacher education is, however, exceptional and is reflected in a proliferation of government documents issued since 1980, and in the advent of the Council for the Accreditation of Teacher Education (CATE) invoked in 1984 as a monitoring body for the approval of all teacher education courses. The links between government action in direct relation to local education authorities (LEAs) and schools, and its action in relation to teacher education, are explicitly intended to achieve a raising of educational standards whilst ensuring value for money from the school system, purportedly to enhance the economic prosperity of Britain (DES, 1985a, paragraphs 1–12). Perceived weaknesses in economic prosperity, it is asserted, would be overcome by tackling weaknesses in schooling, which themselves would be solved in part by the action and 'duty' of the government to secure improvements in 'the professional effectiveness of teachers and the management of the teaching force'. Such action would be in concert with the lead taken in relation to the clarification of objectives and content of the school curriculum; reform of the examination system; and reform of school government (DES, 1985a, paragraph 29).

In the application of central control and the curriculum proposals associated with it (both for schools and teacher education) it is possible to identify contradictions and inconsistencies which illustrate the difficulty of defining 'appropriate' teacher education. Indeed *Better Schools* (DES, 1985a) recognizes divergent and conflicting views about the nature of education and provision of 'appropriate' experiences in schools, and makes some attempt to reconcile them. The extent of the details of policy discussions and prescriptions is somewhat overwhelming. The list below represents the major official documents published since 1977 relating to the school curriculum, and since 1980 relating to teacher education and teaching.

DES/HMI Documents Related to Curriculum of Schools, Teacher Education, and Teaching

	1977a	*Education in Schools: A Consultative Document*
March	1977b	*Curriculum 11–16*
September	1978	*Primary Education in England — A Survey by HMI*
November	1979a	*Local Authority Arrangements for the School Curriculum* (Report on Circular 14/77 review of LEA arrangements)
December	1979b	*Aspects of Secondary Education in England — A Survey by HMI*
January	1980a	*A Framework for the School Curriculum*
January	1980b	*A View of the Curriculum* (HMI Matters for Discussion)
	1980c	*PGCE in the Public Sector*
	1981a	*Teacher Training in the Secondary School*
March	1981b	*The School Curriculum*
March	1981c	*Curriculum 11–16: A Review of Progress*
May	1982a	*Teaching in Schools: The Content of Initial Training* (discussion paper given limited circulation)
March	1982b	*Education 5–9: An Illustrative Survey by HMI*
	1982c	*The New Teacher in School*
November	1982d	*Teacher Training Circular Letter 5/82*
January	1983a	*The Treatment and Assessment of Probationary Teachers, Administrative Memorandum 1/83*
March	1983b	*Teaching Quality*
March	1983c	*Teaching in Schools: The Content of Initial Training*
	1983d	*The Work of HM Inspectorate in England and Wales*
December	1983e	*9–13 Middle Schools: An Illustrative Survey by HMI*
December	1983f	*Initial Teacher Training: Approval of Courses* (Draft Circular)
December	1983g	*Curriculum 11–16: Towards a Statement of Entitlement*
April	1984a	*Initial Teacher Training: Approval of Courses* (Circular 3/84)
September	1984b	*The Organization and Content of the 5–16 Curriculum*
March	1985a	*Better Schools*
March	1985b	*General Certificate of Secondary Education — The National Criteria*
	1985c	*The Curriculum from 5 to 16*
June	1985d	*Quality in Schools: Evaluation and Appraisal*
July	1985e	*Education 8–12 in Combined and Middle Schools: An HMI Survey*

Making sense of this plethora of documents needs to be attempted within a view of the wider context from which they have emerged — the political and economic context of Britain in the final quarter of this century. The enigma of teacher education today resides in the political and economic tensions which loom over education in general, a spectre of turmoil and confusion which reaches out in the encroaching difficulties from beneath tight control of public expenditure in search of the more optimistic and expansionist period, 1955–

1975. It is an enigma which has confounded teachers and teacher educators since 1975, a puzzle of confused and changing ideologies related to confused and unpredictable economic and educational conditions and policies, compounded by acute changes in the number of pupils in schools. Confusion and disagreement about the kind of education which western countries should pursue, among education ministers from twenty four countries of the Organization of Economic Co-operation and Development (OECD), was summed up in the *Times Educational Supplement* as 'The Ministers' Bleak New World' (October 1984). At the institutional level the characteristics of the puzzle appear as a series of critical shifts in the forces of conflicting and rising expectations in the name of accountability, tensioned by diminishing resources.

The rise and demise of teacher education provision from the early 1960s to the mid 1970s is a matter of historical record (Lynch, 1979; Taylor, 1984). The further closure and amalgamation of public sector teacher education institutions into the 1980s as cost-cutting exercises clawed back yet more provision, resulting in continued dissipation of resistance to 'cuts'. The 1981 attack on the universities signalled for their departments of education not just the fingering of institutions which might have thought themselves out of reach of government cuts and curriculum control, but a hefty, thrusting grab. The grasp of the Treasury, mediated now to both public sector and university departments through the Department of Education and Science (DES) and the University Grants Committee (UGC), and reinforced by the 1985 Green Paper on higher education has been matched by far-reaching and swift developments in the control of teacher education curriculum. A shift to centralized sponsorship of policy-related research into teacher education, leading to greater control over the levels and kinds of understanding of its processes has also occurred (Reid, 1985). That has been accompanied by the announcement of new legislation extending the power of the Secretary of State for Education and Science to control grant aid for the in-service education of teachers (DES, 1985a). The power will be deployed through a requirement to local education authorities to submit for ministerial approval their in-service plans. The same legislation will provide ministerial power to require the regular appraisal of the performance of individual teachers, upon criteria so far unspecified.

Central government has a long history of direct control of teacher education via examining (including practical teaching), finance of institutions, manpower planning, and the length and structure of courses. Before the establishment of area training organizations and the further devolution of some controls to the universities following the McNair Report, (Board of Education, 1944) a century had passed in which teacher education was more closely controlled from Whitehall than other parts of the service were (Gosden, 1984). Since the Robbins Report of 1963, policy and planning in academic, administrative and financial realms has been devolved through structures of committees and advisory bodies — the Universities Council for the Education of Teachers (UCET), and the Council for National Academic

Awards (CNAA) holding major roles in defining the content and quality of courses; the Advisory Committee on the Supply and Education of Teachers (ACSET) and the University Grants Committee (UGC) in planning and administration. In a period of rapid expansion in student numbers, the changing of courses in moves toward an all-graduate intake into teaching, and compulsory certification for graduates who wish to teach, the role and stature of these various agencies grew in the 1960s and 1970s. Even within these arrangements, however, and before the 1982 cuts which excised further teacher education institutions 'a "shift" in the agenda of national discussion on teacher education ... from numbers to content and quality', was identified by Taylor (1984). He notes: 'Perhaps most significantly of all, HMI began to take a more active interest in teacher education' (p. 29). Not only was that interest soon to be strengthened, with considerable political muscle exerted by the Secretary of State, but it would operate in particularly new ways. The Minister's publicly announced intention in 1982 to bring into full use his existing statutory powers to deny entry to the profession to anyone who had not undergone a teacher education programme and selection procedure accredited by him was the watershed. Discussion had not only turned from numbers to content and quality in the various agencies and professional bodies involved in national debates, it had shifted 'towards ways in which more effective advice could be given to the Secretary of State on the content and organization of courses and on the criteria on which professional recognition should be granted' (*Ibid*, p. 29).

Decisions about the content and quality of teacher education courses, their conduct, and the criteria for their approval, were at least in part the outcome of departmental considerations in which the Inspectorate has become more immediately involved in the exercise of power (Gosden, 1984). This, according to Gosden, has occurred because senior inspectors, who were in any case influential in the formulation of policy because of governments' long-standing role in teacher education, play a more crucial role in advising non-permanent DES officials. The exercise of power by the DES is being exerted more stringently through the role of HMI in the application of the criteria laid down for the approval of courses and entry into the profession. Executive and bureaucratic decision-making processes are extant to such a degree that the Minister announced an intention (later held in abeyance) to disband the Advisory Council for the Supply and Education of Teachers, and removed from the National Advisory Body (NAB) their powers in deciding public-sector provision of teacher education places. Outcry about the visitations and reporting procedures used by HMI and the associated operation of CATE in relation to colleges and universities has been widespread. However, the relationship between education policy and economic policy becomes displayed with increasing clarity. With commands from HMI for improved quality in schooling and advice about how to achieve it there are riders that no additional resources will be available, despite their own assertions of a clear relationship between greater quantity and better quality of resources and better standards in learning in individual schools, and within specific subjects (DES, 1983e and 1985b). From the Department of Education and Science meanwhile the demand not only for better but for more in teacher education, as predicted numbers of teachers required for primary schools are set to rise, is accompanied by severe financial cuts to institutions, orchestrated centrally by the Treasury and played out through the DES, UGC, and LEAs.

While HMI's advisory role to the Minister in relation to teacher education has been considerably changed, and while their relationship with institutions of teacher education has changed dramatically since the founding of CATE, official re-emphasis in the broader function of HMI has slipped by relatively unnoticed. That function has itself been subject to 'the scrutiny', out of which it was delineated as 'explicitly policy related' within an 'overall thrust of . . . achieving an education system more actively concerned with the standards of its products and more cost conscious' (DES, 1983c). The value-for-money function, strengthened by a sharper focus on the Inspectorate's audit tasks, is explicitly to ensure standards achieved and effectiveness and efficiency in the way resources are being used.

The legitimation of cuts in provision linked with greater accountability and a redefinition of curriculum has been happening in relation to schools and the performance of serving teachers since 1976. But the control of what goes on in schools cannot be complete without redefinition at the point of entry into the profession. For while it may be that student teachers' former school experience and subsequent induction into teaching act as powerful influences towards conservative schooling, it is reasonable to suppose that particular kinds of initial teacher education may facilitate particular kinds of subsequent professional practice and development. That is certainly the assumption of the opening statement of *Teaching in Schools: The Content of Initial Training:*

> The education and training of teachers . . . is liable to change as our system of education, and its task in our society, also change . . . (DES, 1983b).

The implication is that teacher education will follow a path laid by central control and trodden by schools, the emphasis distinctly on training to follow that path. The irony is that demands being made upon teachers require them to aspire to and be prepared for excellence in curriculum leadership. In teacher education many had come to believe that schools were liable to change for the better only if the education of teachers could change to provide an effective avenue of school reform. Indeed that sentiment is retained in the aspirations of the DES. We need to be clear therefore about what kinds of teachers we want, and provide the kind of teacher education most likely to produce particular qualities of professional practice and leadership. It is not obviously apparent that the shift to closer central control and the curriculum assertions associated with it offer the prospect of such change or the likelihood of producing professionals capable of bringing it about. Unless, that is, more careful consideration is given to the development of teacher professionalism.

The 'New' Curriculum of Teacher Education

The recent conventions of teacher education curricula have included academic subject studies followed in their own right for the 'personal' development of individual students; subject teaching methods; classroom practice; and education studies in which the principles of education, based more recently in the disciplines of psychology, philosophy, sociology and history have provided for a wider understanding of pedagogy and curriculum.

For students following a 'consecutive' route of a subject degree followed by a postgraduate certificate in education the subject study accommodates three-quarters of the preparation time for teaching. The other three parts are squeezed into one academic year. In the 'concurrent' route of a three or four-year Bachelor's Degree in Education the proportions of time allocated to the four parts has varied in different institutions. Usually at least equal emphasis has been given to method, practice and education studies combined as compared to the study of a subject. Both routes assume that the year of induction into full-time teaching will be supported by some systematic form of learning guidance before confirmation of certification.

Education studies has experienced its own problems of definition and place in the teacher education curriculum in attempts to integrate theory from the four disciplines with the practical problems of classrooms and schools. Nevertheless it was within education studies that critical theory developed in search of a better understanding of education and of teaching. It was here that conventional practices were opened to question, and innovative alternatives for the improvement of schooling sought. Educational reform was born of the thoughtful scrutiny of ideas and practices, within a vision of educative experiences for student teachers and teachers. Informed critical appraisal as a basis for professional development by teachers became a major goal of the professional community. School experience for teachers and student teachers, however, remains focussed mainly on teaching technique, the gaining and maintaining of practical competence in methods courses and classrooms, with relatively little regard for critical scrutiny. For student teachers the learning of practical classroom skills has often remained a distinct and discrete agenda within their programmes, usually achieved in short periods of teaching practice in schools; sometimes through simulation and microteaching in the lecture room; and occasionally through classroom observation and analysis. For much of the learning a tacit supervision partnership between teachers and tutors has been ritually rehearsed. Though there have been some attempts to capture the potential of classroom study as a means of professional development for all concerned (Ashton *et al*, 1983) relationships between tutors, teachers and students amount to an uneasy alliance conducted often at a physical, let alone professional, distance (Yates, 1982). Partnership mostly occurs in relation to sporadic bouts of teaching practice for students, during which survival strategies and professional prejudice against theory combine to eliminate analysis and understanding of classrooms by way of study and reflection. The idea of partnership and critical scrutiny of classroom practice has very limited meaning in the conventions of initial teacher education. The limitations are confirmed by a lack of enquiry by teacher educators into their own activities and the experiences of their students. The opportunities for student teachers, teachers and teacher educators to develop cooperative, critical and innovative dispositions which might lead to flexibility, participation and professional self-development has not generally occurred (Alexander, 1984; DES, 1982c and 1983b; Sanger and Tickle, 1987). Rather, the apprenticeship mode of learning teaching has predominated, in which basic performance in conventional classroom technique is learned during brief encounters with teachers and children in schools, and more likely after entry into teaching through induction into existing practices. Those practices and the induction into them have been associated with a 'technician' mode of teaching which assumes the mastery and repetition of basic classroom technique for instructional transmission of pre-learned subject content towards prescribed objectives. In that mode of teaching there is a predilection to whole-class instruction to those prescribed objectives. The reassertion of the apprenticeship mode of teacher training, and of teaching as a technical act learned and conducted in a context which is increasingly subject to the performance appraisal of individual teachers, currently holds the political high ground in issues of teacher education, teacher accountability, and financial remuneration of teachers. It is towards confirmation of that hold that initial teacher education policy could move, by defining the kinds of experiences which student teachers will have, and the kinds of teachers to be admitted to the profession. But such a view of teaching hardly holds the educational high ground, where there is increasing concern for the development of professional codes of practice. Professional codes, it is argued, would incorporate autonomous action by teachers which will lead them beyond the level of competent technician (Sockett, 1980). There are aspects of recent policy documents, however, which suggest a return to the basics of past practice in teacher training and which in my view miss an opportunity to develop radical alternatives. Indications of the nature and direction of central policy began to emerge in 1982, and it is worth considering some aspects of those documents which currently are having a major influence on the design and conduct of teacher education courses.

The DES firmly established primary/secondary age-range distinctions for teacher education in its *Teacher Training Circular Letter 5/82* (DES, 1982d). Primary is defined as age 5–12 years, sub-divided between the early years and the later years. Intending primary teachers are required to be prepared to deal with the whole range of the primary curriculum, with substantial elements of English and mathematics, and consideration of the development of specialist subject expertise. Secondary courses are designated according to conventional schools' subjects. 'Junior/secondary' and 'middle years' courses are firmly discouraged in favour of courses which are clearly directed to secondary or primary phases of education. In its issue date, the letter was sandwiched between a discussion paper and a formal version of *Teaching in Schools: The*

Content of Initial Training (DES, 1982a and 1983c). Within a stated intent to be advisory, not prescriptive, 'institutional freedom in professional matters' is tempered by demands for acceptable levels of subject preparation and minimum standards of effective mastery of the main teaching subject, to be studied for a minimum of two full years by all students, including intending primary teachers. The assumptions and conventions of academic secondary schooling are apparent in the form of single-subject specialisms and instructional methods linked to them. The paper explicitly does not deal with developments in pre-vocational education in schools, the implications of the 1981 Education Act for children with special educational needs, or the curriculum of the 16–19 age group. The means to convey subject knowledge, not only through personal teaching performance at all school age levels, but also through consultancy for non-specialist colleagues in primary schools, is required to be given substantial time allocation within initial teacher education. A close knowledge of related subjects to the 'main' one, consideration of links with other subjects, and understanding of the contribution of the subject to pupils' development and to the whole curriculum are further specific requirements. With 100 taught hours for maths and language, matched by 100 hours of private study or practice in those subjects, the content for intending primary teachers is set. Yet time for the early years student is still to include 'all the main areas of the first school curriculum' — art, craft, drama, music, movement, environment, science, geography, history, and religious education. Middle years (note the slip since November 1982) students, however, will be more specialist. Competence for them as class teachers will only develop, it is said, through in-service and private study after qualification (DES, 1983c, p. 9). The content of their proposed initial teacher education is a mixture of learning activities which include reading, writing and mathematics, observation and constructional activities, practical skills in science and art and craft, and statutory obligations of religious education plus moral awareness.

I am not suggesting that we should fill in the gaps in this attempt to define teacher education curriculum, though clearly if it was a serious view held by HMI they ought to make a better job of constructing a case for it. But it demonstrates the packaging of prescribed content and the assumptions therein which form the prop of policy. It is a prop which has stood in the curriculum of the elementary school since the nineteenth century, now conjoined with a push down the age range of a conventional secondary school subject approach based on academic tradition. There is little suggestion of schools changing, nor any that they should change, towards a constructive, imaginative, and innovative view of education or society for the future. Nor is there a suggestion that teacher education should lead such change. Couched in broad generalizations about understanding learning, the principles of assessment, processes of interaction, and broader frameworks of educational meaning and purpose, the education disciplines of psychology, sociology, and philosophy are granted recognition in *Teaching in Schools* as contributory towards 'professional skills (which) lie at the heart of the training process'. Training is to be achieved in a partnership with practising teachers, with assessment of class-room competence and selection for entry into courses conducted equally by teachers and tutors. Minima for school practice time are also set out. Personal qualities which are deemed to be at the centre of successful teaching are cited as essential to new entrants to the profession, with a view that these are in some way pre-ordained and require assessment rather than development (Alexander, 1984a).

Despite the prescriptions, experimental and practical approaches by students in a context of a spirit of enquiry and independent study, in courses of training which should be 'undertaught rather than overtaught' remain on the agenda. Didactic teaching of course content is to give way to 'well controlled and assessed guided study and experiment'. Thus HMI define content, course structure and pedagogy in ways which, like their assumptions about school curricula (DES, 1978, 1982b, 1983e and 1985e) display a mixture of advice and prescription based in the traditions of subject-based teaching, yet which maintain a vestige of aspirations towards innovation and institutional freedom.

The White Paper *Teaching Quality* affirmed the age-phase/subject links in terms of 'relevance' to schools' conventional subjects. It set criteria to be applied in the approval of teacher education courses, including two years minimum subject study, adequate attention to teaching method in main subjects, substantial language/mathematics for primary teaching, and closely linked school practice. These broad requirements, to be imposed by the Secretary of State, would be effected in part by 'recent, substantial and relevant' school experience by tutors, including continuing regular contact with classroom teaching. Substantial involvement of practising teachers in the selection, teaching and assessment of students is also required. In the context of continuing reductions in resources, particularly staffing in schools, colleges and university departments of education, the means of achieving an anyway problematic set of requirements has generated intense debate in the profession. The intention to move towards partnership between institutions of teacher education and schools is, however, explicit and clear. The form which that partnership might take is not clear. In the attempt to meet the concerns about quality in teacher education there is more than one potential paradox. For example, there is the paradox of doing more of what is concurrently heavily criticized by HMI in their findings in schools, and by critical educationalists in their research of schooling. There is the reimposition of strict proportional time allocations to subject studies, professional studies and classroom practice, potentially reinforcing the fragmentation of courses. The tenuous position of education studies leaves recent reforming inroads into classroom practice by way of critical appraisal, innovation and development largely displaced. Concerns with epistemological issues, the social contexts of differential achievements of pupils, education policy, and other extensive issues in the domain of education studies do not figure in the demands of *Teaching Quality*. Its concern is largely to ensure that academic (i.e. subject content) and practical competence are achieved through course structures and controlled by the employers' application of amended obligations under the Education (Teachers) Regulations 1982 to match the suitability of formal qualifications of employees to the staffing requirements of schools.

Teaching Quality's criteria for course approval were embodied more fully in *Circular 3/84 — Initial Teacher Training: Approval of Courses* (DES, 1984a). This was accompanied by the mechanism for the application of those criteria. The Council for the Accreditation of Teacher Education (CATE) was born, to review all existing courses, to scrutinize new proposals, and to recommend (or otherwise) approval to the Secretary of State. Appointment of members of CATE is by the Minister 'on a personal basis', and evidence about whether courses meet the criteria provided largely by HMI inspections of institutions, with supplementary information being collected by the Council directly. The ascribed intent of the introduction of CATE and its operational criteria for improving the quality of schooling itself proves problematic, particularly in relation to primary schools. By now, relevance of PGCE candidates' initial degrees to the primary curriculum, in level and content is imposed (*Ibid*, annex, para 7). The two full years minimum subject study for undergraduates becomes a muddle of 'a wide area of the curriculum' which might constitute 'the chosen subject specialism' including the 'application of the subjects . . . to the learning and developmental needs of young children'. The particular subject in which a student expects to make a special contribution to the curriculum of schools is to be complemented by preparation for the wider role of class teacher. The by now 100 hours demanded for each of maths and language can be acquired by cumulative means via taught time, school experience and private study. Educational and professional studies are conscripted to provide 'adequate mastery of basic professional skills' defined in terms of classroom management and control, together with a list of content coverage which Alexander (1984a) has suggested can be interpreted as either sinister or bizarre, but in any case as quite inadequate to serious consideration of the primary teacher's role and long-term professional development (Alexander, 1984a, p.142). The nature of the curriculum required and the practicability of demands for partnership has resulted in confusion and disarray from this policy as CATE has got under way. The failure of institutions scrutinized to meet the criteria on subject studies and partnership with schools (particularly recent, successful, relevant classroom teaching by tutors) has been widespread. The expectation that subject studies should be at a level appropriate to higher education has been reformulated for primary courses within the concept of a wide area of the curriculum, in which coherence; relevance to the primary school; the effectiveness of links between subject and 'application' elements; and the level of 'applications' studies, will be judged 'on their merits' (correspondence from CATE, 1985). The measure of intent to improve, rather than simply control, initial teacher education might be judged by the requirement that PGCE courses must last for a mimimum of thirty-six weeks — an increase of a few weeks in some institutions, and none in others, for a course which is widely regarded as far too short, within reducing resources.

Given impending increased numbers for primary places in teacher education courses and real resource reduction, then the problems of declining quality noted in schools by HMI might well be anticipated in teacher education. When one couples further potential decline in quality in both schools and institutions with the criteria for close partnership between the two, bringing excessive additional demands on teacher education practice and on teachers, the educational rhetoric of standards and quality is exposed, indeed replaced by crude economic rhetoric of efficiency and productivity.

The White Paper *Better Schools* (DES, 1985a) sets out the government's conclusions following the review of its policies for school education in England and Wales, incorporating threads of policy for teacher education from the earlier documents, especially *Teaching Quality* and *Circular 3/84*. It weaves a fabric of policy which covers aspects of the school curriculum, teacher education, teacher appraisal and the government of schools. For initial teacher education the document restates the essential content of *Circular 3/84* as providing the means to achieve 'solid expertise in one or more curriculum areas' by individual teachers, training and practice in classroom skills, and the expression of personal qualities. These characteristics of training, it is said, will enable teachers to meet the complex demands made upon them. Those demands include the use of a repertoire of teaching styles, from the traditional instructional to the informal guidance role which promotes enquiry and involves sharing discoveries with pupils; 'professional attitudes . . . constantly concerned to increase effectiveness through professional development'; and participation in the corporate development of schools. The latter explicitly includes curriculum development as a professional activity which falls directly within the responsibilities of classroom teachers. The ways in which these characteristics of professionalism are to be developed during initial teacher education, in order that they might inform practice after entry into teaching, are not at all clear from the White Paper. The assumption is that solid subject expertise, professional courses, the involvement of teachers in student selection and training, more classroom experience for tutors, and the pre-ordained personal qualities and professional attitudes of students will somehow combine with classroom teaching skills to provide for these wider responsibilities of teachers.

The challenge of developing processes (beyond meeting the prescribed criteria for course approval) by which the complex professional demands can be met is left to institutions. That challenge is also made to LEAs for the long-term professional development of teachers, from the point of entry into the profession. There is a clear commitment to in-service teacher education as a managerial responsibility by employers:

> to support and encourage professional development at all stages of the individual teacher's career. A newly-trained teacher needs structured support and guidance during probation and his early years in the profession; other newly appointed and promoted teachers, not least

those appointed to headships, need to be able to draw upon induction and training programmes directly relevant to their new tasks and responsibilities; all teachers need help in assessing their own professional performance and in building on their strengths and working on the limitations so identified; and all teachers need to be able to engage in in-service training relevant to their teaching programmes and professional needs. (DES, 1985a, para 178)

For initial teacher education, the combination of subject studies, instructional methods, and practical experience form the core requirement for developing competence in classroom teaching. Education studies maintains a tenuous position as contributory to adequate mastery of basic professional skills on which teachers may build their careers. The elements of course structure, together with rigorous selection of candidates on criteria of personal characteristics, intellectual qualities, and professional commitment are presented as the means of ensuring standards of entry into teaching. The tone is often a minimalist tone, particularly in *Circular 3/84*. The striking of benchmark minimum time allocations, prescription of content, and requirements for particular qualities of intellect and commitment are basic. The problematic conduct of initial teacher education and further professional development, however, needs careful consideration if the standards of entry at the basic level are not to be translated into a standard entry into teaching. *Better Schools* displays a measure of intent to transform professional practice by spelling out conceptions of professional excellence and recognizing where it already exists. To transform the concerns about the basic quality of teacher education, which were outlined in the introduction, into constructive recommendations for the means of achieving changes in the processes of teacher education is a considerable challenge. The challenge is laid down in recent policy. Seen in these terms, teacher education is required to develop the means to achieve high standards in academic subject qualification, personal qualities, professional commitment and classroom practice. The means include:

(i)   the application to classroom practice of relevant theoretical studies for the improvement of professional practice;
(ii) participation in school activities by teacher educators, and in teacher education by teachers;
(iii) interrelationships in teacher education programmes between academic, professional and practical elements;
(iv) effective induction into teaching careers;
(v)   adequate approaches to career development and in-service education.

The question remains as to the most appropriate conduct and the most effective processes for the practice of these means to ensure high standards of professionalism.

The Nature of Control and the Curriculum of Schools

The connection between the education of teachers and the curriculum of schools which they are being educated to teach in is clearly an important one. As I suggested earlier, it is not sufficient to assume that teacher education will simply follow changes in schooling; rather, it needs to provide the means of developing teacher professionalism and leadership which can advance curriculum reform in schools. Recent changes towards centralized control of the curriculum of schools, through increased bureaucratic mechanisms, run counter to that aspiration. The irony is that greater teacher professionalism is being demanded at the same time as opportunities to exercise professional participation are being removed. The direction of change in school curriculum policy during the period since 1975 can be clearly discerned, and it is important to this discussion to locate those changes briefly. They have been most publicly manifest as a swing of the pendulum from the progressivism which was said to be at its height following the Plowden Report's recommendations (Plowden, 1967) and which accompanied economic and educational expansion and the growth of comprehensivization in secondary schools. The shift towards a more 'basic', industrially relevant, cost-effective education intended to ensure an improvement in 'standards' of skills, knowledge and understanding which will result in better economic performance by a future labour force summarizes much of the political tone of 'official' redirection. In that earlier period curricular notions of pluralism, integration, openness and innovation with egalitarian and individualized opportunities became noted characteristics in the search for a new ethos of comprehensive education. Middle schools, for example, themselves a by-product of comprehensivization, arose on a crest of optimism which Nias (1980) identified in the literature of the period 1966–76, much of it DES policy-related material concerned with changes to comprehensive education:

> a hopeful exciting educational world, full of dynamism, innovation and social justice, a world in which conflicting value systems, individual development and common need are joyfully reconciled by the organic processes of exchange and growth. (p. 81)

There is evidence that the seeds of the educational Utopia barely germinated into classroom practice, that political and educational rhetoric remained just that (Bennett, 1976; Boydell, 1981; Galton *et al*, 1980; Ginsburg *et al*, 1977; Hargreaves and Tickle, 1980). Nevertheless, primary/middle school policy and practice were seen by policy makers and policy implementers to be out of control, along with the rest of education but perhaps somewhat more so. Middle schools in particular were perceived as expensive, ironically having been devised as a cheap means of going comprehensive. The 1976 speech by the then Prime Minister James Callaghan (Callaghan, 1976) which led to the inaptly named 'Great Debate' on education has been identified as the point of implementation of policies which would at once check and then reduce opportunity expectations which had developed among the population in better economic times (prior to the 1973 oil crisis and the intervention of the World Bank and International Monetary Fund in the British economy). Those expectations could no longer be met in the job markets. Reducing expectations, it is argued, needed to be accompanied by reductions in educational provision, which in the state sector constitutes a major spending commitment from the public purse. To achieve that change of direction, setting up of bureaucratic controls to ensure the effect of policy changes while gaining acceptance by the population of policies of reduced provision provided a major challenge (Kogan, 1978). Centralized control of education, redefined in basic, core, industrially-relevant skills training flourished on the new rhetoric of control of standards and the monitoring of the work of teachers to ensure that those needs are met in a cost effective way. The legitimation of less expensive basic education, with reduced expectations by and increased control over the products of schooling was necessary, it is suggested (Salter and Tapper, 1981) to avert a crisis of expectations. Administrative intervention to redefine and restructure the system for efficiency and hierarchical authority over teachers and pupils provided the means. Such changes require legitimation, in order that they should be accepted. Salter and Tapper suggest that changes sparked by macro-economic influences, leading to social, political and bureaucratic pressures for educational change, need to undergo ideological and legitimating stages which must be negotiated prior to the expression of changes in the classroom. The legitimation of change is necessary to maintain power, they argue, and winning the ideological argument is necessary to ensure the legitimation through acceptance by the population. In the name of accountability, therefore, this relatively brief period has seen the political and bureaucratic impetus to establish mechanisms for tighter control and prescription in five areas of education: curriculum content and design; the assessment of pupil performance; appraisal of teacher performance; the government of schools; and the education of teachers — both initial and in-service. Bureaucratic and policy controls have been traced directly to the DES (Campbell, 1985). It seems clear that behind this source lies the Department's accountability to the state for the efficient production of manpower (Wallace and Tickle, 1983).

The complex nature of the ideological shifts in curriculum policy for schools within the exertion of those controls is difficult to summarize, since the documents which manifest policy contain inconsistencies and contradictions. The plethora of discussion documents, reports, surveys, and legislation offer the detailed evidence (listed on page 8). Campbell (1985) describes these as indicating a concerted production of a common curriculum whose framework for primary schools was set in the *Primary Survey* (DES, 1978). Its secondary school equivalent was published a year later (DES, 1979b). Their characteristics are summarized by a concern for 'standards' in the 'main subjects' of the curriculum, to be achieved through the more effective use of teachers' specialist subject knowledge and the differentiation of pupils' learning experiences. The ideological tones of the *Primary Survey* were more fully rehearsed in *Education 5–9* (DES, 1982b) *9–13 Middle Schools* (DES, 1983e) and *Education 8–12* (DES, 1985e).

The former claimed (para 4.7) standards of performance in the early acquisition of language and mathematical skills to be satisfactory, but 'variable' in later development and entirely 'variable' (i.e. unsatisfactory) in other parts of the curriculum. More effective 'guidelines' in all parts of the curriculum were 'urgently needed' especially in geography, history and science. The role of teachers as leaders in areas of the curriculum is reiterative of the 1978 *Survey*. If there is a degree of hesitation in *Education 5–9* about the use of subjects as the basis for defining curriculum there is none in *9–13 Middle Schools*. The assertions that the quality of education in the form of 'standards' can be assured by increased use of specialist subject teaching with children younger than 11 are explicit, even though the cause-effect relationship (para 8.11 and Appendix 2, fig. 1) is certainly not established. Indeed the evidence presented from this sample of forty-eight schools asserts a clearer relationship between better quality of work (standards) and 'above average resources' (Appendix 1.29). Further: 'The quality and quantity of resources was also associated with the strength of the head's influence, a second factor strongly associated with standards of work.' (DES, 1983e, p. 139). *Education 8–12* makes no claims for links between subject specialist teaching and standards in its findings, though it demands that more specialist teaching should occur. In its sample of schools, resources and headteachers' influence are joined by the quality of pastoral care to form the three most important influences on standards of work. Many of the surveyed schools were deemed to be inadequately resourced, the rest 'generally adequate'. The relationship between resources and standards in specific subjects in 9–13 schools was subjected to statistical analyses with the same association drawn especially for geography, science, French and CDT, and also for needlecrafts, mathematics, history, home studies and physical education.

One framework of the curriculum therefore in all five surveys is explicitly subject-centred in a narrow range of conventional academic (secondary) school subjects, with an assumed transmission of knowledge via experts/specialists. The reassertions of the curricular assumptions in this view are accompanied by a growing expression of concern for a more effectively differentiated curriculum, taking account of 'less able', 'average' and 'able' pupils. Demands for better provision for the latter especially concern HMI. (DES, 1982b, paras 4.11, 4.12 and 4.13; DES, 1983e, para 8.10; DES, 1985e, para 8.8). While a framework of measured standards in a subject-centred curriculum predominate, there are calls for the exercise of choice, responsibility and initiative by pupils, linked with a greater diversity of teaching and learning approaches (DES, 1983e, para 8.8; DES, 1985c, para 8.6). Children's interests and individual teacher decision making are recognized as in some way appropriate in first schools. But these characteristics are overwhelmed by issues of ensuring progression, continuity, transition, differentiation, subject specialization and frameworks of common practice controlled through guidelines and checklists. Policies for a hierarchically defined (in terms of both knowledge structures and pupils' 'abilities') compartmentalized transmission of a narrow range of subjects have a strong advocacy in this range of reports. Moreover the *9–13 Survey* cites the White Paper *Teaching Quality* on the issue of lack of fit between some teachers' initial qualifications (i.e. main subjects studied in initial training) and their tasks. Indeed, while recognizing that staffing cuts in schools exacerbate the lack of fit as specific subject expertise is lost and not replaced, HMI insist on staff deployment which will make optimum use of teachers' subject knowledge, and a more careful match of new appointments to subject tasks. The links between resources, specialist teacher activity and quality of learning leave the rhetoric of 'standards' exposed amid questions of expense, provision, and efficiency. While economic cuts actually cut those links in individual schools, we see a realignment of resources away from educational provision in the state schools, and a reassertion of a curriculum in which teachers are charged as control-technicians with the efficient transmission of subject knowledge.

The timing and tone of HMI reports was matched by the publication of policy documents and discussion papers, initially following the report on local authority arrangements for the school curriculum (DES, 1979a) which had followed 'Circular 14/77' which required LEAs to submit details of curricula in their schools. The assertion of a need for national consensus, for LEA formulation of policies and objectives which meet national needs, and the application of policies in ways which suit local, school circumstances were set out in *'A Framework for the School Curriculum'* (DES, 1980a); *'A View of the Curriculum'* (DES, 1980b) and *'The School Curriculum'* (DES, 1981b). This need was reasserted in the call for explicit definitions of objectives for each phase and each subject made by the Secretary of State for Education in 1984 (Joseph, 1984) and in *The Organization and Content of the 5–16 Curriculum* (DES, 1984b). A curriculum for secondary schools based on the clear definition of specific aims and objectives was concurrently being defined through the newly-constituted Secondary Examinations Council and the devising of the General Certificate of Secondary Education (GCSE). National criteria have now been set to which pupils' grades in each subject will be matched, and towards which 'approved' syllabuses will be expected to be implemented (DES, 1985b). Syllabus content will thus be defined in specific ways, in relation to what pupils must do to achieve particular grades. That in turn will ensure that teachers need to perform specific tasks towards tightly prescribed objectives in a curriculum which differentiates pupils 'efficiently' (according to their performance in tasks) and allows similarly efficient measurement of the outcome of teachers' work. The assessment of teacher and pupil performance against specific criteria, and in relation to defined content objectives, enhances the effectiveness of bureaucratic mechanisms for the control of education. The potential effects of such mechanisms on the work of teachers and the quality of education will be discussed later. The HMI discussion paper *The Curriculum from 5 to 16* (DES, 1985c) and the White Paper *Better Schools* (DES, 1985a) coordinate the review of policy in relation to the organization, content, and conduct of the school curriculum. Standards of education linked to economic prosperity and achieved through value-for-money schooling are a manifest concern. The means to achieve better schools is seen to rest within a consensus 'partnership' between central government, LEAs and individual schools working from a common policy towards the achievement of national objectives. There is space for local variation in the methods used to achieve them:

> Curricular policy at each of these levels would thus be directed towards the same objectives. (although) ... diversity is healthy ... (it) accords with tradition.... (and) makes for liveliness and innovation. (DES, 1985a, para 34 and 37)

Objectives are set down in 'broadly agreed' terms as:

(i) to help pupils to develop lively enquiring minds, the ability to question and argue rationally and apply themselves to tasks, and physical skills;
(ii) to help pupils acquire understanding, knowledge and skills relevant to adult life and employment in a fast changing world;
(iii) to help pupils to use language and number effectively;
(iv) to help pupils to develop personal moral values, respect for religious values, and tolerance of other races, religions and ways of life;
(v) to help pupils to understand the world in which they live, and the interdependence of individuals, groups and nations;
(vi) to help pupils to appreciate human achievements and aspirations.

The fundamental principles set out for the design of curricula require that all pupils should experience a curriculum which is:

Broad	language and mathematics closely associated with art, craft, history, geography, music, science, physical education and religious education (plus a foreign language at secondary school level)
Balanced	each area allotted sufficient time
Relevant	to pupils' experience and valuable for adult life
Carefully differentiated	to match pupils' abilities and aptitudes as individuals.

While *Better Schools* implicitly adheres to a curriculum defined by subject content, its authors are at pains to point out that this is a matter of descriptive convenience, and that other analyses and designs of curricula are both possible and legitimate:

> The fact that their (content and teaching methods) application is ... expressed in relation to subjects should not be misinterpreted ... Curriculum can validly be analysed and described in a number of ways. ... Such a description (by subjects) implies no particular view

> of timetabling or teaching approach. Nor does it deny that learning
> involves the mastery of processes as well as the acquisition of
> knowledge, skills, and understanding. (*Ibid*, para 52)

Those processes, including active rather than passive learning, less teacher direction, more oral discussion, posing and solving of practical problems, and greater responsibility for pupils to pursue their own enquiries and make decisions, are high on the list of *changes required* toward the achievement of better quality education. The charges that currently teachers do too much work for their pupils, leaving little opportunity for pupils to learn for themselves, to express their own views, and to develop their own ideas, are explicit. They are linked with criticisms about the over-use of class teaching 'to the middle' irrespective of the kind of ability grouping, and the under-expectation of pupils based on teachers' stereotyping of them. Teachers in primary and middle schools are represented as holding a 'mistaken belief' which underlies the predominance of basic skills, and leads to too little scientific, practical, and aesthetic experience, and little relevant application of literacy and numeracy skills. Diversity, liveliness and innovation, the involvement of teachers in curriculum management and planning, and the implementation of curriculum processes which are consistent with many of the ideals of primary education, and with the aspirations of much of comprehensive secondary education, are an important development on what was widely regarded as a 'back to basics' movement in the late 1970s. The processes of learning incorporated into the criteria of new GCSE examinations reflect similar concerns to enhance the quality of learning for pupils.

Swings of the pendulum and the predominance of particular ideologies of curriculum, and the balance between conflicting views at any one time or among any group of educators, are, of course, constantly in momentum and tension. *Better Schools* itself recognizes such conflicts as unavoidable. It seems that the implications of this document with regard to the complex demands placed on teachers in the organization, content, and conduct of the curriculum clearly require a high level of professional expertise capable of activating and sustaining reform in schooling, in directions which certainly do not conspire with notions of 'basic' education. Such expertise will need to be on a level higher than that of proficient technician, and involve professional *participation*. While *Better Schools* sees systematic career development of teachers and the effective induction of new entrants as a responsibility of LEAs towards that aspiration, its other major inroad — control of initial teacher education — is left as a restatement of *Circular 3/84*. That, in my view, is an inadequate response to its own challenge. Furthermore, increased bureaucratization — of initial training through the operations of CATE; of teacher performance through an 'effective management' approach to appraisal; of professional development through direct funding of in-service teacher education; of the curriculum through control of syllabi; and so on, does not hold the prospect of greater professionalism for the improvement of education.

Training and Assessment of Practising Teachers

Demands for the accountability of teachers, which were launched formally in the Callaghan speech of 1976 have been discussed widely since (for example, Alexander, 1984a; Graham, 1985; Elliott *et al*, 1985; Holt, 1982; Sockett, 1980). It is not necessary here to address the detailed arguments, but sufficient to suggest that there are two approaches to the question of what should be done in order to ensure that professional standards and qualities are enhanced for the improvement of schools. Optimistic views which see teaching as a profession, with professional responsibilities carried out in a framework of self-determination and commitment to education, hold to ideas of accountability and responsibility conducted in mutual trust and partnership between those concerned with education. Those ideas are explicitly critical of the external 'management of the teaching force' approach which is espoused in recent policy, legislation and proposed legislation. The 'management' view has gained in momentum in mechanisms being used to ensure that particular kinds of curriculum will be implemented, controlled and safeguarded at the direction of central government. The initial thrust of accountability, which centred on school-wide self-evaluation and curriculum reviews, has taken a turn firmly in the direction of individual teachers' performance and its assessment.

It is argued that the deprofessionalization of teachers is likely to result from centralized control with increased bureaucratization turning teachers into technicians charged with specific skill tasks. In such a system teachers' work would be specified by others; teachers would participate in policy- and decision-making in only tightly-defined realms. They would be accountable to technical managers. There is an implicit concern in this argument that teaching would be judged according to the 'efficient' instruction of pupils, who would be subject to receiving pre-packaged knowledge of a kind that could be readily assessed in pupil performance. It is feared that the alternative approach, in which education is regarded as a process in which enquiry, judgment, questioning, and discovery lead to the personal development of individuals, would be devalued or even excluded.

The 'management' view of teacher appraisal stems at its extreme from a concern to weed out incompetence. The 'professionalization' approach aspires to move teachers well beyond competence towards codes of practice which would ensure excellence through autonomous, professional accountability (Sockett, 1980). What is crucial to the debate is the issue of criteria upon which competent or excellent teaching would be judged, the ways in which judgments would be made, as well as questions about *by* who and *for* whom they would be made. It appears that the management approach to control assumes that there is a consensus about what constitutes good teaching, and that the mechanisms of controlling and developing it are understood. Those who seek professional excellence do so by seeking new means by which it can be developed, with aspirations towards better understanding of those means (Graham, 1985).

Later I will consider the issues involved in seeking professionalism through self-development, outlining opportunities which are needed at least to complement the contrasting 'effective management' view. The move to effectively manage teachers through 'accurate knowledge of teacher performance ... based on assessment' is the clear bureaucratic control message of *Quality in Schools: Evaluation and Appraisal* (DES, 1985d). The rationale for assessment is:

> based on the belief that knowledge of teacher performance results in teachers being helped to respond to changing demands and to realize their professional potential. (p. 5)

There is acknowledgement of two levels through which this is reported to have begun to happen — school self-evaluation of curriculum, and LEA systematic teacher appraisal. The ways in which the ideology and practice of teacher assessment have taken hold since 1976 was promised in the White Paper, *Teaching Quality*:

> HM Inspectors are collecting evidence about the extent and effectiveness of practices for teacher assessment and self-evaluation in schools and will make this evidence more widely available. (DES, 1983b, para 92)

More recently we are told:

> there appear to be no fully established models of teacher appraisal, initiated by LEAs, which have gone through the full cycle of assessment, staff development and follow-up action as appropriate. (DES, 1985d, p. 7)

Quality in Schools recognizes a quickening pace and sets out to identify some of the possibilities and problems of evaluation/appraisal, based on such a rate of development that 'at least five (local) authorities are now in the process of establishing schemes for teacher appraisal'. There are 105 LEAs in England and Wales. A quickening pace can be anticipated, however, given impending legislation which will require regular appraisal of the performance of individual teachers. The managers' charter is in place, with employers' inspections to identify workforce efficiency and 'inform managerial decisions in schools'. Of the criteria to be deployed there is little to be learned from DES publications. The mechanisms and procedures by which the aspiration to improve schools is to be achieved offer generalized prescriptions and conditions: evaluation and appraisal must be linked to in-service training; teachers should have time, support and goodwill for their development; and a healthy perception of status and good morale are critical! (*Ibid*, p. 47). In these procedures, we are told, roles need to be understood; expectations need to be clear; trust between management and workers is as essential as good communications, a shared sense of purpose, and a state of readiness for the implementation of schemes of teacher assessment.

What is important in the context of this book is that there is a clear intention that classroom observation will play a central part in providing evidence of teaching skill, coupled with interviews of teachers which are said to require skill and sensitivity in the management of evaluation and appraisal. Training for both is said to be necessary. For that, it is suggested, industry and other countries might provide the expertise. There is no recognition of the infant-state of our understanding of classroom processes and the complexities and methodological difficulties involved in investigating classrooms. The problems of studying the perceptions and beliefs of teachers, pupils, parents and others about what constitutes effective education are ignored. Theoretical problems involved in explaining classroom phenomena are even more difficult. When one combines all these with the difficulties of assessment generally, and of teaching particularly, it is perhaps understandable that the DES steers a cautious course. The assumption that outsider expertise from industry might produce management training which can be imposed on teachers who are themselves unprepared in the skills of classroom observation, interview techniques, and analysis misses important opportunities for professional development. The alternative of classroom and school-based initial and in-service education of teachers, motivating professional self-development through consideration of relevant practical issues is not explored in official literature. Yet there is an increasing body of experience and understanding available within the curriculum research and evaluation field.

Consequences of Changes in Teacher Education

The production of teachers on the cheap, in a form defined according to standard basic competence in subject knowledge and classroom skills could be anticipated as the potential outcome of recent policy. The production of such teachers would provide a mechanism for ensuring particular educational experiences and curricular provision in schools to complement those changes which are already occurring through direct control of schools themselves. For intending teachers the potential outcome could be a fixed career route bound by particular subject knowledge, age range, and instructional strategies. This might be reinforced by a passive mode of appraisal, in-service education and career development. Management control of longer term professional development may well be set within similarly narrow limits of a subject/content centred curriculum.

In initial teacher education policy the value of variety and experiment in curriculum, alternative pedagogies involving underteaching rather than over-teaching, and opportunities to develop modes of teacher education (DES, 1983c) seem to have been relegated in favour of conventional training and modes of assessment. It is training which seeks to impose a subjects/content/ skills rationale for the curriculum of teacher education as well as further down the age range of schooling, potentially regenerating the mechanistic means whereby 'objectives', 'standards' and levels of 'ability' can be efficiently measured. Through the rhetoric of accountability and the stress on the technical/managerial functions of teaching, it fits well with the political and economic ideology of the time.

The model of teacher training in partnership with conventional schooling would have a knock-on effect in schools for generations. Its consequences would be to reinforce those practices in schools which HMI have so eagerly criticized — the domination of English and mathematics and their separation from other subjects (DES, 1985b); too much reading and writing (DES, 1983e); insufficient opportunity for initiative taking, exercise of choice and responsibility, and enquiry learning (DES, 1983e and 1985b). One is bound to ask again: what kinds of teachers and teaching do we want? Here the contradiction and anachronism of DES policy comes home to roost. Basically competent technicians grounded in a narrow range of knowledge; or educated professionals capable of generating and accommodating new knowledge with the capability of long-term professional self development to bring about change in schools, is not too strong a polarization. The latter is clearly the *aspiration* of policy, but I would contend that the means of achieving that goal requires a detailed and considered answer to the question about the most appropriate conduct for the education of teachers.

One is still left to wonder why the curriculum shift has taken the direction it has. Clearly the DES nor anyone else can predict the manpower needs and the particular educational capabilities required in the next century when incoming primary children will matriculate. The preparation of teachers for the implementation of curricula as they serve the profession well into that century is no less problematic. The problematic nature of teacher education leaves a gap to be filled by recasting and redefining educative experiences for student teachers and teachers in alternative forms to that which assumes a training model limited in conception to competency-tested, mechanically performed teaching skills for the transmission of 'fixed' knowledge. It means opening a way to a better and clearer view of alternative teacher education which looks to a vision which will stimulate pro-action and lead potentially to constructive radical reform of schooling. That involves seeing professional development and the improvement of classroom practice through the study of teaching and learning, with the participation of teachers in research processes — the proposition of research-based teacher education (Stenhouse, 1975; Elliott, 1980; Fox, 1983; Nixon, 1981). Such participation in the process of teacher education, as I have shown, has barely emerged in DES policy. Yet it has much to offer to the aspirations of policy in their coordinated expression in *Better Schools*.

To suggest a return to a model of professional training which is deemed to have failed to adequately prepare many of today's teachers for their current responsibilities, is unsatisfactory, especially when it is widely recognized that the professional community has an inadequate understanding of teacher education processes. Nor will a move to more adequate mastery of subject content in itself do, particularly if it is at the expense of students' understanding of educational principles, procedures and practices. There have been some detailed attempts made to improve the processes of professional development, through individual research and development projects. Despite their successes and the contributions they make to understanding how teacher education can be enhanced, we are a long way from thorough and comprehensive knowledge. There are claims and demands, sometimes complementary and sometimes competing, for means of improving the qualities, characteristics and competences which teachers and aspirant teachers are required to demonstrate and acquire. There is less evidence about the means by which acquisition and demonstration can be achieved and judged.

Research and the Search for Educational Excellence in Professional Preparation

The education of teachers, like most aspects of education, is subject to folklore, anecdote and personal response rather more than it has been subjected to extensive critical analysis which has become widely available for the improvement of practice. When Wragg (1982) reviewed teacher education research internationally his work indicated that the practical application of the research in improving the quality of learning teaching for individual students is likely to be negligible. The need for funding to conduct the review; the use of research assistance and secretarial and librarian help to uncover many of the sources, followed by extensive work in judging the quality and potential value of research studies; and the difficulties in classifying their content, give that indication. For findings to be useful they need at least to be readily accessible in order that students, teachers and tutors may take them into account. The theory-practice relationship is as much a problem in educating teachers as it is in educating children.

The nature of the research reviewed by Wragg is grounded in the conventions of positivism, presenting a particular problem for 'application'. For example, reporting a project on student teacher attitudes which concluded that British trainees are more child-centred than their American counterparts, but less favourably disposed to administrative and school personnel, the implications for action are obscure. In a citation of his own work in which Wragg asked thirty-five tutors to rate a videotape of a student's lesson, he concluded that there was little agreement among them, and a wide range of grades awarded. Compounding the inference that what research does tell us is that teacher education is wallowing in the realm of the deeply problematic, Wragg cites among others work by Povey (1975). This study investigated the reliability and validity of different methods used to assess teaching practice with college of education students. The methods studied were:

Analytic: assessment using a rating scale of uniform and specifically defined criteria;
Profile: using less specific but uniform criteria;
Global: the assignment of grades without reference to set criteria.

The results noted that the highest correlation with final teaching practice grades were obtained for tutors using the analytic method, but points out the unsatisfactory nature of correlation coefficients as a measure. It is also said that disagreement between tutors was more marked among supervisors of secondary trainees in relation to classroom organization and management. The problems exist in the substantive issues to be considered in learning teaching, in the research procedures and methodology available for investigation, as well as in the implications and applicability for practice.

What we have is confusion and disagreement among professionals about assessment criteria and their use, so far as research techniques can show. The outcome is reported in an academic journal which is unlikely to be read by subject and method tutors and especially by teachers in schools responsible for assessing students, and where it is read the potential consequences are unclear. Students themselves would almost certainly remain objects of assessment unaware of such reports and discrepancies in practice, and the difficulties of defining criteria for assessing teaching.

The extremely thorough and detailed review by Wragg has tracked down and uncovered research reports on student teachers, their backgrounds, attitudes, personality and learning styles; the content of courses; teaching practice and school experience, including student attitudes towards it, their behaviour and their assessment; and experiments in training, including apprenticeship models, micro-teaching and self-instruction. For researchers and research purposes the value of such a review may be considerable, given the need in the positivist tradition to take account of previous research studies. For the practice of learning teaching and teaching teaching, the theory-practice gap gapes openly. It remains a major problem.

Despite the problems of positivistic descriptors of the characteristics of students, their programmes, and their preparation and assessment for practical teaching, the review excluded many published accounts of 'innovative and experimental training programmes'. Those which were included focus on the ways in which student teachers model themselves on experienced-teacher behaviours; on the use of micro-teaching for skills development; and on the extent to which student teachers can teach themselves. The latter is said to be confounded by difficulty in research methodology greater than in the other areas studied, even though investigations were concerned mainly with how students and teachers handled packages of 'teacher-proof materials'. Wragg also notes the difficulties of evaluating experimental courses which are radically different from conventional teacher education programmes.

The distinctions in these accounts between 'objective' research, evaluations of programmes by funded evaluators from outside the programmes, and innovative practice which is internally monitored by those directly involved, are evident in Wragg's classifications of studies reviewed. The differences between these types are profound, even though they may be used in combination. 'Objective' research in the empiricist tradition of quest for 'pure' knowledge can occur without concern for its dissemination. The research and development tradition of programme evaluation incorporates a central rationale of application and change through dissemination and training by evaluators for key practitioner personnel. Internal evaluation requires that the tasks of teaching, of investigating and understanding that teaching for the sake of improving practice, and the conduct of actions to bring about improvements, are the combined responsibility of professional practitioners. In each of these approaches to research, the assumptions about how knowledge is acquired and transmitted differ; the methodological problems vary, each with its own range of complexity; and the criteria by which quality and value are judged cannot be the same. What is the same is the attempt to identify better ways to educate teachers, based on understanding of teacher education processes. That research concern of all traditions has more recently become the national concern to identify elements of teaching skills training and teacher appraisal systems. (DES, 1982c and 1985a; Wragg, 1984)

In the form of quantitative research very little is being done currently which is likely to enhance the quality of learning of student teachers and teachers in-service, let alone those purportedly out of touch and outdated teacher educators. That is not surprising given the scale of the tasks, the methodological problems, and the lack of research funds. The most extensive recent research and development project is the *Teacher Education Project (TEP)* reported by Wragg (1984) with associated volumes of training materials (Kerry, 1983). The Project's identification of teaching skills, classroom management techniques, questioning and explaining strategies, identification of bright pupils and slow learners, and so on, goes a long way toward providing much needed analysis of student teachers' and teachers' complex tasks and responsibilities within the classroom. It seeks to respond to the recognition of a need for a 'highly skilled force of professional teachers who are able to nurture and facilitate learning for the next generation . . .' (Wragg 1984, pp. 3–4). The combination of *skill* and *professionalism* is aspired to by the identification of significant teaching skills, subsequent provision of training materials, and the stimulation of 'trainee and experienced teachers to analyze and determine their own strategies'. (*Ibid*, p. 4)

Eschewing the extreme of objectives-based, competency-tested approaches to teaching skills training, in which discrete behaviours are expected to be identified, mastery-taught, and mechanically performed, the *TEP* also recognized the sustained debate about teaching, and that teacher education and training 'has not crystallized around any single viewpoint' (*Ibid*, p. 8). On a middle road between detailed classification of teaching performance skills and an holistic view of teaching action, the project seeks to provide 'a modest contribution to the understanding and nurturing of the teacher's professional art and craft'. That contribution, funded, extensive and detailed as it is, self-consciously leaves many aspects of teaching unstudied.

The project adopted inductive methods in which school experience provided the base for raising both practical and theoretical issues. The problems raised by theory based teacher education courses and the theory-practice gap were confronted. The practical base proved attractive to experienced teachers who were not involved in the research, as well as those who were, confirming that teaching is, and is seen by teachers as, based in 'intelligent action'. Preparation for intelligent action is in its infancy both in practice and understanding. There is no rush reported for knowledge based in research reviews: 'We decided that our own and other researchers' findings would inform training materials, not dominate them.'

A clear interpretation here is that teachers were ill-equipped in professional skills, and saw themselves so, and were also ill-equipped to analyze and determine their own strategies. The sale of training booklets on specific teaching skills — class management, questioning, explaining, and so on — is both laudable and presumably profitable in professional terms. But what of that professional accompaniment to such skills, the reflective, analytical and active? Does the provision of training booklets by outsider researchers lead to an enhancement of the learning strategies of these teachers and intending teachers, and their teacher 'trainers'? Certainly the TEP sought a partnership in consulting and involving headteachers and teachers, teacher trainers and students in its research. It reasserts the absence of consensus about what constitutes effective teaching. The consequence for improving practice, it claims, is the need for practitioners to use their 'senses to appraise situations and their intelligence and imagination to respond'. The qualities of sensitivity, sensibility, intelligence and imagination, and other qualities in the affective realm of learning teaching, come from educational processes more complex than training alone. Educational understanding from humanistic studies of learning which attempt to deal with those realms is even less advanced, because it is more problematic, than the knowledge we have from behavioural outcomes and instructional effectiveness approaches to the study of teaching competence. Not only does the TEP open up this complex affective element of teacher education, coupled with its somewhat greater emphasis on skills training, it also espouses learning from a professional partner. That partnership is defined as one in which students work with fellow students, teachers and tutors to analyze and modify the students' practice, a model which is said to 'come into its own' at the point when the student has failed to effect the rudiments of classroom control. A call for students to reflect back at later stages of development on earlier lessons is founded on the project's view that such reflection was sometimes very crude (Wragg 1984, p. 194).

If the state of reflective action is so poor among practitioners, it is likely to remain poor among new entrants to the profession unless the conception of partnership incorporates cooperative analysis of and reflection upon the work of teachers and tutors, and the contexts in which teaching occurs. It is hardly surprising that learning teaching without the capacity to analyze, reflect, and modify practice has left teachers feeling insecure, in search of guidance from training manuals. Yet the potential of reflective partnership is in no doubt:

> When teachers and students analyze their own and each other's teaching the dividing line between in-service and initial training becomes so thin as to be almost non-existent. Indeed, if student teachers did not exist, one very effective way of influencing the practice of experienced teachers in a school would be to invent them. (Wragg, 1984, p. 199)

Concurrence with this sentiment may be widespread. One wonders, though, why Wragg did not assume a similar partnership principle for the analysis and reflection of the work of teacher educators. Perhaps the analytic/reflective problem stems from the model of the 'crude' evaluation by teacher educators of their own work, and their lack of real practical contact with the issues and problems of investigating and understanding teaching for improved practice. A greater concern with academic theorizing in the traditions of positivistic constructions of knowledge is the context in which 'standards' in teacher education have been sought.

Partnership based on observing life in classrooms, analyzing the data of observations, and modifying practice, provides the central rationale of the IT-INSET Project (Ashton *et al*, 1983). The purpose is to weld initial and in-service education of teachers through implants of student teacher groups and their tutors into classrooms for up to one day a week for at least a term. Teachers decide the issues to be studied and developed, within which it is intended that the group would theorize and draw on external theory to inform changes in practice, in a cycle of evaluation and development. The emphasis is on training with 'qualitatively enhanced classroom experience' for student teachers, classroom centred in-service training, and consideration of 'real classroom problems' for tutors. There is an explicit intention to advance further the emphasis on professional components of initial teacher education programmes which had, in the 1970s, begun to take seriously the rigorous intellectual demands of classroom and school practice to complement the subject, method and theory components. Bringing 'academic' tutors into that professional orbit is one of the 'enormous problems for training institutions and schools' alluded to but not fully reported and analyzed. Aspirations are also clearly towards a form of more relevant, problem-centred INSET which might overcome the difficulties of centralized courses in which content does not match the needs of teachers, and from which the application of theory-based learning in classrooms proves unsuccessful. The marriage of theory and practice; a shift to more school experience for student teachers and school-based curriculum development by teachers; connections between pre-service, induction and in-service; and bridging the organizational gaps between initial and in-service teacher education are the project's central intentions. The implications for partnership are clear:

> training institution tutors (and even their students) have a role in INSET, and teachers have a no less important role in initial training. There is therefore a need for closer cooperation between schools and colleges. (Ashton *et al*, 1983, p. 18)

The principles of the project assume this partnership to be readily achievable for the advancement of a second need: to improve the quality of education provided in schools through systematically and continuously:

1 Analyzing practice
2 Applying theory
3 Evaluating the curriculum
4 Developing the curriculum
5 Working as a team
6 Involving other teachers in the school

It is recognized that implementing these activities requires the learning and use of a cluster of professional skills which are not commonplace. Indeed, the associated work of *Curriculum in Action* (Open University, 1982), which set out to develop classroom observation and analysis skills for teachers, displays something of the internal complexities of analyzing practice, the first principle of IT-INSET. The struggle with the methodological and theoretical problems involved make the aspirations of both projects adventurous and ambitious. The evidence of evaluation, however is sparse, represented in a few pages of discussion about implementing the six principles, and based on problematic written responses from participants. If one looks beyond the principles to the premise of partnership there is no analysis of the pitfalls and possibilities incurred. The definition of partnership and its operation remain unexamined.

The realities of teaching practice supervision partnership are often far removed from the school experience partnership assumed by Ashton *et al*. In a report of a national survey of teaching practice supervision in BEd courses in England and Wales, Yates (1982) showed that the average length of teaching practice was 4.8 weeks in years 1 and 2, and 7.6 weeks in year 3 — a total of eighty-six working days over three years. Supervision visits by tutors averaged 12.2 for each student during the three years in institutions using a single supervisor system, and 16.3 where two supervisors per student were used. One hour 38 minutes was the average time allocated to each visit, including travel, observation of teaching and consultation with teachers and students. Yates concluded:

> There is evidence to suggest that the contribution of school-based personnel in the supervision process is of greater value than that of college-based personnel. (p. 213)

Teachers were seen by students as being of greater help than supervisors, giving more time for observation and discussion and offering 'more valid' evaluations of students' teaching. Supervisors were perceived far more as assessors. More than half the teachers in the sample perceived an institution-school communication problem; only a quarter of supervisors shared that perception. In particular, only 18 per cent of teachers had a clear view of their role in relation to the students, yet 64 per cent of tutors thought the teachers had a clear understanding. No regular training in supervision skills appeared to be available for teachers working with students.

Set against the aspirations of *TEP* and *IT-INSET* this report provides an indication of the scale of the partnership task to be tackled. It indicates the need for an understanding of the complexities involved, in order to implement effective practice which pays more than lip service to the rhetoric of policy for closer cooperation between schools and teacher education institutions. Even between students and supervisors (whether they be teachers or tutors) it is clear from Yates' work that there is a long way to go towards effective two-way partnership. That view is shared by at least some tutors. Rudduck and Sigsworth (1985) sought a solution to their dissatisfaction with teaching practice supervision and their own performance of it, by establishing class-room study and reflection as a basis for improving student practice. They saw the possibility of laying the foundations of professionalism through a mechanism of partnership using a contract between supervisor and student. The contract set out to provide conditions for dialogue between the partners, recognizing their unequal power. In the dialogue students defined the focus of observation/discussion, the tutors responding in confidentiality. Instead of critical scrutiny and assessment of students' classroom skills the tutors provided 'evidence' as observers of events which the student could not see because of their involvement in classroom tasks. In discussion 'classroom life' rather than 'student deficiencies' provided the agenda for confidence building and the readiness of students to engage in a form of grounded theorizing. Rudduck and Sigsworth discuss the problems of shifting from conventional 'prescription and advice' approaches to supervisory dialogue, including: the need to develop observation skills; the requirements of classroom skills training; the unequal power relationship; the aspirations of students to measure up to conventional teacher competence; and so on. Yet they assert that it is in partnership supervision that the potential lies for laying the foundation of 'proper professionalism':

> i.e. the capacity of a teacher to remain curious about the classroom; to identify significant concerns in the teaching-learning process; to refine his/her understanding of the structure of those concerns through empirical study; to value and seek dialogue with experienced col-leagues as support in the analysis of classroom data; and to adjust patterns of classroom action in the light of new understanding. *(Ibid,* p. 170)

Recognizing the possibilities offered by recent moves toward closer partnership and the problem of engaging teacher-supervisors in shared roles, this remains a report of the supervisor-student connection as if teachers were not involved. Given the evidence of Yates' report, partnership supervision defined by Rudduck and Sigsworth may well be innovative and exploratory, with considerable potential for the development of professionalism. But the implication is that it is necessary to take account of the influence of classroom teachers on students, and to consider the quality of teacher-student partnership and its contribution to professionalism. For instance, the illustration of observation-dialogue-action offered does not explain how the student engaged fully in handling classroom management tasks during a lesson should or could develop the skills of observation said to be needed for classroom analysis. That is deemed a supervisor skill, leaving a severe inadequacy in the development of 'proper professionalism'. Citing an analogy between the teaching process and the artistic process, i.e. speaking of good teaching as exploratory, interpretive, flexible, reflective and responsive, they imply that we know how most of the learning of these activities happens. We do not. There are tensions between instructional training for skill competence and exploratory self-developmental learning and performance which are difficult to reconcile. In the absence of adequate understanding of the way teachers learn and practice professional dispositions which incorporate yet subsume competent classroom management, we need to explore how student teachers can acquire the qualities of good teachers, and how good teachers and tutors maintain a commitment to achieve professional and educational excellence.

Research has paid little attention to the teacher and the effect of teachers' actions on children. Recent studies in the sociology of education, social psychology, and classroom observation which pave the way out of ignorance with potential for improving the education of teachers face the problem of how they might be used in learning classroom practice. Alexander (1984a) is critical of the three modes of teaching practice used in conventional teacher education courses: the apprenticeship of block practice; micro-teaching and simulation; and the use of sporadic classroom observation. He calls for four shifts in initial teacher education to surmount the problems:

(i)   a substantial focus on the work of teachers and their impact on aspects of children's school learning;

(ii) exploration of learning behaviour in the contexts of interaction between teachers and pupils;

(iii) willingness and preparedness by teachers to analyse the reasons for classroom actions and interactions;

(iv) the application of 'practical study' by way of 'self-exploration' by teachers and students. (Alexander, 1984a, p. 95)

Such shifts require substantial amounts of time, over prolonged periods, to be devoted to the practical and theoretical elements of teaching and learning. They equate with the aspirations and the challenge of recent policy to link practical and theoretical studies; increase participation in schools by tutors and in teacher education by teachers; to interrelate subject, professional, and practical elements of courses; to achieve effective induction into teaching; and to develop adequate means of achieving effective in-service education for long-term career development. It must remain a deep concern that the requirements of CATE and the policies of the DES do not open the way to explore how these aspirations may best be met.

Preparation for Professionalism Beyond the Classroom

Teacher effectiveness studies are based largely on a view of teaching limited to the technician/instructional function. Even within that limited view the work of Peterson (1979) showed that 'closed' instructional techniques leading to higher test performance depended on external control over the learners, while 'open' enquiry approaches led to increased independence, curiosity and creativity and depended upon an internal personal control sense being developed in students. If a derivative hypothesis could be applied to learning teaching we might well enquire as to the effects of instruction leading to technical competence, and whether enquiry-based curriculum experiences might lead to competence associated with, and enhanced by, the capacity to remain curious about the classroom. But the responsibilities of teaching neither begin nor end within the confines of classrooms. A classification of the activities of teaching, based on an interpretation of demands made of teachers, includes administration, counselling, policy-making, curriculum leadership, curriculum development, and community relations, in addition to classroom competence (Mulcahy, 1984). The insufficiency of conventional views of teacher effectiveness is clear, and so far, Mulcahy points out, teacher education has failed to prepare student teachers for effective functioning in the wider professional tasks. If we are to anticipate change, towards new forms of schools and new roles for teachers in the future as the DES demands, attention to the broader elements of practice needs to begin with vigour.

For teacher education, alternative forms of effective practice need to be developed which can take account of the criticisms of schooling. The preparation of new teachers and those in service would need to lead the way in responding to criticisms and new demands. For example, student teachers and teachers will need to be prepared for roles in curriculum leadership. To be effective that leadership will need to be based on understanding of curriculum — not only on a knowledge of one's subject. Understanding will need to be acquired through self-motivated study and professional commitment, and the use of learning techniques which will serve to nurture the quality of teachers' own long-term education. It is no use arguing that these wider competences can be acquired in schools through conventions of training and induction when it is being demonstrated that such dimensions of professional practice are in short supply in those places. It is necessary to approach with radical alternatives, to find ways to develop particular competences which new teachers will be required to use on entry into the profession. Campbell (1985) in research on the work of curriculum subject coordinators in primary schools suggests that the profession is in a 'transition stage' towards greater collegiality for curriculum development. That transition has been a long one. Comprehensivization of secondary schools, the raising of the school leaving age, the recommendations of the Newsom Report, the advent of the CSE and other developments of the past quarter of a century all brought about such expectations. Pace may certainly have increased with more recent events of the GCSE, AS levels, TVEI, information technology, craft/design/ technology, links with industry, school curriculum reviews and teacher performance appraisal. Legislative events affecting the governance of schools and closer participation by parents, and provision for children with special educational needs in ordinary schools, have affected teachers since 1980. Yet, as Campbell points out, teachers are not trained for the wider professional responsibilities nor equipped with the skills, knowledge and capabilities required by them.

For classroom competence, wider school responsibilities in curriculum development, and professional participation beyond the school, set in a process of long-term learning, it is necessary to develop an alternative mode of teacher education to the conventional one implied in recent policy. In particular that mode of teacher education must face up to those calls for partnership between students, teachers, and teacher educators and recognize that:

> ... it must be clear that the reality of partnership is less easy than the rhetoric; it requires very fundamental shifts in traditional attitudes towards teacher education by both teachers and trainers, and involves changes in structure and procedures at the institutional level and between schools and colleges/universities. (Alexander, 1984a, p. 97)

We are some way from the development of radical alternatives which offer practicable means of meeting the criticisms of current practice in teacher education, and which offer a way of achieving the aspirations of policy-makers and professionals for improving it. That way is available, though not in itself unproblematic. I will outline some of the principles on which it is based, before reporting examples of its practical implementation within *Student Attachment to Schools*.

Part Two

Towards Research-Based Teacher Education

Changing Orientations to Educational Research

Educational research faces a major problem of application to practice. There have been moves on the part of the research community towards a devolution of research activities in recognition of the inherent difficulties of educational research as a derivative of social science, and in response to the practical difficulties of dissemination. The view that research findings and curriculum proposals have a limited effect on the practice of teachers and teacher-educators has become widespread. Ways in which researchers have attempted in recent years to promote a more favourable relationship with teachers and to effect the implementation of research findings in classrooms have included strategies of:

(a) 'effective dissemination' — a harder try to get teachers to respond;
(b) 'experimental intervention' — using practical approaches through the in-service education of teachers, with trials of teaching techniques based on research results;
(c) 'collaborative research' — in which teacher involvement in the research is expected to effect the practical use of results. (Bennett and Desforges, 1984)

There have been some fundamental reconsiderations of the nature of educational research and the possibilities which it offers for understanding practice and improving the quality of education. Often these ideas have arisen from the reflection of researchers about the responses of teachers and student teachers to research, as a practically moribund contribution to classroom experience. McIntyre (1980) recognized the failure of research on teaching to produce a body of general, theoretical principles on which practice in teacher education could be based, and argued that the production of such a body of knowledge is not possible:

My conclusion, therefore, is that there is not, nor could there be, *any* systematic corpus of theoretical knowledge from which prescriptive principles for teaching can be generated. (p. 296)

This conclusion is based on the problematic nature of research in classrooms, in which it is impossible to validate descriptions; to capture whole events; to generalize contexts; to account for the meanings and purposes of teachers and pupils in specific situations; to generalize findings deriving from manifold and unstable variables. Taking as a starting point the impossibility of attaining firm and lasting generalizations, McIntyre sought ways in which the practical, experiential knowledge of teachers might complement and be complemented by *interpretive* and *action* research. He also sought ways to use student teachers' experience for the formulation and testing of their own hypotheses for improving classroom practice. Through a conception of dialogue and collaboration he suggests that current classroom practice and teacher education would be subject to critical examination in which research would 'elucidate, examine, explain and extend' teachers' and teacher educators' working knowledge and the perspectives and strategies of student teachers. In these proposals for a practice-research partnership McIntyre makes a plea for dialogue which will help in our understanding of teacher education and improvement of its quality, as well as improving classrooms. This involves a dimension of educational research which does not try to ape a seemingly unattainable positivist model of science.

Alexander (1984a) has also shown how shifts have begun to occur in the evolution of solutions to the theory-practice gap. The gap itself is considered in detail from the rise of education theory in the form of 'disciplines' for academic study, to attempts to maintain professional relevance. Persistence of the problem, he suggests, may be because the proposed solutions have been inappropriate *or* because the problem has been incorrectly defined in the first place. The idea that positivistic research credentialled by a university base should or could be taken and applied to teaching practice is questioned. Educational research, based in the social sciences, is problematic in terms of the application of general principles to specific cases. Educational action and research are also value laden. The implantation of 'knowledge' into 'practice' is seen as failing.

While teachers can be seen sometimes to respond by attempted applications, more usually the response is active rejection of theoretical approaches. Interpretive ethnographic research of schools and classrooms (for example Ball, 1981; Hammersley, 1985;) is usually the province of the outsider-researcher, including teachers and students studying each others' classrooms. Bases for formulating practical hypotheses for teaching and for discourse about teaching, it is argued can be built from such activity. Yet there is still a difficulty in the relationship between outsider research and the work of practitioners. Changing orientations to the problem in the recent past have included various attempts to blend academic study with practical experience, including 'practical theorizing' or forms of 'grounded theory'. Action research is centred in that attempt and offers the core of a radical alternative for the development of professional excellence which meets the call for 'a genuine theory-practice integration on the basis of parity of academic and professional/ experiential perspectives'. (Alexander, 1984a, p. 148) Action research derives from the challenge that teachers should engage in the research of their own practices and the school experiences of their pupils championed by Stenhouse (1975) and developed by Elliott (1980), Fox (1983), Carr and Kemmis (1986), Nixon (1981) and others.

A central implication of proposals for action research is that curriculum research and development, leading to the improvement of schools, ought to belong to the teacher, and to *all* teachers, working individually or cooperatively with colleagues in the education service. It is argued that well-founded curriculum research and development, based on the study of classrooms, rests on the work of teachers and that the study of their work should be undertaken by teachers themselves. A main prop of the argument is that research which treats teachers as objects of study and potential 'recipients' of research wisdom assumes that professional development and the improvement of classroom practice is to be treated independently of teaching activity. Action research offers a radically different view of the study of teaching and learning through the participation of teachers in research processes. Such participation provides a process of teacher education in itself, through the development and application of appropriate methodologies for the study of teaching/learning; knowledge of substantive issues; and the generation of theories of teaching/ learning.

Action Research as a Form of Professional Development

Central to the premises of the research model which Stenhouse (1975, p. 123) explored is the assumption that curriculum decisions and development will take place in individual schools. Curriculum research conducted by teachers would provide the information needed for decision-making, leading to organic, continuous change and improvement in action. It is the relationship between investigation and action which makes the location of both within schools so important, and which provides the shift from other forms of curriculum research and development so thoroughly (and expensively) tested in the 1960s and 1970s.

The distinctions between 'pure' empirical research conducted by professional researchers without necessarily having cause to consider the application of findings; the evaluation of programmes in which curriculum practice/ development is critiqued by observers to inform project developers or those who teach; and practice which is internally researched by those responsible for it were discussed earlier. The research model of curriculum development initially adopted by Stenhouse, involving teachers directly, aspired to incorporate elements of each into 'a more scientific procedure which builds action and criticism into an integrated whole' (Stenhouse, 1975, p. 124). That procedure would need to assume that curriculum policy and practice is problematic, its deficiencies identifiable. The identification of problems and the detailed study of them thus becomes the necessary starting point for improvement, with the curriculum developer cast in the role of investigator/enquirer as well as practitioner. While the concept is based in the empirical tradition of research, it challenges the conventions of curriculum development and evaluation in which policy and practice are prescribed by outsiders and performed by teachers, to be monitored *post hoc* by evaluators who are also outsiders.

This kind of professionalism, incorporating integrated action and research extended to the individual activities of teachers, raised for the *Humanities Curriculum Project* team a number of questions about teacher participation in a unified research approach to curriculum change. Practical questions about the capability of teachers to sustain teaching and researching as complementary activities, and the availability of time for research work were uppermost. The issue of time constraints on even the practice of many of the required activities of teaching, let alone the possible avenues of research deriving from it, has remained the most contentious of these questions. That constraint exists in all teaching situations, but it is often argued that it is especially difficult to find time for reflection and enquiry for teachers of young children in small schools, where preparation and marking time are at a premium, where curriculum 'leadership' time is in short supply, and where dual responsibilities for aspects of school life have to be undertaken by each teacher in the distribution of tasks. The question of constraints is of course impossible to 'answer' in terms which are applicable to all teachers, and many examples now exist to show that teaching and research can be combined to advantage. Such activities certainly require time.

Practicability also depends on questions of the span, form, and methods of research adopted, estimated costs and resources available, and the nature of the problems to be investigated. It was clearly acknowledged that to get a majority of teachers adopting a research stance toward their work would need a generation of effort, not least to change teachers' professional self-image and conditions of work.

The basic image of research-based teaching which Stenhouse conveyed still needs clarification in practice, even though the vision has been realized by a growing number of individuals. In the more recent climate of school self-evaluation and in-school curriculum development, as well as through in-service courses which use a teacher-research approach to learning about classrooms and schools, the adoption of this mode of professional development has continued to grow. In contrast, some aspects of recent DES reports on schools and recommendations about what teachers should do imply that both the content of the curriculum and teaching methods simply need changing as centrally prescribed for all to be well in schools. If only teachers would give less reading and writing, more choice and responsibility (DES, 1983e and 1985b); if only they knew their subjects better (DES, 1984b). The difficulty of this approach is that it faces the same problems as educational research findings: it is external prescription capable of being rejected by practitioners upon whom implementation depends.

Action research assumes that curriculum proposals are to be treated as provisional and worth testing. That concurs with the learning experiences of teachers, operating on a basis of practical knowledge and experience, constantly testing out ideas to be assimilated into a repertoire of practice, changed according to circumstance and rethinking based on further experience. The challenge of action research is to establish a commitment to systematic questioning of teaching and a concern to test theory in practice, with the development of skills to enable enquiry and the implementation of effective practices. The fulfilment of its promise depends upon the conditions for professional development to include opportunity for involvement in curriculum research for the systematic improvement of practice. It also requires from policy-makers, researchers and teachers a recognition of the potential of research-based teaching and the aspiration of teachers to develop professional skills of enquiry which equate with conventional conceptions of professional practice. The first need among teachers themselves is the recognition of curriculum as problematic. Second is the disposition to seek understanding of specific curriculum events. Third is the need to master investigative skills to provide the data and means of analyzing it in testing hypotheses or theories (or in constructing hypotheses and generating theories upon which better-informed practice may be devised). Fourth is the capacity to effectively conduct that practice. These provide the essential characteristics of autonomous professional self-development.

Experience of research-based teaching has already raised some of the issues which need to be considered by those wanting to implement the approach. A major problem with the initial conception of teachers studying their own teaching, apart from that of having time to stand back and observe, think or read, was the question of finding appropriate research techniques. There are problems inherent in all social science research methods used in the study of education, as well as different possibilities to be derived from them. Discussions of the range of methods, their possibilities and problems, are widely available and it is not necessary to rehearse them in detail here (see, for example, Cohen and Manion, 1981; Hopkins, 1985; Walker, 1985a).

It was argued by Stenhouse that the ethnography of classrooms based on the methods of anthropologists held most attraction to research workers engaged in curriculum development, and held out possibilities (as well as problems) for the teacher researcher:

> At the theoretical level the approach is a complex one, methodology is subtle and debatable, generalization and summary are difficult. But the product, the study which emerges and is presented to the reader is vivid and generally speaks very directly to teachers. (Stenhouse, 1975, p. 151)

The exploration of this research model was conducted within the

Humanities Curriculum Project, staffed by full time university researchers concerned to create a curriculum which also advanced knowledge on a particular issue — how to teach about race relations (Stenhouse, 1975). It was possible to establish extensive investigations into the work of teachers and the project team, ranging over forty schools. The sensitivity and complexity of the topic were matched by the adoption of a range of investigation techniques, including measurement of the effects of the programme providing quantified data, and field study of specific situations. For the research programme, methodological techniques were subject to the same investigative stance as the topic itself. It was from this combined concern for action and investigation that the challenge of the unified research model was adopted.

The measurement programme required verification by being translated into hypotheses which teachers could verify in classrooms, and by providing theory about schools as educational contexts which could be checked in other school settings. Case study data complemented the research by considering the variability of schools and classrooms, recognizing that the generalization of curriculum research is restricted by the specificity of teaching situations. The development aspect of the Project included a consideration of teachers as decision makers in the design, control and implementation of the curriculum in race relations. Teacher participation in the action and the research of the curriculum became intrinsic to the work:

> The key to the whole approach is the role of the teacher as a researcher. Not only is the project a study of teachers who are studying themselves: the application of results depends on teachers testing its tentative hypotheses through research in their own situa-tions. A particular kind of professionalism is implied: research-based teaching. (Stenhouse, 1975, p. 141)

It was argued that successful innovation and change would be conditional upon the research being conducted within individual teachers' classrooms/ schools, and that the research roles of teachers and university researchers should be complementary, relating closely to the teachers' teaching role. Within those conditions it was assumed that the research responsibility would be held largely by the teachers, who would define which aspects of their classroom might prove most worthwhile to investigate. Steps were taken towards constructing case study profiles of classrooms based on teachers' views of their teaching and its context. Measurement of the effects of teaching, and case study evaluation by outside researchers combined to provide a triple approach to research, in which a major element was provided by teachers investigating problems defined by them from within their own practice and specific situations.

Since that time much has been added to the educational research com-munity's understanding of ethnographic approaches to the study of schooling, though even now its application to the study of curriculum is limited (Hammersley and Hargreaves, 1983; Hammersley, 1985). Published work is often about teachers rather than by them. Though the methodological issues in self-study by teachers are different from those arising from observer research, the two can be complementary, with advantages of cooperative identification and refining of research problems; combined techniques of data collection; joint analysis and interpretations; and supportive dissemination of work through the example of enhanced professional practice. Observer research and independent teacher research are also closely connected in purpose: to discover what is done in teaching, either one's own or someone else's; to describe how it is done; and most crucially to understand why features of the curriculum are as they are.

Decisions about appropriate methods depend upon the nature of the research question, the kind of data accessible, and the opportunities available to conduct the research. Intellectual questions have to be met by practical opportunity. The potential of ethnography was recognized because of the interest in researching teachers' work and thoughts which grew out of the sociology of education and the curriculum research and development movement. The interest was based on a recognition of teachers as 'situated actors' — creative agents for potential change, but who are not free agents to simply act as they wish. The intention of research was to explain school processes, moving towards changing its less desirable aspects and achieving innovation in a period of change in the curriculum. It was recognized that teachers' perspectives and practices, and their physical, social, political and economic contexts, need to be examined and understood to rectify the lack of study of teaching. In order to describe and explain teachers' organization of pupils' learning, and the context in which this takes place, it is necessary to examine teachers' perspectives and practices in particular social settings. The growth of case-study techniques emerged in response to that need, providing empirical methods which could describe and explain the interpretive process by which teachers act:

> Analysis must recognize human beings ... as persons constructing individual and collective action through an interpretation of the situations which confront them ... which ... means that in order to treat and analyse social action one has to observe the process by which it is constructed. (Blumer, 1962 and 1969)

To be concerned with particular individuals or groups, within particular social locations or with regard to particular types of social action (for example, teaching) Blumer (1969) points out that we must:

> see that action from the position of whoever is forming the action. ... should trace the formation of the action in the way it is actually formed. This means seeing the situation as it is actually seen by the actor, observing what the actor takes into account, noting the alternative kinds of acts that are mapped out in advance, and seeking to follow the interpretation that led to the selection and execution of one of these prefigured acts.

The methods available to achieve this include observation, participant observation, unstructured interview, reflective dialogue and written account. At various times these might include the use of field notes, audio-tape, video-tape or photographic record, and documentary evidence in the collection of data. The ethnographic approach of the outsider-researcher is but a step removed from the idea of teacher-initiated classroom analysis, reflection, and self-analysis. The essential difference is that in seeking to explore teaching acts by these means, the purpose of the teacher within a unified action-research mode would be to reflect upon and enhance ones own practice. The approach serves an essentially practical need and provides professional self-development.

A Knowledge of Teaching

The notion of teachers studying themselves derives from the 'interpretive' view of knowledge, which seeks to understand the world from the perspectives of individuals. It assumes that knowledge is constructed actively and subjectively by the individual, and used in accordance with interpretations of problems or situations by the individual. A personally located view of the world and of ways of seeing and understanding is based on different assumptions from the 'empiric-analytic' form of knowledge, in which regular patterns of events are sought which might lead to laws or predictive theories, which could then be learned and applied. That positivist view is encased in the more dominant traditions of research to which social science and educational research are mostly attached. A 'critical' tradition stemming from the development of grand theories which aspire to explain social phenomena, and which adopt explicit value positions in their judgmental demands for change, is also discernible in the assumptions adopted by some educational researchers and commentators. The critical analysis of education as an institution of the wider society has sought to stand back from practice, to theorize, explain, and potentially to change practice by changing the consciousness of teachers.

These three approaches to understanding teaching — the interpretive, the empiric/analytical, and the critical — derive from fundamentally different perspectives on the way knowledge is constructed, held, and used. In teacher-research an emphasis on the acquisition and use of 'personally held' knowledge as a means of changing assumptions held by individual teachers, and hence changing their practice, is accompanied by a 'grounded' attempt to understand more generally what teachers do in order to derive theories of teaching from its common features. This approach to the study of schooling processes and the achievement of change in them has been criticized by those who take a 'critical' view of the social and economic structures in which teaching occurs, who argue the need to understand and change structures rather than individual action. (CCCS, 1981; Sharp and Green, 1975). However, action research offers a form of professional development within a conception of teacher education curriculum as a learning process capable of empowering individual action and contributing to the dialogue of dialectical change.

Recognizing the importance and inescapable fact of teachers' subjective perceptions as crucial in the control of classroom practice, Stenhouse accepted the need to develop a 'sensitive and self-critical subjective perspective (through which) illusion, assumption and habit must be continually tested' (Stenhouse, 1975, p. 157). The place of theory is explicitly contained within the world of the teacher conducting that testing, rather than generalizing beyond it. Theory is a matter of the systematic structuring of the teacher's understanding of his/her work:

> Concepts which are carefully related to one another are needed both to capture and to express that understanding. The adequacy of such concepts should be treated as provisional. The utility and appropriateness of the theoretical framework of concepts should be testable; and the theory should be rich enough to throw up new and profitable questions. (*Ibid*, p. 157)

By such means, and through a network of teachers who would share in the task of generating a common language of theory, producing accumulated case-records out of which general theories might emerge, it was assumed that generalizable systematic structuring of our understanding of teaching would be possible. In the proposition of research based teaching the generation of curriculum theory would thus arise from practice and its analysis on two levels: independent structuring of understanding by individual teachers; and the collective view which would need to be coordinated to serve the educational community. Together these would constitute an educational community involvement in what Glaser and Straus (1967) termed 'grounded theory'. The task first is the development of conditions to extend the practice of research based teaching through the recognition of its potential for professional development and the improvement of practice. That would be followed by the development of dispositions, field-work skills, and analytical approaches which teachers would be capable of sustaining, developing and incorporating into normal professional practice.

Resolving Some Problems in Teacher Education and Curriculum Reform

Recent policy implies that the solutions to perceived problems in the quality of education in schools and teacher education lie in the central prescription of content and teaching methods, with 'effective' monitoring of 'efficiency' and 'standards' within reduced budgets. Opportunities to research the problems and effect informed solutions are correspondingly curtailed. Paradoxically teachers are required to move further in the direction of teacher professionalism with responsibility for self-evaluation in schools and self-appraisal of practice. This requirement is to be met from a position of inexperience in conducting such activities. Bureaucratic management control and the asser- tions of 'consensus' curriculum in which teachers operate merely as competent technicians ignore the vision and the potentials of research-based teaching as a form of professional development for individual teachers and cooperating school staffs. Research-based teaching provides a means of meeting current demands and extending well beyond those requirements through a creative, intelligent role for teachers. In assuming that teachers are not mere objects of study for the benefit of researchers nor mere technicians engaged in working other people's proposed solutions, it is clear that teaching needs to be studied and understood from the point of view of the teacher responding creatively to situations. Teachers need to be seen as active participants in complex activities which they want to understand and improve. It needs to be recognized that they are engaged in constructing knowledge of the curriculum.

The conditions needed to enable observation, reflection and analysis by teachers are different from those needed by researchers. The motives and purposes overlap with distinctions between research as a contribution of public knowledge, and enquiry as an avenue of individual professional development becoming blurred. Professionalism incorporating integrated, unified action and criticism provides a means of improving the practical knowledge which is the concern of teachers. It also offers the opportunity to improve the map of understanding of teaching/learning processes. The desire to develop practical knowledge based on understanding arises from the perspective of the teacher in a specific situation, concerned to find solutions to problems for the benefit of pupils' learning. Practical, experiential knowledge gained through the formulation and testing of hypotheses in classrooms lies at the heart of research-based teaching. It proffers the means of learning teaching. That can be distinct from the act of teaching, (i.e. performance based on the acquisition of learning) and from learning about teaching. Action research seeks an integration of all three: learning teaching, teaching, and learning about teaching.

In these ways several problematic aspects of professional development, curriculum development and educational research can be solved. The nature of learning, teaching, and school contexts, and the relationships between them, would be better understood in order that all three might be improved. The theory-practice relationship in the education of teachers would be clarified. The relationship between short-term certification and long-term professional development would be unified by the learning dispositions and skills which accrue from research-based teaching. An action research approach also seeks to understand the learning of teachers, to develop the learning capabilities needed for bringing competence to the realm of excellence within a spirit of change and improvement in schools, and to understand improved practice which results from those capabilities.

Provision of appropriate conditions for the conduct of such professionalism is of paramount concern. The general lack of support for those who might want to conduct systematic questioning and improvement of their teaching has already been discussed. The best way forward may well be within funded research and development projects in which full-time researchers provide support for the advance of research-based teaching. Profit from the work of an observer and consultant would be gained that way through the learning and improvement of research techniques. Such opportunities have all but dried up along with the funding of educational projects. The *Teaching, Handling Information and Learning* (THIL) project funded by the British Library from 1983–1986 at the University of East Anglia is building on the action research experiences of a group of teachers from first, middle and secondary schools, further education and teacher education, developing self-examination of aspects of their teaching and their pupils learning within the theme of information handling (Sanger, 1986). The recently completed *Teacher-Pupil Interaction and the Quality of Learning* project has also pursued the development of practice through enquiry into the quality of pupils' learning experiences (Ebbutt and Elliott, 1985).

While opportunities through funded projects have decreased, and in any case may only be available to teachers within reach of universities, there has been a steady growth in the use of research-based teaching approaches within taught courses, in the development of school-based in-service education, and in self-evaluation of schools. No doubt developments in teacher appraisal will lead to further interest as teachers respond to demands to examine their individual practice by taking initiatives which demonstrate their professionalism. Whatever the impetus for developing a disposition for critical self-analysis there are now numerous reported examples which show how widespread that disposition is (see, for example, Hustler *et al*, 1986; Nixon, 1981; Rowland, 1984). There are many more which remain in the records of individual schools, and in the files of individual teachers who have attended courses or kept log books of their own teaching. And there is growing recognition in the academic community of the value and need for such work. Recently, Professor Wragg, Director of the *Teacher Education Project*, was quoted as saying:

> I think one of the most important things for the remaining part of this century is for teachers to do research and inquire into their own classrooms and pupils. They shouldn't become library bound but there should be more systematic scrutiny of what happens in the classroom. (*Times Educational Supplement*, 'Professor Primary', 14 June 1985)

The opportunity for widespread implementation of research-based teaching among a large group of professional scrutineers exists in provision for INSET, with priority being given within educational funding to support for serving teachers' professional development. The extension of that opportunity to future generations of teachers can be achieved by the preparation of student teachers for this wider professionalism through research-based initial teacher education. The potential for INSET and initial teacher education to combine, and the influence of experienced teachers and student teachers working together in this mode of enquiry are considerable. Where this combination can work within a conception of partnership in which teacher educators also adopt a research view of their practice, confirming the model of systematic enquiry for the improvement of practice, partnership can capture the potentials of professional impetus. That would lead to further clarification of the place and practice of research in teaching and in in-service and initial teacher education.

The means of shifting from competence to excellence in teaching, for both student teachers and practising teachers, are available. Their promise can be realized if an authentic partnership for professionalism is founded.

Principles for Partnership in Learning Teaching

To take seriously this view of research as a basis for professional development means that teacher-educators need to adopt the action-research stance towards their own teaching, and a stance towards research in that teaching. Research-based teaching asks teachers to share with pupils and students 'the process of learning the wisdom which we do not possess so that they can get into critical perspective the learning which we trust is ours' (Stenhouse, 1979). It is argued by Stenhouse that knowledge taught in universities, which is won through research, cannot be taught correctly except through research-based teaching. An understanding of the research process is crucial to the transmission of knowledge, which is 'questionable, verifiable and differentially secure' (*Ibid*, p. 5).

To present knowledge as otherwise — i.e. as established authoritative results of research — is seen as error. What is more, that error is seen as widespread, and in danger of remaining so if teachers are educated in such a way that they will transmit it to their pupils. Further, 'taught knowledge' is seen as qualitatively different from, and inferior to, knowledge gained through research, and transmitted through a sharing of the research process. The former assumes that research belongs to researchers, to be conveyed as 'results' which might be learned and, in the case of knowledge concerned with professional practice, applied in the workplace. Enquiry-based knowledge is a matter of experiencing the learning process. Central to the process is the view that the aim of teaching is to offer opportunities and provide facilities for learning and understanding; that the learner is active; and that the teacher's responsibility of enabling the development of understanding by establishing appropriate conditions of learning must be matched by student responsibilities for the pursuit of their own understanding.

None of these claims devalues the findings of 'others' in a research-practice community. Research 'literature' on substantive, methodological, and theoretical issues would not only remain as a resource for informing practice, but would become more accessible to students, teachers and teacher educators by being grounded in educational experience and practice. The claims do question the assumption of the conventional research-practice relationship in education, and ask that that relationship be reconstituted through educational process, defining all members of the educational community, regardless of formal status, as enquirers-in-partnership into the substance, methods and theory of educational practice. The assumption is that the application of understanding through process will lead to long-term professional self-development, the improvement of practice, and the propensity for change, within an enquiring and professionally committed community.

Research-based teacher education assumes coming generations of student teachers and the regeneration of practising teachers and teacher educators created in forms which subsume competence in teaching within more intellectually rigorous, critical enquiry modes of professional self-development. This requires fundamental shifts in attitude towards teacher education, involving changes in structure and procedures within courses. It means in particular reconceptualizing the nature and the place of practice and research in the education of teachers. While it has been pursued in the in-service education of teachers to some effect the ways in which an action research stance towards learning teaching might contribute to the conceptualization and practice of research-based *initial* teacher education, and the kinds of teachers which that might produce, is yet to be fully explored.

Research-based initial teacher education assumes that from the start of a professional career student-teachers should, together with their tutors and practising teachers, be committed to the ideals of a unified research model. Constructing initial competence to a point which is minimally accepted as 'good' will occur by formulating and testing hypotheses through the conduct of the necessary performance skills, monitoring, reflecting upon and analyzing practice (either one's own or that of others), and placing the analysis within wider theoretical understanding of classrooms and schools. When teaching is deemed to be competent at least in some of its facets space will be found for learning other skills to a point where the range/repertoire of classroom skills becomes extensive. Those skills will be based on insight and understanding gained through the complementary use of enquiry. The critical assumption is that teaching, investigating teaching and understanding teaching are inextricably linked (Fox, 1983) and that therefore *learning* teaching must incorporate all three. Technical classroom competence would not only be subsumed within understanding, it would be considerably enhanced by it.

This form of initial teacher education would equip practising teachers with the skills and attitudes needed for research-based teaching. Research agendas would be set by the teachers, students, and teacher educators to develop both practical and research competences around substantive classroom concerns. Research-based initial teacher education would go further in asserting that classroom practice by student teachers should be the subject of self-reflection and analysis or collaborative enquiry. It would include the premise that the curriculum and pedagogy experienced by student teachers should be subject to staff and student enquiry/research. It would also require that classroom practice should be learned by student teachers within a commitment to research their own work by practising teachers and tutors. Those principles have been the foundation of the undergraduate teacher education programme at the University of East Anglia since its foundation in 1981.

In summary, then, research-based teacher education seeks commitment to the construction of competent teaching and the reconstruction of competent teaching towards teaching excellence by involving students, teachers, and teacher educators in systematic questioning, with the development of enquiry skills, and a concern to generate questions and test theory in practice through that enquiry. This commitment provides the essential characteristics of professional self-development and educative experience based upon a recognition of curriculum and pedagogy as problematic. It means developing dispositions to seek understanding of specific curricula or pedagogical phenomena or events. And it requires the mastery of investigative skills which would provide the data on teaching and learning, and the means of analyzing and interpreting it. The construction of hypotheses and the generation and testing of theories upon which better-informed practice may be devised and shared in the educational community would be an essential part of the enterprise. To achieve this in partnership means recognizing and reconciling the disparate overt interests of and demands upon students, teachers, and tutors/researchers in order to achieve dialogue in a framework of shared interest. That means establishing relationships between schools and teacher education institutions which will enable student learning of initial classroom competence and the means to transform it to professional excellence; curriculum development and in-service education through research experience for teachers; and research opportunities for teacher-educators working consultatively with teachers and student teachers. The franchise on such opportunities will not be granted readily to student teachers and teachers. They are practically difficult for teacher educators. But the franchise will need to be worked for and acquired in some measure, and supported by resources if informed critical appraisal of teaching, set within wider educational, structural, and cultural contexts, is to prove meaningful.

Part Three

The Practice of Teaching in a Learning Context

Practical Knowledge: The Key to Professional Credibility

Teachers hold the pivotal position in the partnership between research, classroom practice, and the induction of student teachers, and thus in the improvement of schooling. The identification, acquisition, and further improvement of teaching competence is the heart of the professional enterprise. That heart belongs to teachers more than to researchers or teacher-educators. The practice of those skills/competences is the key to professional self-respect and credibility among the many clients and sponsors in the educational enterprise. Such competence is the necessary basic characteristic of being professional. The value of practical knowledge as competence, and beyond competence to professional excellence, needs to be faced by researchers and teacher educators, in a way which so far it has not been, if a meaningful partnership based on mutual respect and understanding is to be achieved. The complexity of practical knowledge, which grows as experience increases, and which is used to shape and direct the work of teaching through decision-making and action, has been largely disregarded in the study of education. Its low status in the academic world, where professional credentials are controlled, has resulted in a dearth of interest in developing a body of practical knowledge. There is a profound difficulty among teachers in articulating their experience beyond the intuitive, which may result in part from that disregard, from the low status of practice, from the conditions in which teaching occurs, and from the nature of practical knowledge itself:

> It is hardly surprising that teachers have developed no such articulated body of knowledge, if we consider the context of teaching. To begin with, teachers are trained in a setting which is rarely seen by them as serious or relevant to their future work; thus, whatever conceptual skills they might acquire during their training would tend to be compartmentalized, rather than applied to the understanding of teaching. In teaching itself, while teachers may often rehash and

compare experiences, they in fact have little experience that is shared, and there are few opportunities for them to reflect on and attempt to articulate their experience in an organized way. Finally, the view of knowledge as 'empirical' and 'analytic' which prevails in educational thought tends to place a relatively low value on experiential knowledge, and thus teachers themselves may be unaware of the value of their own knowledge. Certainly there is little encouragement for teachers to view themselves as originators of knowledge. (Elbaz, 1983, p. 11)

To provide recognition of 'everyday' practical, experiential understanding, to learn how it constructed and how it is reflected in practice, requires a shift in the values placed on the kind of knowledge which is admissible in the educational community. That means accepting as legitimate ways of knowing which are different from the empirical/analytical, more akin to artistic knowledge than scientific. In that alternative, experience offers modes of understanding and processes for coming to understand teaching and learning which incorporate individual, emotional and expressive responses, as well as technical proficiency. Teaching is accepted as a non-clinical act; understanding it is subject to non-clinical study. Both teaching and the study of teaching involve intuitive wisdom, uncertainty and ambiguity, and require high levels of intellectual activity. Such a view would incorporate technical proficiency and personal response within a knowledge of the institutional, social and cultural contexts in which teaching takes place. A major obstacle to overcoming the theory-practice gap would be to ignore those contexts which hold such a powerful influence over the work of teachers, and which consistently form the focus of attention when propositions for improving teaching are presented to teachers. But the reconceptualization of experiential understanding needs to begin at the point of initial teacher education, in both formal course structures and the kind of treatment given to practical experience (Alexander, 1984a). Formal structures need to facilitate opportunities to gain that experience in substantial amounts, demonstrating the value placed on it, and to encourage its treatment by students, teachers, tutors and researchers as a legitimate, admissible and valuable focus of investigation. For successful partnership that is required too for practising teachers and teacher educators who have an experience base to work from, but who need the opportunity and inclination such that they would treat practice as problematic and contemplate it through self-study and collaborative research.

Practical teaching can be seen as the spinal chord in this reconceptualization, with introspection, analysis, and change in practice operating at various levels within the professional responsibilities of those engaged in partnership. For the student teacher embarking on the initial endeavours of classroom practice, the nature of the learning experience is concerned with gaining and proving practical competence in a range of skilled activities. The quality of such practice incorporates and depends upon technical competences which can be disentangled into constitutive elements of instructional skills, the mastery and use of which are central to good teaching. The development of personal qualities and professional commitments is also a constituent part, which proves much more problematic to disentangle. Gaining knowledge of subject matter and the development of skills in its use are also critical features of the early stages of teaching (and later change) as students are required to fit themselves into teaching syllabus contents with which they may not be familiar. Understanding the characteristics of children's learning processes is another part of the range of practical knowledge which underpins the development and operation of instructional strategies.

Given this complexity of the content of practical knowledge for teaching and the fact that in the act of teaching these many factors are brought together, orchestrated by the teacher in holistic acts, it is not surprising that student teachers should find a sense of challenge in learning teaching. Much of that learning and all of its orchestration is achieved by doing — i.e. through practical activities in the classroom, conducted independently within the guidance of teachers and supervising tutors. Such is the nature of learning any practical skill. Understanding the nature of the practical knowledge of teaching is important to our appreciation of the way it is acquired and improved. Elliott (1978) considered the nature of teaching as practical knowledge, and its relationship to theoretical knowledge:

> Polanyi (1958) and Oakeshott (1962) have both convincingly argued that 'knowing how' to engage intelligently in an activity does not depend on a knowledge of propositions about that activity ... we have all recognized those 'good intuitive teachers' who could not tell us 'how to do it' ... even if they tried, they wouldn't be able to specify their concrete knowledge of how to teach, completely in words. Oakeshott argues that this irreducible and unspecifiable practical knowledge springs from being on the inside of a tradition, or what he calls the 'idiom' of the activity. From this position the initiator's acts spring from his unspecifiable sense of 'the coherence' of the concrete activity he is engaged in. His practical knowledge can never spring directly out of a knowledge of propositions about the activity. In fact the reverse is the case. Propositions about the activity are 'abridgements' of the practitioner's practical knowledge, and are therefore only fully comprehended in the analysis of the activity. They cannot be grasped *a priori* merely by studying 'literatures'. Theoretical understanding springs from the analysis of the activity. (Elliott, 1978, p. 4)

The recognition of this relationship for partnership in teacher education is profound. In current practice, student teachers who expect propositional rules for teaching in their education courses are deeply disappointed. Teachers are critical that *their* training barely equipped them for the practical 'realities' of classrooms. Teacher educators and researchers pursue the academic respectability of the realms of theorizing. But where does this view of practical knowledge leave the student teacher, whose problem is in its acquisition? It goes some way to explaining the adoption of conventional practices of 'sitting with Nelly' and master-apprenticeship approaches to teacher training. Those approaches, I have argued, are not sufficient for the development of teaching excellence, though they may, through a process like osmosis, lead to some learning of classroom competence in its basic forms. The view of practical knowledge as stemming from coherent action also goes some way to displacing faith in microteaching and simulation as a means of practice teaching in non-classroom contexts. Further, it makes observation and analysis of teachers' practices — often a student's first encounter with teaching — of questionable value. These means of learning teaching, which are conventionally used in pre-service courses, do not take sufficient account of the nature of the practical knowledge to be gained and do not provide the best means of gaining and proving it. So where does the student teacher begin, and how does he/she get within the 'idiom' of the tradition? According to Elliott, the view of practical knowledge above means that skilled performance can only become possible by 'looking from' rather than 'at' the constitutive elements of teaching, to produce an integrated and meaningful activity. Analytical breakdown of the activity into its various parts by way of theorizing cannot in the first instance help in the learning and practice of the whole activity of teaching. The elements of practical knowledge are orchestrated in practical performance in ways which are not readily susceptible to analytical, rule-driven activity. The constituent parts need to be gained, then, by a process of accretion. For student teachers that process has considerable impact when it happens from 'within'.

The acquisition of teaching skills — the everyday, taken-for-granted practical knowledge of the teacher — is high on the students' learning agenda at this stage. Negotiation of the opportunities to acquire such skills is a key factor. For the student that acquisition has to be real, not simulated. And the trauma of learning can be offset by elation, even over matters which may appear banal or mundane to the experienced teacher. The initiation of beginning students into taking registers, receiving messages from pupils, doing marking and conducting routine classroom maintenance — i.e. becoming 'real teachers' — is very significant, recently described to me by a group of students as 'brilliant' and 'a way of looking into the secrets of the trade'.

> The novelty/opportunity of doing marking and other things which teachers clearly do not find novel or rewarding were rated as highly important initiation rites, much valued by students ... Doing such things also helped students to observe, it was assumed, on the basis of *participant* observation. The problems of purposeless observation were reiterated, and benefits of immediate action in teaching again raised. (field notes from discussion between students and teachers, February 1985)

The secrets of the trade are an important first step in the direction of acquiring practical knowledge, as the discussion below indicates. This is a first-year undergraduate student, after a few weeks of her course during which one day each week has been spent in school:

Student: I've reached the stage where I do consciously take the class when they arrive. I do register them, and give the messages, and everything that might have to be done. And I suppose I'm running the class for the first half-hour.

Teacher: I think that's interesting, the way they look to you when they come in on a Tuesday morning. They tend to go to — instead of come to me, although I'm around. And so do other children in the school when they come for things. Obviously its part of sitting at the teacher's desk. We've got two desks in the classroom, but the one where I'd normally be. You get that kind of acceptance which is very valuable, and I think is necessary.

Student: From my point of view, and from the class's point of view I'm not so much a visitor now. I'm someone that belongs to them, doing the basic things rather than just the special things, that was what worried me from the start. I don't want to be seen as someone that just came in and did different things, because I don't think it gives me the right view of teaching and it doesn't give them the right view of me either. I think they still do have that view a bit, I think that's inevitable because I'm not here all the time. But I think I've got my feet under the table. (taped discussion, February 1985)

The adoption of responsibilities for teaching at an early stage in a teacher education programme, and the setting of expectations and guidance for the conduct of those responsibilities, offers the prospect of early acquisition of basic professional competence. Paradoxically, the process of accretion of experience can only be achieved with some analysis and selectivity in the guidance, learning, and performance of teaching skills. It is unrealistic to suppose that students should perform widespread unified acts of teaching from the beginning, or learn to handle every skill with uniform confidence at the same time. Conventional teaching practice is conducted often within a context and with a range of problems such as those identified by Yates (1982) and HMI (1982c) discussed earlier. The potential of practice for the development of competence remains unrealized for many students and new teachers, the relationship between action and analysis limited to the 'dialogue' between students and teachers or tutors, often in the form of post-hoc tutorial comment such as in the examples below:

Date	Time Seen	Class/Group	Age	Activity
26.5.83	**From** 11.00 **To** 11.50	3rd year	10	English

Comments

This was a well planned, well prepared lesson. Your intentions were clear, specific for this lesson within a sequence of lessons, and the expectations were conveyed to the pupils. Resources were well organized. Your relationship with the pupils is firm yet allows an active working atmosphere. (Perhaps you can relax your sharp reprimands now and achieve control in a more gentle way). The use of praise for good work was apparent and your concern to foster that praise-giving is positive. There are various ways to achieve it, and perhaps you should beware over-selective use of it for just *some* pupils i.e. the *lack* of a positive message has its effects also. How you balance this is critical to motivation.

Classroom manner is authoritative and affords clear instruction and comment to the pupils. Your directives are well-defined and pupils responded well. The major point to consider is: how can you analyze what the children were learning, and how can you conclude the lesson so that the pupils see the point of it (in learning terms) and see where they will 'go to' next. The central purpose of the lesson needs to be explicit and can be made so at appropriate points — for example, when using examples of good work you might ask 'what is good?' or in ending a lesson you might consider more than just organizational procedures.

Date	Time Seen	Class/Group	Age	Activity
7th June 1983	9.00–9.45 discussion **From** 11.00 **To** 11.45	Year 2	9–10 years	Science

Comments

Four weeks ago you expressed some surprise at the suggestion that 'whole-class' instruction was not the *only* way to teach! Today you have planned, prepared for, and implemented a very complex lesson of practical group work for a class of twenty-nine individuals. They responded exceptionally well to your teaching. The strengths on which to build include:

1 Your manner with the class — authoritative, but directed to *learning*, with a sense of excitement, of mystery even, of problems to be solved and experiences to be encountered. This was supported by clear organizational intentions.
2 Your preparation and distribution of resources — which was thorough, complicated, and extremely well managed, so that you could be involved in the learning and active as learner *with* the pupils.

3   The group organization — with four different activities which encouraged cooperation between pupils, involved them in discussion and required elements of social learning as well as scientific!

4   The content — which was 'active' and involved the pupils in learning processes. It is the sophistication of engaging pupils in their *own* learning processes towards which you could strive. Your *understanding* of what went on in this lesson can now be developed.

5   The learning atmosphere. Despite the complexities, the opportunities for pupil misbehaviour, and the possibility of such lessons 'going wrong', there were *no* problems. Ask yourself why? Not once did you have to be authoritarian. Pupils moved freely, had reasonable control over decisions and actions, and had the opportunity to develop responsibility.

6   Your instructions and demonstrations — a real problem in relating these to different groups. You managed this in a way which kept all pupils interested in what the lesson was about, as well as being specific about what each group would do.

7   The conclusion of the lesson, drawing together the 'results' was sufficient to bring the activities together. This could be developed to involve pupils in analysing their work — relating the processes of 'science' to their activity.

In all, this lesson demonstrates a considerable development on your earlier sound start. You will — and should — adjust the fine detail as you feel necessary. The overall impression is extremely encouraging. Your task now is to reinforce such good practice and move forward to sophisticated evaluation of learning and teaching.

This characteristic approach within short bursts of teaching practice is inadequate for a conception of research-based initial teacher education, barely representing dialogue. Dialogue needs systematic support, within partnership, in ways which enable students' learning to be actively pursued by them. That also means enabling initiative and responsibility to be adopted for increasingly complex commitments in teaching, and in reflection upon teaching. Theoretical research-based initial teacher education is one thing; its practice is another. In this section I will show what its practice begins to look like, and how it works, using examples of reflective thinking, enquiry and analysis as characteristics of student dispositions in the acquisition of teaching competence and the development of technical proficiency. The data which follow demonstrate the possibilities for dialogue and partnership for learning in the very early stages of students' teaching encounters — their first contact with classrooms as student teachers. The experiences and issues are common in learning teaching, illustrating the ways in which student agendas are focussed upon a range of complex matters in their own active pursuit of learning. That learning I have broadly analyzed to illustrate the ways students:

adjust to the professional expectations of becoming a teacher;
come to know the context of school, community and society;
master subject knowledge within the demands of teaching;
acquire instructional strategies and classroom management skills;
develop professional attitudes and responsibilities.

The treatment of the issues and the acquisition of the capacity to learn independently are my immediate concern across all of these. It is experience, reflective and investigative capabilities, and professional wisdom gained within a spirit of flexibility and enquiry which provide a basis of the culture of the educated and educative community. It is that culture which allows the dimension of change through critical enquiry, for individual teachers and for schools. The foundations can be laid at the very beginning of initial teacher education:

Adjusting to Institutional and Professional Expectations

Adjusting oneself to the institutional and professional expectations of teaching confronts every student teacher in the initial encounters of school experience. It is a major negotiating stage for learning practical knowledge of other kinds, as well as for determining one's whole orientation toward teaching. Professional support from headteachers, teachers, and tutors may be abundant but the immediate and traumatic experience cannot be easily mediated. The 'secrets of the trade' can present themselves rather more as mysteries among the 'hidden' curriculum of learning how to conform, as this group of students show:

> H introduces for discussion that the values of the hidden curriculum which teachers/students convey in the classroom will affect pupils future lives; 'do we think about them or are they so inherent in our values ... are we quashing the individual to fit into the system.
>
> 'S' relates this to his experience; he is fitting in to what he thinks the school wants. 'They're very aware that we're students'.
>
> H: What do we do then, do we walk in and fit in or do we strike a balance between ...
> L: I don't want to (fit in). As a student I'm prepared to fit in to a certain extent but if I go into teaching and people keep on telling me that I've got to do what they want me to do and not what I think is right, well in the end I'll end up giving up teaching.
> H: How much freedom have we got? The content is decided for us, the method is.
> S: The content of our course?
> H: Of what we teach.
> L: It depends on the individual school and how neatly packaged the

curriculum is. I would say your freedom's limited but it's limited in life anyway. You've got a fair amount of freedom ... two teachers might operate on the same timetable and work out different relationships with the children.

Though the discussion shifts to curriculum content and method, the concerns initially are less specific. They are about personhood: about how to relate to children, how to conduct oneself in staffrooms, how to dress, how to cope with staff conflicts, and so on. The discussion of curriculum provides an *example* of a concern which is a fundamental and long-standing matter of contention in education, one which goes much wider than individual students' adjustments.

The students discussed at length a series of major dilemmas faced by teachers. Conformity to the prescription of curriculum content and the administrative and bureaucratic institutional controls, against freedom with professional responsibility for making decisions and exercising initiative, with a view to being in control and creating change, recurred. At the heart of the concerns is the motivation and learning of the children, as well as the teacher. 'Being oneself' in direct interaction with pupils while being compromised by institutional requirements is seen as a key factor in the dilemmas of teaching:

> H: You've still got to be sincere haven't you? They'll see through it if you're putting on a false face. If it would be insincere you've got to try to make lessons of interest in a genuine way to yourself or otherwise some things you could never present to them, and it would be wrong to present them in a way that was down in the mouth and saying 'well we've got to do this this morning, I really hate doing this lesson but we've got to cover it'. That's what turns children off straight away isn't it. I'm sure that everything we do have to cover if we put enough effort into it we'll find some method that appeals to them.
>
> L: Actually I might actually say to kids God I hate this subject but I think I've found a way to make the best of it. I mean I would try to make the best of it but I might admit to them ...
>
> H: You wouldn't say it as strongly as that, you'd say it more mildly ...
>
> L: Oh sure.

At this very early stage it is possible to see the emergence of reconciliation between a desired, active avenue of professional development and recognition of the passive technician role of teaching in which the teacher is the instrument of other people's decisions. Unquestioning conformity, potentially leading to dull curriculum experiences for children and teachers alike creates deep concern. Professional responsibility in which teachers maintain high levels of motivation and commitment is already an assumed characteristic of these students. It is a characteristic which cannot be fostered by mere conformity to existing practice, by learning through apprenticeship. It requires that the issues of curriculum and schooling context in which these students are immersed should be open in professional dialogue.

Knowing the Context of the School

Knowing the milieu within a school, identifying its underlying philosophies and organizational patterns, or recognizing inconsistencies and contradictions within them, presents a further learning challenge to students. Adjusting to institutional ethos, by fitting in or negotiating a place within it, depends on that knowledge, which can be elusive and slippery. Of course there may not be a sense of ethos within a particular year group, department, or school, in which case affiliations and associations with ideas may need to be negotiated with individual teachers. If one recognizes that in any case the articulation of ideas and of practical knowledge is relatively undeveloped in professional practice, and that adjustments have to be negotiated within the severe time constraints of student and teacher contact, it might be anticipated that this aspect of student learning may present itself as a daunting experience for individuals. Making sense of a curriculum in its total complexity for the group of students below presents different problems for each of them, even though 'J' and 'A' are attached to the same school.

J: So you've actually got a structured timetable.

M: Yep.

J: Our school says it (the timetable) is too flexible, they won't give us a structured timetable. We walk in every day and we don't know what we're doing.

A: They just do varied things every day when the teacher feels he wants to do them.

M: So presumably you are working on that basis yourself, or are you going to?

A: Well, no, we'll have to be more structured than that because ...

J: My teacher won't have that, my teacher just will not have it.

The other teacher, though, agreed to a fixed timetable for the student in which 'set subjects' will be presented to the children.

A: I think what will happen ...

J: I've got lessons prepared, and I'm just going to have to go in ...

A: We're just going to have to have set days prepared, and go in and do set subjects, otherwise how will our supervisor know when we're doing what?

J: I just can't get that at all. I can't.

Observer: Does it worry you?

J: It does because you go in ... we've both gone in before now and we've both been really panicking because you haven't got a clue what you're going to do. Then you can go in and you can plan, but you'll be really just a loose end, on the end of the school, there's just no need for you to be there. O.K. you're an imposition most of the time anyway, but when you go in on a day when they don't . . . I mean, I went in last week and O.K. the teacher's really nice to me and will offer anything I want, and I went in all morning because we have to go in a whole day and she just did not need me before break. So I came back to the University.

The question of negotiating a way into teaching as students entering the teachers' domain, making sense of oneself in relation to new responsibilities in a world which is strange to these recent pupils, illustrates the problem of the person in confrontation with school milieu as a part of the complex prospect of learning how to teach. In this instance, for 'J' the selection, adoption and conduct of specific teaching responsibilities had not happened. Learning from within was not possible until access had been negotiated, to enable the student to make decisions, to engage in dialogue and implement elements of practice which could further that dialogue. Even so, the experiences provide the basis for extensive dialogue and understanding about the dilemmas of the student teacher and of teaching, and the starting point for investigating teachers' perspectives and variations in curriculum management and teaching method. The problems are raised by the students' practical experience. The way in which that experience is treated, drawing out possibilities for investigation, initiating enquiry and analyzing observation data with appropriate reference to literature could establish understanding on the basis of practice in learning teaching. It would also potentially lead to solutions to the practical problems of negotiation and dialogue within the profession as students acquire under-standing and enquiry techniques, enabling informed critique of future encoun-ters.

Acquiring Subject Knowledge Within the Demands of Teaching

Recent suppositions in statements of official policy have asserted the need for the better acquisition of subject knowledge by student teachers. The premise on which this policy is based is that teachers need to hold, at a high academic level, mastery of particular knowledge content. That knowledge content is to equate with the prescribed content of the curriculum of schools. The demands that first degree subjects and 'main' subjects within concurrent teacher education courses should be carefully matched to the schools' curriculum illustrates the manifestation of these suppositions. Prescription of a minimum of two years devoted to the study of the main subject, a central criterion for the approval of courses by CATE, is further evidence. The problems with these suppositions and prescriptions are manifold, not least in relation to the primary school curriculum. The problem is not in the aspiration that teachers should be expert in an area of knowledge. That clearly is a laudable aim. If it is assumed that an area of expertise will be constantly up-dated, that too is not in contention. The difficulty is in the assumption that the particular expertise of individual teachers, gained through academic routes which culminate in higher education, will match the needs of pupils at various stages and 'levels' of learning. It is compounded by the view of knowledge as 'held' by the teacher in advance, to be transmitted presumably by didactic means to the pupils, whose role is passive.

The challenge which student teachers face is of course much more problematic and complex than that. Subject knowledge and its acquisition within the demands of teaching and in direct relation to the curriculum experiences of pupils, presents an active stimulus for students' learning. It is part of the acquisition of practical knowledge, particularly for those intending to teach in the primary or middle years where knowledge of a range of subjects is expected in teaching. That acquisition is required, and occurs, concurrently with the learning of other elements involved in teaching:

> D: The main issue that bothers me is the teaching of subjects in which I'm not reasonably expert — talking about music for example, my class teacher is a music teacher.
> P: And you've got to teach it.
> D: The way the timetable works out there are a lot of things on one day which are not my strong points, so its a question of taking music not as the least ... worst option ... but em ... tossing a coin and deciding which one of those I missed out on as preparation time during the day. So music — as I say, the music, that's bothering me, how I'm going to present music to the kids, especially bearing in mind that the class teacher is an expert.
> T: Have you been given any guidelines?

The substance of this concern is not restricted to students wrestling with the unfamiliar elements of a broad primary school curriculum. It is also the concern of, say, the secondary school historian whose particular specialist period is not included in the teaching timetable, or the artist whose painting expertise does not meet the needs of teaching ceramics. Thus in the case above music is only one of the 'subjects in which I am not reasonably expert'. Every student and most teachers at some point face that problem, particularly with the introduction of innovations such as microcomputers, or craft/design/technology. The curricular issues it raises, about whether knowledge is fixed and pre-digested, for regurgitation to students and eventually to pupils, are important for understanding the nature of schools. This student assumes the need to be prepared as an expert in subject content in order to instruct pupils adequately. His position as a *student* teacher, and the opportunity available to acquire expertise while working with a specialist music teacher, is over-

64

shadowed by his concern to demonstrate competence. We can reasonably speculate that students are led to believe that their task is to demonstrate competence, rather than show that they are capable of acquiring it. Assessment, not learning acquisition, predominate in their agendae. In this case, the music teacher could adopt the role of expert consultant, making explicit a contract for learning which the student would pursue. The criteria for judging the student's capabilities would be different from those implicit in his concerns, and would need to be agreed between student, teacher and tutor. The expectations and responsibilities of each of the partners then changes considerably from that of conventional supervision assessment. Prospects for learning subject content for teaching could then be faced within a context of long-term acquisition and change. Recognition of the provisional nature of knowledge, and an individual's provisional understanding, would be better conveyed to student teachers and pupils such that the assumptions about the fixed nature of knowledge could be overcome, without a sense of threat.

The prospect of extending knowledge content and the relationship between educating oneself at the same time as educating other people — i.e. of mutual enquiry — were discussed by another group of students:

L: If there wasn't that interesting relationship I wouldn't be trying to do it. If we weren't learning as they were learning we wouldn't be interested in teaching. I mean we just wouldn't be here. That's the foundation.

H: We're beyond the level of ... we don't have to worry about the knowledge (that children learn) well, it doesn't tax us too much does it?

L: J. F. Kennedy did but time doesn't. You know, it depends on the topic.

Tutor: How did 'Time' face you, H (ref to a shared experience in PPP).

H: I hadn't got the knowledge. Once we know ... Well, I struggled with it you know I did. Because I hadn't got a sufficient knowledge of it.

Tutor: But you just said that you'd got that behind you ...

H: Em. Time. Science, don't remind me. We're all capable of ...

A: Somebody came up to me with an SMP card and asked me what vertices were. And I just couldn't think. My God. I had to; I just couldn't think ... for the life of me. (The child was sent to consult another who had 'done it').

L: I didn't know what Hogmanay was last week.

Tutor: Did it worry you.

L: No not really, I knew somebody else did. There's other means of discovery than just through me. I'm sure that other child enjoyed telling them ... they probably learnt more from them than they would from me. There's no reason why that should be a last resort. It could be a first reference couldn't it?

A: Well, you just can't know everything. Later I looked up what vertices were. I might have been taken aback if I couldn't give any reference to it.

L: We none of us knew what Hogmanay was ... It's New Year's Eve isn't it? (describes graphically sending child to discover meaning) We were in a joint situation. None of us knew. We were all ignorant, so I didn't mind. It's when you're the odd one out that I worry about it ...

Learning Instructional Strategies and Classroom Management

There is a similar tension between the acquisition and the demonstration of instructional strategies which is characteristic in the situations faced by student teachers. For learning teaching the treatment of practical knowledge needs to be enabling, encouraging reflection and analysis rather than distorting that knowledge by prescription and externally applied assessment of performance. That is not to say that judgments about performance should not be made. As part of the process of reflection and analysis those judgments are crucial to professional development. They facilitate the explication of criteria and principles underlying practice in ways which inform and enrich the dialogue and the understanding upon which further action can be based. In the case below the first encounter with teaching is recounted by a student with such reflective quality. It illustrates the tension between the desire to act competently and the realization of the extent and complexity of the practical knowledge to be gained before that is possible.

Janet teaching fractions

J: Funnily enough though I'm maths I found the (teaching of) fractions hard. When I first thought about it seemed to me quite easy ... it's just, add this, multiply that, but then when I talked to a couple of people (adult teacher friends) about it it occurred to me that I didn't know because, emm, when I had to teach them (the children) I had to go back to the basics which I'd already forgot ... emm I suppose really I'd forgotten how to look at it from their point of view. That was the main thing I suppose ...

Tutor: What do you mean by the basics? Can you give an example?

J: I'm now used to the abstract form of the fraction, adding, multiplying, I don't think about it. But they're used to just day to day things and when I started to teach them I cut up an apple to show them what fractions were, a part of the whole, but that's the sort of thing I'd already forgotten. I'd forgotten that fractions, I just took them at face value. I'd forgotten that they were actually, sort of half, a half of *something*. I know that sounds silly but I just took them as they were, numbers, meaning nothing just, I knew how to manipulate them but I didn't think what they actually stood for.

Tutor: What did you actually do in teaching the children in the first place?

J: I asked my teacher where shall I start, 'cos I hadn't seen them do any maths. He said he wanted me to start right at the start even though they knew a little bit. He wanted me to reinforce what they already had. And so I took an apple in and I cut it up and I'd made some pictures out of coloured paper with different shapes cut up into halves, and quarters. Halves and quarters was what I did first of all. And just showing them how it was written, and showing them halves and quarters.

Tutor: Showing them how it was written?

J: Showing them how it was written as well as cutting an apple up and saying, they'd obviously heard 'half' before, but actually showing them as well as cutting it up at the same time and trying to ...

Tutor: Do you mean how it was written '*HALF*'?

J: Yeah, er No I mean 1 over 2 er, I mean, you know ...

Tutor: Did you show them *HALF* as well?

J: Ermm, yeah, err, on the coloured pictures I did put that but I didn't really think about that as intentional. No ... I suppose maybe I should have done to make sure that they did know but I'd already written it. I'd written both half HALF and 1 over 2 with the pictures; and pointing them out and talking about the *pictures* I suppose I must have made it clear, but em ...

Tutor: I wasn't sure whether they know how to read the word, I'm just asking you ...

J: Yeah, em ...

Tutor: You didn't think of it?

J: No no no no no (hesitantly)

Tutor: Do you see a connection between the apple cut into pieces, the picture, which is a representation of that, the word, which is a representation (symbol) of one part, but it's abstracted, and the mathematical symbol? Do you see a link?

J: Yeah I suppose there ... I didn't consider the word very much although I'd written it.

Tutor: Do you think the children see a connection between the different ways of representing?

J:	I think that they did. One girl in particular who was having most difficulty, she did find it quite hard in going from the apple to the pictures. Although some of the others were a little bit more advanced than that, I found that I had to tell her quite a few times, and try to tell her different ways, to try to make her understand.
Tutor:	Was it a picture of an apple or was it just shapes?
J:	It was shapes, different shapes, I did halves and circles.
Tutor:	Do you mean semi-circles?
J:	I mean circles and squares, and semi-circles, on different sheets, and I showed them at different times. I showed them a circle first ...
Tutor:	So were you asking her to translate from half an apple to half a square?
J:	I suppose it's quite an obvious thing really, trying to see it from their point of view, seeing it in simple terms and not taking too much for granted about them ...
	refers back to the introductory comments and reiterates 'I didn't think ...'
Tutor:	What will the consequence of that be?
	J talks of 'seeing from the children's point of view', making the work as easy as possible. Describes reinforcement lesson done.
J:	I was mainly trying to get them to grasp that fractions are equal parts of a whole, and that when you write it out the denominator tells us how many equal parts. That's what I was trying to get over first ... The teacher wanted me to do simple addition of halves and quarters, and introduce them to thirds, sixths and eights. I did the simple addition in the third week, with the apple as well; and I started to use counters then with numbers, showing them half of a number, and this week I made some worksheets for them cos they are all at different stages. I found that by the third lesson ... he asked me to start right from the start, by the third lesson I had some children that were getting bored, some that were only just keeping up, then the in betweens; even though there were only five, but em, I thought, if I do a worksheet then I can give them individual attention when they come to their difficulties ... I found it hard, once I got a little bit further in the subject, I didn't know ... without either getting some ... one bored, there were five of them, one was particularly ahead and one was particularly slow, I didn't want to leave them out, and so I thought I'd get on to worksheets. The worksheets start off quite simple, I did pictures like I did

when I first started with the halves and quarters and the idea is trying to encourage them to think of a way themselves . . . I say first of all if you draw the pictures and it's up to them to colour it in, so it can help solve the addition problems; and later I say solve, which is about as hard, solve the questions, em, draw pictures or use counters depending on the question to help you, trying to get them to think of a way of solving it . . .

The encounter is common enough. It could be any detail of a vast array of content, the academic knowledge having to be translated in the teaching encounter, where pedagogical problems are multiple. The ability of this student to describe and reflect on those problems displays sophistication and competent intentionality towards solutions. In solving the practical problem a range of theoretical issues arise through that reflection. Relationships between concrete and abstract thought, questions of iconic and symbolic representations, matching tasks to pupils, the relationship between individual and group learning contexts, for example, are centred in practical, experiential understanding. For this student the assumptions about teaching a particular content were transformed into an intellectual and practical challenge. Problems are not always identified so readily, and lack of perception can thwart the promise of understanding through reflective action. In McIntyre's (1980) terms, though, Janet is clearly on the way to being able to 'elucidate, examine, explain and extend' her practical knowledge on the experience of her first ever encounter with teaching. That encounter occurred within three weeks of embarking on a four-year programme of study in which practical teaching opportunity is extensive.

Within this single experience and the consequent deliberations the range of issues raised and practical problems to be solved by Janet is extensive. Learning instructional tactics suitable for short-term learning of specific contents by particular children involves a complex set of variables. These tactics need to be incorporated into longer-term strategies, of even greater complexity, suitable for whole programmes of learning and a wide range of children's needs, across the breadth of curriculum content. For her second encounter with the class Janet was asked to teach the basics of pottery to the whole class. By her own account she knew nothing about pottery. Not only did the content present a different set of problems for her, but so did the planning of resources, classroom organization, the management of the pupils, and her own expectations for the children to be 'imaginative' and 'creative'. Within those challenges for developing her own teaching competence, the specific skills of demonstrating, instructing, explaining, stimulating, questioning, and praising, were all raised within a precise context. Within a short time Janet had experienced first-hand the practicalities of teaching, from which she generated a meaningful agenda for reflection, for discussion and for practice.

The agenda became part of the long-term acquisition of practical competence and of its development to professional proficiency. The way in which the agenda is cultivated towards that aim is crucial.

Developing Reflective Dispositions

The development of professional attitudes and responsibilities, and in particular the capacity to reflect upon and critically examine one's own teaching in order to move toward proficiency are rather intangible areas to examine in the professional development of teachers. Policy documents, as I pointed out earlier, seem to assume that such matters are preordained and simply need to be tested for at the point of entry into teacher education courses. The adjustments to professional expectations and the knowledge of curricular contexts, subjects, children, and classroom strategies will be determined, it is assumed, by the personal qualities, professional attitudes and dispositions towards learning teaching. We know little about the development of those characteristics. The development of proficiency in classroom and curricular practice and the enhancement of knowledge of subjects and children depend upon our generating an understanding of those qualities, attitudes and dispositions and working out ways in which they can be fostered. At the present time in teaching we are a long way from that understanding. The following discussion among students shows that a commitment to teaching and to being a competent teacher at a very early stage in the programme can be enhanced in a profound manner. These students had completed one year of a four-year programme:

> L: Really, I mean there's a really strong idea of professionalism I find. I've really extended my idea in the last year about what that professionalism is ... there's something implicit that gives you this idea that there are these strong codes ...
>
> *Observer:*   What is this professionalism that you're talking about?
>
> L: Extended professionalism is not just doing it but knowing the whys and wherefores and the hows and what next of your doing it ... it's going below the surface of walking into the classroom and doing that lesson because that's what you feel like doing, into all the issues around it. And I think the professionalism comes into thinking and working out those issues.

L explained that at this stage she is now finding time to think about what she is doing, whilst at first she was too busy 'doing' to notice other incidents or to reflect. She was asked if she could elaborate her view of extended professionalism and explain how she had arrived at it.

> L: I had a notion (before the course) that I might learn teaching techniques as well as things other than. It's really funny because

we did a first course with A ... and he was talking about something to do with our part in the developmental process ... sometime after he'd gone through all the Piaget bit it was, and emm. I went back home and I'd got an essay to write and I actually read a definition of what the extended professional was and it kind of occurred to me at that point that what he'd been saying today was related to that. I mean it was just pure coincidence that what he said that day related to what I read that evening. And then as we went on people kind of picked up on that idea of going in there (school) and doing more than just get on with it. And it developed. But maybe it developed more by pure coincidence, I picked up the impetus.

Observer: It wasn't integrated in the School of Education, you just happened to integrate it because of your experiences?

L: Sure, but I think everybody's done it. I mean, a lot of people seem a lot more involved now than they did at first.

So I think somewhere along the line someone's definition and someone else's action have met for everybody else ...

Tutor: What kind of involvement?

L: I don't know how involved they are, but when we go into seminars they seem to have a grasp of the arguments.

H: Well, last year, if you were going into school on Friday you started dreading it round about Tuesday evening, and you even, you know, if you had a cold you'd turn it into flu, and ring up the school and say you weren't coming in.

L: Oh dear.

H: Yeah, it was that bad. But like this morning Sarah got up at half past six to catch a bus to get to school. She couldn't get there quick enough.

The analysis of these concerns of students beginning to learn teaching, and the data used to illustrate those concerns and that early learning, arise from activities which were part of *Student Attachment to Schools*. Those activities will be described in more detail later, but it is important at this point to note that the incidents and discussions recounted occurred outside of the formal requirements of 'teaching practice'. In the undergraduate programme at the University of East Anglia these initial encounters with teaching began in the first week, with one day a week of school activities for the first two terms. The formal requirements of practical teaching began in the third term. *Student Attachment* at this early stage was seen particularly by students as a forerunner and preparatory opportunity to formally supervised activities. I will now describe how the formal elements of practical teaching fit into the context of the programme, and the way in which dialogue has been developed among students, teachers and tutors for the acquisition of teaching skills throughout the programme.

Practical Teaching in a Formal Programme

Formally in the BA (Hons) Degree in Education (including a Certificate in Education) at the University of East Anglia the dialogue has been approached by incorporating conventional supervisory activity into long-term discussion of the elements of practical teaching, supported by seminars, and with a commitment to partnership with teachers for learning teaching. The design of the degree programme is based upon a set of *principles of procedure*, the conduct of which will be discussed in Part Four. Here I will describe the coursework elements of classroom practice which lead to the recommendations for the award of the certificate of education incorporated into the degree award. Those elements are designated as Practical Professional Preparation (PPP) in recognition of the limitations of the term teaching practice, and in an attempt to establish cognizance of the importance of professional activities and responsibilities beyond the conventional conception of teaching. In these activities the partnership between students, teachers, and tutors has been pursued particularly through the development of a 'schedule' of practical teaching's constitutive elements, and through the persistent use of that document as an aid to dialogue.

Practical professional preparation, with four courses in the four years involving preparation for classroom and school practice, practical experience in schools, and the evaluation of teaching, represents a central thread in the pattern of courses for the degree programme. Each PPP course has its own focus, reflected in course titles:

PPP1　The classroom as a context for teaching and learning.
　2　Teaching and the curriculum.
　3　Practice in classrooms.
　4　Analyzing classroom practice.

The development and assessment of practical professional preparation has been approached as a problematic yet central issue. It is recognized for example that criteria of judgment with respect to practical teaching are complex and contentious; that practical difficulties of access to evidence are common; and that variations in school contexts affect performance, as well as the quality of students' learning. These problems are themselves subject to continuing enquiry, through the development of the 'schedule'. Properly designated the *Professional Preparation: Discussion and Assessment Document*, it was devised, piloted and implemented by practising teachers, students and tutors as a means of making explicit for discussion elements of professional practice which are deemed important. (See appendix 1, p. 85) It serves two purposes. Discussions between tutors, teachers, and students sought to agree the best way to identify and pursue the range of goals in learning practical teaching. The impetus came also from the problems and complexity of *assessing* practice, for the formal needs of course assessment and recommendation for certification for entry into teaching. The recognition that assessment presupposed effective modes of *development* in which students, teachers and tutors co-operated in dialogue was a feature of the principles of procedure according to which the degree was designed. Together, these led to the devising, piloting, and implementing of the 'schedule' as the document became known. The document, supported by an account of how its use is envisaged, together with partnership meetings in individual schools where its content and use are discussed, forms the focus of activities by, for and with students. This was particularly important to the students, given the policy decisions about the assessment of the degree and the place of practical teaching within it. First there was the problem of identifying and agreeing upon the characteristics, qualities and skills which are required at the formal assessment stages towards certification for teaching. In this programme, a *preliminary* assessment after the first year judges whether students are thought capable of proceeding successfully through the *honours* programme of the degree, including the recommendation for certification for qualified teacher status. The preliminary year is diagnostic, as well as formative. The diagnosis and performance needed to be based upon the same range of criteria used at the point of recommendation for qualified teacher status. Recommendation at the end of three years (subject to satisfactory completion of the degree) for certification is based on a judgment of competence for entry into the profession across the range of criteria, on a pass/fail summative assessment. That summation follows extensive formative learning which will be discussed below. Year four permits re-assessment or consolidation of classroom performance where that is needed in individual cases. For the majority it offers the opportunity to envelope recognized practical competence within systematic analysis of teaching and learning, emphasizing the implementation of evaluation and enquiry method through individually negotiated activities. At the end of year four practical knowledge gained through the honours programme is accredited in such a way that it is reflected in the classification of the final award. For example, competence in practical teaching confirms a class of award; proficiency in teaching enhances it. This final assessment is derived from PPP courses 2, 3 and 4, across the range of criteria set out and with the addition of individualized criteria for PPP4. A profiling mechanism for the purpose of classification was incorporated into the design of the 'schedule' in relation to groups of characteristics and criteria.

The complexity of summative assessment is matched by the formative development of students and the place of the *discussion* and assessment document within it. (See appendix 2, p. 94) The impetus to work with teachers in the devising of the document, with the unearthing and consideration of similar work from other institutions, led to the intention that the document would operate systematically for the acquisition of teaching competence. Discussion between students, teachers and tutors about the elements of teaching occurs before any profiling or recording of judgmental comments, and the document is used as the vehicle to reflection and dialogue throughout each PPP course and within some 'theoretical' courses. Between planned verbal dialogue in seminars and schools and the written account at the end of a course, interim written accounts by students and teachers/tutors on specific lessons are recorded in detail. In the document profile judgments are complemented by extensive space for comment, made at the end of each course to serve as a record for dialogue into ensuing years. Supervising teachers and tutors each complete a written account in each PPP course. For everybody involved in the partnership this complex dialogue makes explicit what is required of students, including ways in which competence can be enhanced to proficiency. This document for 'middle years' students has an equivalent devised for use with 'early years' students. Similar documents have been developed for the PGCE programme. The use of the documents has increased the sense of shared understanding, cooperation and involvement in decision-making about how best to reach the goals of competence and proficiency. It has also uncovered fundamental conflicts of view about teaching, and about the education of student teachers. Most importantly discussions have shown that for tutors and teachers as well students the nature of teaching is a complex and problematic matter in which learning within a shared sense of enquiry can be cooperative and mutually supportive, even though it may be contentious. They have also highlighted rather than hidden the importance of decision-making about the development of individuals and the best means of achieving it, while at the same time grasping the nettle of how to handle failure and come to terms with difficult decisions about future personal careers.

Each PPP course has a particular emphasis related to concurrent or associated professional courses in each of the years. The first, for example, is linked with foundational studies about the nature of children and their learning, and about the schooling context in which that learning is organized for formal compulsory education. The second is associated with 'methods' courses which deal with curriculum matters in the range of the primary curriculum. The third builds upon the first two through closer consideration, in a professional course as well as in the PPP course itself, of teaching and learning strategies across the curriculum. Each course entails requirements that students should adopt responsibility for a substantial amount of the children's learning during the period of time in school. Usually the adoption of those responsibilities is based on preparatory experience in school gained through *Student Attachment*, which has tended to develop as cooperative teaching with teachers:

> *Teacher:* Most of the things we've been doing have been fairly cooperative haven't they, rather than, you know, one of us watching the other.
>
> *Student:* Yes.
>
> *Teacher:* We feel now that we should do more of that, more actually withdrawing and being critical. What we've done up to now has been perhaps me starting things off . . . sometimes working with (student)'s ideas. But then I've been working

with her; rather than 'I'll do it today, you do it tomorrow' we've been together as much as anything ... Which has helped us, to get to know each other, how things work, and the children have got used to us working together. We were saying yesterday that we need to think about watching each other and being more critical now.

Student: I would find that very valuable, to sit and observe. It would have been easy when I first came in to say that was what I wanted to do, but I've done it the right way round. I've got in and I've got involved. I know the children and I know their personalities and I think that now to sit and observe would be more valuable than having done it without knowing anything about them and not knowing a lot about (teacher) either.

I do not want to imply that the power of formal assessment of individual students is diminished. Judgment of competence in this document on a scale of 'outstanding' to 'weak' over a wide range of capabilities is a powerful mechanism which dominates the concerns of students. It is only in part alleviated by making explicit the expectations for practical teaching and discussing the criteria which underly those expectations. The involvement of teachers in that process changes the relationship with students, as the teachers become much more overtly assessors of the students. Yet within this context classroom skills are acquired in cooperation with teachers' and tutors' commitments to consider their own practice and to develop ways of researching it. Where that happens the models of practice available to students are more consciously articulated, and models of professionalism also become accessible to students in the early stage of their own professional development. Through those experiences the capacity to initiate, plan, prepare for, implement, conduct and evaluate teaching and learning experiences for pupils can be more adequately developed. Data selected from one set of lessons by a student embarking on a third course of practical professional preparation show how that capacity is used in practice. The data also shows the complexity of practical knowledge required for just one part of the teaching responsibilities adopted. This proposal shows a clear awareness of the context in which the teaching will occur, including previous learning by the pupils and the material resources available; it demonstrates capability in the instructional, organizational and managerial skills to be deployed by the student; and it shows that subject knowledge and knowledge of the children are incorporated within wider and fundamental understanding of the need to develop responsibility and independence in pupils' approaches to learning. A further ten lessons on this topic were conducted in addition to the three detailed here (see appendix 3, p. 96). They were developed from the student's capacity to evaluate the events of the classroom and his own part within those events, which this data also reflects.

From the early tentative steps of first year students embarking on their first encounters with teaching it is a long path of learning which leads to the complexity of activity and level of proficiency which these extracts represent. It is not possible to convey fully the ways in which that learning occurs or to adequately display the texture of experiences within the teacher education programme which contribute to it. Formal lectures, seminars, workshops, school experiences, discussion groups, tutorials, reading literature, presentation of written assignments, and so on, each add dimensions to the construction of that learning. The construction contains members which are made of the material of professional adjustments, knowing school and curricular contexts, subject knowledge, understanding of children, acquisition of instructional strategies, and the development of professional responsibilities. It is made possible in part by analysis and dissection of these constituents, such as is represented in the *Professional Preparation* document. I would contend that the proficiency is achieved through the orchestration and integration which occurs with the active reflection of students upon those constituents and their relationship to classroom practice. The mechanisms of that integrative learning, discussed with 'L' as the development of extended professionalism, would seem to be enhanced when reflection is not only personal and individual, but also an explicit feature of partnership through dialogue between students, teachers and tutors. Both levels of learning activity — contemplative individual reflection and group dialogue — are likely to be achieved more readily where reflection on practice and the further application of learning through practice occurs on frequent and regular occasions. The aspiration for good practical teaching will only be achieved, I believe, where that learning process is fostered.

In the case of the BA programme reflection and the further acquisition of skills is helped by the long term attachment of students to schools, the details of which will be discussed in Part Four. In the formal course structure the analysis of classroom practice is also a substantive element in PPP courses, and is the central focus of the fourth course of practical professional preparation. With recommendations for certification (subject to final satisfactory completion of the degree) already decided, students are in a status position similar to that of new entrants to the profession so far as recognized classroom competence is concerned. The fourth course therefore provides formally for the extension of competence or proficiency, through systematic questioning and the development of enquiry skills. Its intention is to equip the intending teachers with some of the skills and attitudes needed to conduct research into their own practice or that of others in the schools in which they will work. Its rationale and purpose acknowledges the 'recommended for certification' status of fourth year students and enables them to study substantive issues of teaching, learning, and curriculum development. The issues may be proposed by the students themselves, or may be 'commissions' by schools with particular concerns which they want researched. The course aspires to develop the capacities required for professional contributions to the development of teaching, learning and the curriculum of individual schools or groups of schools. The kinds of issues studied are represented by the list of topics below. An example of the 'products' in the form of written reports is included in the final section of the book, though it should be clear that the outcome of the research and curriculum development activities does not rest in written reports alone. The practical activities which are generated within the schools, and the involvement of teachers in those activities form a major part of the course.

Developing Curriculum Guidelines for Physical Education

Developing 'immersion' teaching materials for middle years French

Using computers in classrooms

An investigation of the development of social relationships in class-rooms

Teaching strategies for beginning readers

Strategies for dealing with pupils' spelling problems

Curriculum provision for high ability children in rural primary schools

Teachers as Learners: Practical Action and Reflective Understanding

In all partners — student teacher, teacher, teacher educator — though from different amounts and kinds of experience base, the relationship between practical action and reflective understanding is likely to be similar. Learning is in large measure a reflective activity which takes place through the actions of the learner. In the case of learning practical teaching most of that activity occurs in independent circumstances — some would say in isolation. It also occurs in a condition of threat and insecurity, increasingly so in the climate of imposed external assessment, appraisal and accountability. It is necessary to establish and maintain the right conditions for learning through dialogue and partnership in order to ensure an effective process of teacher education. Process in the teacher *education* sense — the exploration of learning, the working through of tentative ideas, and the solving of problems — is as important as the quality of the learners' performance. It is through a grasp of the process and the development of the capabilities which lead to further learning that the acquisition of competence, the development of proficiency, and their enhancement to excellence, can best be achieved. Quality control of teaching performance based on minimum competence criteria may be necessary, but it is insufficient for professional practice. Reconciliation is needed between the learning of craftsmanship and the development of reflective capacities. If teacher education processes and their outcome in terms of professional performance in the widest sense are seen as problematic, the re-emphasis of instruction in basic performance skills, judged at minimum competence level for certification, offers no advance on past practice. We need a view of conditions which will enhance long term learning, which will promote professional development by ensuring that students acquire the disposition to question, enquire, and solve problems within their own teaching and the wider school activities of their future careers. That includes conditions of dialogue and collaboration in professional partnership. The question of establishing conditions of cooperation and community in learning are central to proposals for an effective educational process. Those conditions are crucial in relation to the 'content' of teaching activities, for the experience of teaching action is inherently uncertain, open ended, and speculative, involving spontaneous, intuitive and direct-practical responses and judgments.

To seek a process view of learning teaching means questioning the convention of training in teaching skills. It does not preclude the mastery of crucial technical competence, but incorporates technique and makes it subject to enquiry along with other features of classroom activity, and hence subject to change and improvement. Bruner (1960) has said that the most general objective of education is that it should cultivate excellence, i.e. helping each student achieve his or her optimum intellectual development. His concerns are with the nature of learning and the means by which the aspiration of the full development of human capacities can be achieved — the facilitating of the education process. He is concerned not simply with 'objectives' in the sense of goals to be reached, but with making the primary intention of any learning act that it should help future learning occur more easily. 'Ability' then would be judged in terms of the application of understanding in new situations, and the further acquisition of knowledge in incremental progression. Bruner's ideas about an education process intend that students should pose questions; explore and research sources for possible solutions; share actively in their learning in conditions of trust, where false avenues can legitimately be followed; and gain support from teachers. Learning, and the further application of understanding in those conditions, can be achieved on the basis of principles of procedure which provide a framework for enquiry. Within that framework the point is not *only* to have learned a set of skills, it is rather to develop capacities which can be applied to future experiences, problems, and situations. That is the essence of Bruner's 'learning how to learn'. The achievement of technical skills is not disregarded. On the contrary, they form part of the content of learning and are improved by motivation, use, and further enquiry.

At the INSET level, where it might be assumed that competency has been adequately demonstrated, the question of the relationship between practical and reflective knowledge has been explored by Elliott (1980). He argued for reflection on practice as the basis of dialogue to overcome the research-practice gap, in which researchers study teachers and teachers are expected to 'apply' their findings. He linked that problem of teachers as passive recipients of research wisdom with the inadequacies of the instructional mode of teaching, in which teachers pass on appropriated knowledge to passive pupils, whose task is to produce preconceived results. Recognition of the inadequacies of these approaches to learning is the heart of Elliott's case, for such teaching, he argues, is necessarily power-coercive and the learning necessarily power-dependant. Both presuppose a bias against self-directed enquiry learning and the development of autonomy.

Student teachers, teachers and teacher educators are assumed to be active, self-motivated learners. Elliott (1980) examines how their learning occurs:

> As Karl Popper claims, we make progress by reflecting about our errors rather than basking in our strengths. However, the identification of enabling acts may have the pragmatic merit of giving a teacher sufficient confidence in his strengths to face up to his weaknesses ... the task is that of identifying and describing the problems teachers have in enabling the development of their students' understanding ... Such self-knowledge is, in my view, at the heart of the professional development process. By involving teachers in dialogue, classroom action research itself constitutes an educational process ... (p. 317)

Education in this event is deemed to involve understanding in realms of learning such as teaching, which are problematic and not given to simple solutions. In the nature of learning teaching the unpredictability of situations and personal responses, the variability of teaching circumstances, and the likelihood of changing demands, amount to the need for learning to be capable of taking the student further later. In the construction of knowledge and the pursuit of excellence, that requires the development of understanding by teachers as active learners, *and* the means to further that understanding in long-term professional activity, subsuming the acquisition and development of technical skills:

> The process model embodies a radically different set of assumptions about the relationship between teaching and learning from the behavioural objectives model and the process-product research which matches it. The aim of teaching is viewed as 'enabling', 'facilitating' or 'providing opportunities for' the development of understanding. Such aim descriptions specify conditions to be realized by the teacher rather than his students. A teacher can *enable* pupils to perform certain learning tasks successfully without them then actually doing so. The student's task performance is ultimately his or her responsibility. The teaching aim of 'enabling the development of understanding' must be distinguished from the learners' aim of 'developing an understanding'. The teaching aim is concerned with establishing conditions in the classroom which enable students to develop their own understanding of the subject matter. The process model. inasmuch as it specifies enabling conditions, embodies an active conception of learning and does not assume that it is caused by teaching. (*Ibid*, p. 314)

Experiential learning is based on events to which the individual responds with thoughts, feelings and intentions. In the case of teaching the events centre around the intentions and actions of the teacher and the pupils. The teacher shapes the experiences by his or her actions, and perceives and responds to them in particular, unique ways which in turn affect new intentions and actions. From the common pattern of experiential-practical knowledge we can build a shared understanding of teaching. That can be done in part by taking seriously the practical knowledge of teachers and working out ways in which it can be subjected to critical enquiry. In order to uncover and understand teachers' practical knowledge, Elbaz (1983) analyzed the content of knowledge held by 'Sarah', a teacher of English, in terms of her knowledge of herself as a teacher; of the environment and social surroundings in which she worked; of subject matter; of instructional method and learning process; and of curriculum development. The origins of these aspects of the teacher's knowledge in theory and practice, and the way theoretical propositions were transformed into practical relevance were also studied. Most important, the way practical knowledge changed and developed in the light of responses to practices is taken into account by Elbaz. This study of the content, origins, development, coherence and functioning of practical knowledge demonstrates the complexity of the task of learning teaching, teaching, and understanding teaching so that it can be improved. But the major conclusion of the study was to demonstrate the possibility for teachers to become aware of and articulate their own practical knowledge, leading to greater self-understanding and professional growth (Elbaz, 1983, p 170). The process requires formality and rigour, in systematic self-analysis using whatever methods are appropriate, in order to give form to one's knowledge and move beyond the anecdotal and superficially introspective. The study also shows that the various aspects of practical knowledge — self, situation, subject matter, instruction, and curriculum development — are realms within which habitual practice and technical skills occur and are transformed. Those skills are subsumed in the learning process, not simply the objective of it. Thus, Sockett (1985) argues:

> We can shut ourselves in an empty classroom practising our blackboard writing. We can have critics or supervisors watch out particularly for the way we handle children's answers ... but if we must use our judgement when we apply our skills, the route to the improvement of performance lies first in practice with judgment and critical reflection, later in systematic self-analysis accompanied by trials of alternative practical hypotheses ... (p. 15)

One way of perceiving the relationship between the technically competent skills of classroom practice and their acquisition, and advancement through reflective critique is to consider the kinds of thinking involved. In an analysis of repertoires of thinking strategies, Costa *et al* (1985) distinguish between six kinds of thinking:

remembering;
repeating;

reasoning;
reorganising;
relating;
reflecting.

The first two amount to routine memory and the application of rehearsed solutions. The third involves judgments between competing ideas, and the search for solutions and explanations. The fourth and fifth require action to change the relationships between ideas or apply practical solutions from a range of possibilities. The sixth, deemed in the realm of 'metacognition', involves the capability to consider the consequences or possibilities in the thinking and actions associated with the other categories. It is this higher order of creative thought and action which is inherent in higher-order teacher professionalism, and which needs to be supported by the development of a range of investigative skills which are complementary to conventionally held teaching skills. What is even more promising, in my view, is that the partners in the enterprise of research based initial teacher education would come to form better understanding of the place and value of practical knowledge.

Informed and Informing Practice: Learning Teaching in Context

Learning to teach is a process of continual hypothesis testing in one's own teaching. Student teachers (and teachers, teacher educators and researchers) need to be selective in defining hypotheses and substantive foci of enquiry. There is a need for guidance in planning the procedures of study, and in assimilating the learning which results. Yet in the complexity of the performance of teaching there is simply not time to hypothesize, act, reflect and repostulate on everything. It is in the face of practical problems which must be 'solved' without such testing that instrumental practical know-how is both acquired and demanded. We have to accept that craft knowledge gained in the master-apprentice manner will be a considerable influence in learning teaching. The craft of teaching teaching in that manner, passing on what is held to be instrumentally effective because it 'works' and is shown to work by 'experience', should not, however, become predominant. Reconciling the two approaches means working out how to subordinate craft knowledge to professional dispositions so that learning for understanding will be shared by students, teachers, and teacher educators in an approach to acquiring and utilizing professional excellence.

Then the question arises as to how that should be done with regard to substantive issues at the school level, recognizing that the institution should also be a focus for collective self-study and curriculum development. Given the recognition that initial teacher education does not often prepare intending teachers for such tasks, and that in-service provision does not sufficiently cater for the needs of practising teachers in the development of evaluation skills, it is necessary to tackle that question at both stages of professional development. The danger of narcissistic self-appraisal and inferior evaluation require that critical reflection should be respectably honest and conducted with external consultative support. What is more, insular and isolated classroom or institutional analysis is potentially blind to wider cultural, political and economic elements within which schooling and teaching need to be viewed and understood. It is possible, then, to conceive of issues for study at three levels:

(i) immediate classroom concerns — matters of direct classroom practice;

(ii) institutional concerns — matters which bear directly upon classroom practice, or are part of wider professional responsibility;

(iii) cultural concerns — matters which pervade practice.

The substantive foci of teacher research and the contexts in which it occurs will inevitably relate to the problems and situations of individual student teachers, teachers, and teacher educators. Issues will, in the case of learning teaching in the early stages of professional development, be centred on student teachers' concerns deriving from immediate classroom experience. The context may be limited to a particular classroom setting. Further professional development and improved teaching will be contained within the classroom context too. Practical knowledge and skills, analysis of teaching, and the generation of understanding through the development of theories about concrete practices will also be set in wider social, institutional and political contexts which themselves may provide foci for investigation. Understanding the wider contexts is important for understanding what teachers, students, and children are doing in their classrooms. Cultural contexts are also important subjects of enquiry, particularly for achieving understanding of schooling as a mechanism of social and cultural reproduction and the development of constructive critical appraisals of schooling. Critical appraisal at all three levels is necessary to understand the practice of teaching and the processes of schooling. Enabling change through dialogue and empowering practice depends upon an awareness of events at each level and the relationship between them.

Reconciling Induction into and Reform of Conventional Schooling

Treating individual student-teachers', teachers', and teacher-educators' practical experience as worthy of serious, rigorous reflection and systematic self-analysis means that dialogue needs to stimulate the identification of issues for study. Because instruction is the dominant mode in which we experience teaching, the opportunity, facility, and intellectual 'space' for defining one's own learning agenda is not common. The demands of everyday events in classrooms withold the chance from teachers to study their own teaching in systematic ways. When the opportunity is available, such as occurs with cooperation in partnership, knowing how to handle the situation with its uncertainties, vacuums, and sometimes intangible questions, is a difficult task. The identification of problems and defining of hypotheses are subject to difficult emotional and intellectual processes. That stage of the learning process is central to the essence of problem solving through enquiry, and it is a critical stage in the relationship between practice and theory. It is this stage which has traditionally been 'captured' by the providers of propositional knowledge in both initial and in-service teacher education, I believe, overriding the demand for relevance. Working in partnership with student-teachers, teachers and teacher educators from the stage of problem-posing can provide for a developing sophistication in problem awareness and refinement.

Conventionally in educational research, from the point of hypotheses or identification of issues, enquiry would pursue a line of:

deciding on an appropriate design for investigation;

investigation, including the use of appropriate techniques for gathering data / information;

recording and storing data;

interpreting and analyzing data;

reporting (or disseminating) conclusions, leading to;

action to be taken, based on understanding and the development of theory.

In practice this is not a straight line headed in a single direction. False trails, dead ends, and lay-byes, as well as return trips to reconsider what has been done before, are characteristic of the pursuit. At each point decisions are needed to ensure that the techniques used or designed are appropriate to the problem. Various research techniques are available, each with their own difficulties as well as advantages. Questionnaires, interview schedules, unstructured interviews, group discussion, systematic observation, interpretive or participant observation, commissioned prose accounts of ideas or events, are just some of the investigative tools tried by educational researchers. (For detailed consideration of teacher-research methods see Hopkins, 1985; and Walker, 1985a.)

Most of these techniques derive from the tradition of outsider-researchers working on teachers or children as objects of study. The developments of qualitative techniques which avail us of systematic *self* reflection are more recent and innovative. Even these have derived largely from researchers pursuing their own interests and particular theoretical positions, as I indicated in Part Two. The kind of academic, intellectucal and practical shift called for by Alexander have barely begun. Changes in course structures and ways in

which practical knowledge is treated within innovative conceptions of partnership present opportunities to pursue new modes of research which will
potentially reconcile the theory-practice gap and develop a new kind of
expectation about what it means to be a professional teacher.

The argument will be presented, I have no doubt, that here is a recipe for
poor quality research which is incapable of leading to theoretical principles and
which, furthermore, is likely to ignore existing theory. Certainly here is a
different order of research which, pursued rigorously and systematically will
take other provisional theoretical studies into account where they exist and are
appropriate. It is that notion of a practice-research professional community
which makes credible a notion of partnership. It is by developing an
understanding of teaching through theory that professional practice will be
improved. For as practical knowledge is the key to professional credibility,
theory is the key to understanding practice. To achieve these aims of
partnership would result in a reconciliation of the problem of inducting
student teachers into conventional school practice at the same time as
reforming that practice through professional dialogue between students,
teachers, and teacher educators. It requires a reappraisal of research and of
teacher education, with the recognition of the value and mechanisms of
gaining and changing practical knowledge. To this end Alexander (1984a) has
suggested that the use of schools as a way to develop capacities to conduct
research should be more fully exploited, through greater emphasis in teacher
education programmes on:

the actions of teachers and children's responses to them;

teachers' knowledge and its subjective formulation;

self-analysis of attitudes, motivations and knowledge;

respectful and honest scepticism for conventional education disciplines;

extension of the disciplines;

going public in grounding understanding in practice;

exploration of reflexive 'everyday' knowledge.

These, he argues, require a reconceptualisation of professional theory to
provide the substantial changes necessary for more effective processes of
teacher education (Alexander, 1984a, pp. 100–2). The principles and practice
of research based initial teacher education offer the possibility and prospect of
that order of transformation in the professional activities of teachers.

APPENDIX 1

UNIVERSITY OF EAST ANGLIA
School of Education

MIDDLE YEAR SECTOR

B.A. DEGREE

PROFESSIONAL PREPARATION:
discussion and assessment document

Student's name _____   Year _____

Learning Teaching, Teaching Teaching ...

PRACTICAL PROFESSIONAL PREPARATION

MIDDLE YEARS SECTOR   YEAR 1 2 3 4

COURSE: DATES:

School: _____

Student's Name: _____

Tutor/Teacher's Name: _____

_____

Age Range: Location of school:

Age(s) Taught: Village ☐ Town ☐ City ☐

                  Other (specify):

_____

During each P.P.P. course the Schedule will act as a working document for discussion between students, teachers and tutors.
Discussion will be supported by written comment on separate sheets, for individual sessions observed.
Tutor *and* teacher will *each* complete a schedule at the end of each P.P.P. course as an assessment of the student's progress.
Comments pages will indicate specific remarks, and provide guidance in practical professional development.

UNIVERSITY OF EAST ANGLIA
School of Education
Tel: Norwich 56161

Organizational or other features of the school relevant to the student's experience:

Beneath each appropriate subsection one of the numbers will be circled to indicate where the student is judged to stand in the range:
1. Outstanding   2. Good   3. Moderate   4. Weak.
Where specific categories or sub-sections are not considered, or no evidence is available, N/A should indicate this.

1. AWARENESS OF THE TEACHING/LEARNING CONTEXT COMMENTS:

I COMMUNITY
 i. Is aware of the school as part of a wider community.
 ii. Examines the community and environment for potential learning resources.
 iii. Shows a desire to become involved in community activities.

←——————→

Has made no attempt to see beyond the classroom or become involved.

1 2 3 4

II INSTITUTION
 i. Has researched and shows an understanding of the aims organisation and structure of the school.
 ii. Shows a good knowledge of material and human resources available.
 iii. Shows desire to become involved in extra-curricular activities.

←——————→

Complete ignorance of the school as a community.

Has made no attempt to establish the resources available within the school.

1 2 3 4

III GROUPS WITHIN THE SCHOOL
 i. Clearly understands the context of the group within the class and/or school.
 ii. Good knowledge of working space.
 iii. Considers the practical conditions necessary for different kinds of group learning.

←——————→

Is unaware of the nature of the group and accepts it at face value.
Is totally unaware of the opportunities available in the teaching area.
Lack of knowledge reflected in an inflexible approach to organisation.

1 2 3 4

IV INDIVIDUAL ROLES
 Considers evidence and makes assessments about individual children.

1 2 3 4

2. RELATIONSHIPS WITH PUPILS AND STAFF OF THE SCHOOL

COMMENTS:

I COMMUNITY AND INSTITUTION
i. Consults and plans with others. ←——→ Operates in isolation.
ii. Shows tact in relationships. Insensitive and tactless.
iii. Conveys 'presence'. Retires unnoticed.
iv. Takes account of needs of both teaching and non-teaching staff. Inconsiderate to staff needs.
v. Takes responsibility for the learning environment. Makes little contribution to the learning environment.

1 2 3 4

II PUPILS
i. Shows empathy and rapport with children. ←——→ Relationships in conflict with children.
ii. Commands respect and holds the interest of children. Fails to gain respect.
iii. Intervenes and withdraws appropriately to foster understanding and encourage interaction between others. Inappropriate intervention and withdrawal.
iv. Balances individual and group needs within class. Creates situation of conflict between individual and group needs.
v. Balances class and school needs.

1 2 3 4

3. PREPARATION

I OBJECTIVES
  i. Provides evidence of short
     term goals related to
     longer term aims.
  ii. Selects objectives
     appropriate to the needs of
     individuals and groups.
  iii. Considers means of
     assessing learning.

←——————→

Operates on isolated
objectives.

Does not relate
objectives to needs of
pupils.
Lacks foresight in
assessing learning.

1 2 3 4

II METHOD
  i. Selects appropriate
     methods.
  ii. Demonstrates ability to be
     flexible and imaginative.
  iii. Shows awareness of
     available resources.

←——————→

Plans inappropriate and
ineffective methods.
Has limited view of
alternative methods.
Ignores useful resources.

1 2 3 4

III CONTENT
  i. Selects content
     appropriate to goals.
  ii. Takes account of
     individual pupil differences.

←——————→

Selects inappropriate content.

Plans only for 'average' child.

1 2 3 4

IV ORGANISATION
  i. Is flexible but realistic in
     organisation of children.
  ii. Considers constraints of
     time and space.
  iii. Shows prior organisation
     of resources and materials.

←——————→

Uses rigid organisation.

Lacks foresight of constraints.

Fails to organise in advance.

1 2 3 4

V DEVELOPMENT
  Actively utilises previous
  evaluations in preparation
  of work.

←——————→

Is unable to utilize
previous experiences
to modify preparation.

1 2 3 4

4. PRACTICE

COMMENTS:

I MANAGEMENT SKILLS

i. Adapts organisational methods and control techniques to suit whole class groups, individuals.

ii. Uses available space and time to maximum advantage.

iii. Sensible use of available resource material and equipment.

iv. Appropriate management of selected curriculum materials and equipment.

v. Records pupils learning progress and learning process.

←————————→

Inflexible in class management.

Unaware of constraints and unable to pace lesson.
Ineffective use of resource material.

Inappropriate selection/ use of curriculum materials.

1 2 3 4

II COMMUNICATION SKILLS
Spoken

i. Instructions and explanations clear, unambiguous and helpful.

ii. Appropriate and effective use of questioning strategy.

iii. Listens attentively and appropriately to children's contribution.

iv. Uses voice in interesting and appropriately modulated way.

←————————→

Instructions and explanations unclear ambiguous and confusing.
Ineffective use of questions.

1 2 3 4

Written

i. Remarks are appropriate to the aims of the lesson and in language readily understood by the child.

ii. Written comments indicate careful reading of text.

iii. Writes in a legible hand.

←————————→

Makes haphazard and unexplained comments/ evaluation

Written comments generalised and superficial
Untidy to the point of illegibility.

1 2 3 4

4. PRACTICE (cont.)

COMMENTS:

Visual
  i. Displays high standards in
     visual presentation (in
     visual aids, displays,
     blackboards, etc.)
 ii. Imaginative use of visual
     stimuli.

←————→   Poor visual
presentation.

Arid visual impact.

1 2 3 4

Non-Verbal
  i. Displays ability to vary
     manner, facial expression,
     movement etc. as
     appropriate.

←————→   Wooden, with little or
no "presence".

1 2 3 4

**III GENERAL
RESPONSIVENESS**
  i. Is tactful and positive in
     communicating appraisal
     and assessments.
 ii. Is sensitive to the
     emotional needs of
     individuals and groups.
iii. Is sensitive to the
     intellectual needs of
     individuals and class.
iv. Is adaptable, and takes
     advantage of unexpected
     opportunities.
 v. Anticipates problems and
     facilitates solutions.

←————→   Is blunt and insensitive.

Takes little account of
response of individuals
or class as a whole.
Has little or no
awareness of individual
needs.
Unresponsive to
changing situation.

Post-event approach to
problems.

1 2 3 4

5. CRITICAL ANALYSIS

COMMENTS:

Quality of critical analysis in:
1. Preparation:

1 2 3 4

2. Classroom management

1 2 3 4

3. Pupil's involvement in the
    learning process.

1 2 3 4

4. Pupil's progress and
    understanding.

1 2 3 4

5. Record keeping.

1 2 3 4

OVERALL IMPRESSION AND ANY ADDITIONAL COMMENT:

APPENDIX 2

**Professional Preparation: Discussion and
Assessment Document**

The Professional Preparation document was devised in lengthy discussion between teachers and School of Education staff, piloted with a group of students in spring 1983 and used formally for the first time in summer 1983 with Year 1 BA degree students. The original document was modified after that experience to the present form.

It is very new for all concerned. For some, it may be a first encounter with the issues of the assessment of professional preparation.

A summary of important points which emerged during the design of the document is given below.

Day-To-Day Use

The document sets out characteristics of professional development (not solely classroom competence, though that is central) which are considered important in the work of student teachers. One purpose is to clarify, to make explicit, what is expected of student teachers in order to help in *discussing* their work. It has a diagnostic and formative purpose, intended for use *WITH* the student. All items are considered important; it is necessary to select particular aspects for discussion at any one time and to be clear which.

Use in One-Term Courses

Some parts of *each* section will feature in *each* one-term course: (for *example*, aspects of relationships with pupils; and communication skills) are central to activities undertaken by student teachers). But each PPP course has its own particular focus and emphasis:

EDU 105   The Classroom as a Context for Teaching and Learning
EDU 307   Teaching and the Curriculum

EDU 313   Practice in Classrooms
EDU 315   Analyzing Classroom Practice

so that there may be some change of emphasis in each course in the attention given to particular sections of the document. The details of each course will be presented at the time students undertake them, but to illustrate briefly what this means:

Section 1 'Awareness of the Teaching/Learning Context' is obviously a focus
        for EDU 105
Sub-section 1:iv relates clearly to 3.1, 3.11 in 'preparation';
4.1, and 4.111 in 'Practice'; and 5.4, 5.5 on 'Critical Analysis'.
Similarly, section 3 'Preparation' provides a focus for work in EDU 307 in the preparation of curriculum materials, the implementation of them being dealt with in section 4 'Practice'.

The document is not intended to operate as a checklist, and not all items are likely to be considered in a single one-term course.

For those items which are dealt with, specific written comments, indicating a student's progress and giving guidance for further development, should be added at the end of the course. These should be supported by summary comments written in the 'overall impression' pages, and the use of numbers beneath subsections (see inside front cover for explained).

Copies of completed documents will be given to each student and discussed with him/her.

Use through the Degree Programme

Copies of the same document will be used throughout the four PPP courses of the BA degree. No distinction is made within it about which items are appropriate for each year. By year 4, 'coverage' will have been extensive; experience in some aspects will have been gained in each of the four years and thus enhanced; in some new learning experiences will arise later in the programme. It is not possible to be prescriptive, but the previous paragraph — Use in One-Term Courses — indicates how this will work.

The copies of completed documents which are given to each student at the end of each course provide a crucial 'development' link. They will be used for reference by the student and by teachers and tutors with whom the student works in the next PPP course. They will also provide a 'profile' of development for the purpose of recommendation for qualified teacher status at the end of year 3, and for the award of the honours degree at the end of year 4.

Judgments about what should appropriately be expected at each point are a matter for continued discussion, as is the question of how the judgments are applied in a programme of professional *development*, within which the sector is concerned for the development of the maximum potential of each *individual* student.

APPENDIX 3

Environmental Studies

Tuesdays-9.40–10.40am
Thursdays-1.15–2.30pm
Class 5.

19 children, 10 and 11 years old, mixed ability

Intentions

This project work concentrates on 'Communications in the Modern World' with the overall aim of this project being to increase the class's knowledge of the various forms of communication present in the modern world. The work is intended to be largely self-directed within each group, within broad overall guidelines, with the group work concentrating on one particular topic as chosen by the group and studying it under the broad headings: history; the present; the future. Within these headings it is intended that the individual will practice his/her discussion and negotiation skills; will develop further the skills of detailed research, thereby improving his/her use of reference books and note taking skills; will develop the skills of factual and imaginative writing; will produce artwork of a technical and imaginative nature; will increase his/her vocabulary; will prepare work for presentation to others; and above all enhance his/her ability to create a learning experience for themselves where s/he is able to think around a problem to find a means of answering a question s/he personally poses.

In addition, the class will produce two 'editions' of a newspaper and a radio station which are intended to further the linguistic and written skills of the class. In the production of the newspaper the class will develop research techniques, the skill of reporting — both investigation and writing — copywriting, headlining, layout and artwork.

The radio station will develop the oral skills of concise and clear reporting, using language to capture the attention of the audience, research, questioning skills and the use of alternative forms of attention gaining, such as catchy jingles. It is also intended that the skills of play writing for radio and the acting of the same (for example, the use of the voice to portray emotions etc.) as well as production skills such as sound effects — will be covered.

Equipment

Seven folders. Loose paper. Treasury tags. Reference books (see attached sheet 1) and posters. Video and filmstrip on the development of the telephone and Royal Mail. Cassette recorder and tape. Drawing materials. Typing blanks. Any information as obtained by class.

Organization

The class is to work in computer groups as already established. Groups B and E are to form 'Unit Sun', groups A, C, and D to form 'Unit Moon'. 'Sun' are to undertake the first production of the radio station, 'Moon' the newspaper. Each group are to undertake study of one aspect of 'communications', producing a folder of work and appropriate pieces for eventual wall display. (Second production of each units to swap.)

Each child is to have a role within the production team. During each lesson at least half of each unit are to work on folder production. Individual workload to be decided in consultation within group.

Introductions

This work is the continuation of work initiated during attachment and therefore is already introduced to the class. The major task in formally introducing, therefore, will be the designation of topics and units for the activities.

Activities

Week 2: *Instigation of the project.* Dividing into units as above and discussion to decide possible contents for each production. Dividing into groups as per computer work to decide on folder topics.

Recording each child onto tape to allow the class to experience the 'tricks' cassette recording has on a voice.

Week 3: *Decisions* about roles within production units and responsibilities within each folder group. Beginning of project.

Weeks 4,5,7 and 8: *Class to work on folder work and production work*, according to stage reached and requirements set out in 'organization' above. No formal planning is possible at this time.

Week 9: *Rounding off of work on Tuesday. Thursday's lesson* to be given over to group reports on individual topics.

(N.B. production deadlines to be weeks 5 and 9.)

Conclusions

Continual assessment of the oral and written skills according (to intentions above) to be undertaken throughout with remedial action as appropriate.

Initial Resources for Environmental Studies

Posters

Satellite Communications
The Telephone Instrument
The Journey of a Letter

Slides and filmstrips

Spreading the News No 380
Science and Communication. 1 x 2
(plus two films from County Library if available.)

Books (Library)

Television — Caney/Hortsmann.
Newspapers — Siddle/Compton/Wilson/James.
Radio — Goodall.
Telephones — Crush.

also Thames Television's *Understanding Television.*

Ladybirds — *The Story of Newspapers*
           The Story of Printing
           How it works : Printing Processes
           How it works : Television.

Book Titles

Barnes, M.J. (1979), *Telecommunications*, Wayland Publishers Ltd.
Compton, H. (1962), *Newspapers*, ESA.
Crush, M. (1973), *Telephones*, Franklin Watts Ltd.
Edwards, J.D. (1973), *Electrical Machines*, International Textbook Company Ltd.
Howard, S. (1980), *Machines*, Blackwell Raintree.

James, A. (1975), *Newspapers*, Blackwell.

James, A. (1976), *The Telephone Operator*, MacMillan Educational.

Johnson, T.E. *The Post Office and You*, GPO.

Jones, C. *Television*.

Ladyman, P. (1979), *Electronics*, Hodder and Stoughton Ltd.

Page, R. (1967), *The Story of the Post*, Blacks.

Pitt, W. (1975), *Signals*, Franklin Watts Ltd.

Sutton H.T. and Lewis G. (1973), *Words Travel*, Cassell.

Taylor, B. (Ed.) (1972), *Communications*, Brockhampton Press.

Williams, B. (1978), *Inventions and Discoveries*, Franklin Watts Ltd.

Wilson. G. (1974), *Newspapers*, Franklin Watts Ltd.

News

(a) Outline design of course:
  (i) History of communication and study of various forms in modern world.
  (ii) Newspaper)
  (iii) Radio   ) Production of — 2 (every three weeks.)
(b) Communications, for example, Radio, T.V., mail, telephone, newspapers, books, railways and transport. talking. (Production of folder.) Study of medium through research etc.
(c) Newspaper)
  Radio   ) establishment of requirements (see sheet) + role.
  Notes: All children to act as reporters. Details of + continuation of 'headlining'. 'Halve' class — groups of eleven and eight in actuality).
  Roles: (All roles rotate.)
  (i) *Newspaper* (a) Editorial Board (five + self). Responsible for deciding content/headlining etc., layout.
            (b) Typist/scribe.) Remainder of group responsible for
            (c) Reporters/artists.) features.
  (ii) *Radio*   (a) Editorial Board (four + self) (as above).
            (b) Newsreader.
            (c) Pop presenter/interviewer.
            (d) Playwright/story-teller.
            (e) Reporters.

Note: Work on programme/newspaper to work around study of forms — production of folder by group of four. Each child to concentrate on topics of own choice under general headings, no two members of group to study same unless special permission sought, although cross-subject work may be necessary.

Areas of Study to Follow

(a) *Applicable to each topic*:
History — first inventions/applications.
Present form — how important to modern world?
Future — what plans might group have.

(b) *Specifics*:
(i) Radio/TV surveys:	categorization of programmes by time (from *T.V. Times* and *Radio Times*.) Favourite programmes of class/staff/school. (Friday methods of presentation).
(ii) Telephones/mail: TV/radio	Costs including comparison between effectiveness and cost. Networks — creation of mail/telephone service? Processes followed.
(iii) Newspapers/TV:	advertising. Style of presentation.
(iv) Speech/sign language:	language diversification (reasons for, types of etc.) Body language — how does this work — Observation.
(v) Railways/transport:	What uses? Effects of line closure (local 1969) — question family.
(vi) Books:	What type preferred? How made?

N.B.: Each group is to have at least one member working on folder at any time, whilst others may work on 'production'.
Need to keep folder 'ticking-over'.

Newspaper

News from school/home/town
Funnies
Radio page — what's on radio
TV and book reviews
Crossword
Advertisements
'Did you know' (?)
Features — interviews *or* problems
Letters
Sport (?)

Radio

Interviews

Plays/stories
Pop programme (singles)
News — reports (as above -ish)

Group 1 — Radio (SUN)

SUZY TORRICE	CHRISTOPHER RAFFERTY
KIRSTY WOOLSEY	PAUL KING
MICHELLE KEARNEY	PAUL HEWITT
LISA HARRIMAN	MATTHEW BLOOMFIELD

Group 2 — Newspaper (Moon)

MARTIN DEAN	MATTHEW PAGE
ALLAN MILLER	ESTELLE BURTON
RICHARD HAMMOND	LYNSEY READ
MARTIN BEALE	JOANNA FREEBAIRN
JASON LUDLAM	LOUISE MAYER
TIMOTHY LITTLE	

Final Groups for Folder Work

Group A — TV

Joanna Freebairn
Louise Mayer
Estelle Burton
Lynsey Read

Group B — Radio

Kirsty Woolsey
Suzy Torrice
Michelle Kearney
Lisa Harriman

Group C — Railways

Martin Dean
Allan Miller
Richard Hammond

Group D — Telephone

Timothy Little
Matthew Page

Group E — Newspapers

Christopher Rafferty
Paul King
Matthew Bloomfield
Paul Hewitt

Group F — Other Forms of Transport

Jason Ludlam
Martin Beale (formerly part of
Group D)

Lesson Plan: Environmental Studies

Thursday, 2 May 1985   19 children, 10 and 11 years
1.15–2.30pm.   old, mixed ability.

Intentions

This lesson is intended to introduce and initiate the project, 'Communications in the Modern World', and as such will focus on the work scheme as per attached sheet. As this work is largely self-directed the class will be able to practice discussion skills and negotiation strategies during this lesson. In the second section of the lesson, oral English skills will be developed and the fear of listening to their own voice faced.

Equipment

Cassette recorder + tape. Sheets of loose paper. Class readers.

Classroom Management

Class to sit in 'computer groupings'. Each child to be given a sheet of paper. (Martin D to be included in first newspaper group to allow me to aid his usage of the typewriter within normal class situation). List of order of recording to be kept for use during activity three.

Introductions

Initial discussion on communications and their role in the modern world. Class to provide as many examples of communications as possible-list on blackboard. (20 minutes)
Discussion within groups as to which topic to be followed — negotiation on class level to avoid duplication. (10 minutes)
Division of groups into radio/newspaper groupings for eventual productions — discuss eventual outcome. (10 minutes)

Activities

(i)   Class to read silently from class readers whilst activity two is progress. (35 minutes)

(ii)   One group at a time to record about two sentences onto the cassette tape:- rotation of groups until all have recorded. (35 minutes)
(iii) Playback of recordings to whole class, who try to guess who is speaking. (35 minutes)

Conclusion

All children to be asked to act as reporters for next Tuesday's session, any interesting personal or school stories or happenings to be brought in for use. Mode of relaying is not important.

Summary

Titles chosen for production are:
Radio Redgate
Redgate Express.
Class seem interested in project. Attentive to instructions and willing to offer ideas.

Some unwillingness to work quietly when asked to. Planning needs to ensure that Michelle's return does not place her in a position to disrupt the lesson.

Own pacing needs looking at when dealing with such a difficult amount of work.

Lesson Plan: Environmental Studies

Tuesday 7 May 1985   19 children, 10 and 11 years
9.40–10.40am.   old, mixed ability

Intentions

This lesson is intended to continue the project work instigated in the previous lesson. The 'production' units (Sun and Moon) are to begin their work, and as such will practice further their discussion and negotiation skills. In the second part of this lesson the groups (A to E) will begin their folder on their topic as decided previously. The actual skills and abilities which result will be dependent on the order of work each group decides on.

Equipment

Seven folders, loose paper (exercise book size). Reference books and posters as per attached list. List of roles.

Classroom Management

Class to divide into computer groups, but with the two constituting 'production' unit Sun occupying the desks at the far end of the classroom (desks A).

Editorial meetings to be held at desks 1A and 5E (unit Moon). *N.B.*desk 1A to be moved into corner position.

Own role to be that of a resource rather than a director.

Introductions

(i)   Collection of any reports already written as per instructions (5 minutes)
(ii) Discussion within 'production' groups to decide roles in these (see planning sheet) (mediation as appropriate). (15 minutes)
(iii) Discussion within folder groups to decide rough index for work, and individual responsibilities for work within the topic. (15 minutes)

Activities

(i)   Editorial boards meet to discuss contents of production, and)
      designate tasks for group members (nine members of class).)
(ii) Remainder of each 'folder' group to begin work on topic as) 20 mins
      decided in introduction.   )

Conclusion

Reiterate need for all to seek out stories. Suggest that any relevant information from home is brought in if possible.

Summary

No reports as yet.

Class find difficulty with assessing work for themselves, with regard to the distribution of jobs — needed help in all groups.

Some confusion with grouping — remedied with advice.

Activity (1) undertaken by whole group — this undoubtably a better idea at this stage.

Topic work: outline planning caused some problems, with aid required in two groups to suggest ideas within each topic area. Group D split into two by mutual agreement with Martin B and Jason instigating a topic on other forms of transport used for communication.

Lesson Plan: Environmental Studies

Thursday 9 May 1985   19 children. 10 and 11 years old,
1.15–2.30pm.   mixed ability

Intentions

This lesson is the continuation of the work initiated on 'communications'. The aims, therefore, are those common to the course, (see overall plans for these).

Equipment

Various books as per resources sheet. Folders. Loose paper. Paper punch.

Classroom Management

The class are to sit in their seats as allotted on Tuesday 7 May 1985. Work is to be self-directed, with access to the library for groups of up to three. Own role to be prompter/adviser. No more than two people from one group to work on productions.

Introductions

Folder work should be self-directing, therefore requiring no stimulation.

Production units to be begun by collecting reports, and or initiating the same within the individual groups. Work may also be stimulated by the meeting of the editorial boards.

Activities

The class are to begin their folder work according to their agreed plans for Tuesday. (whole lesson)

Meeting of the editorial boards to discuss the responsibilities of their unit, and to initiate same. (20 minutes)

Conclusions

Individually awarded suggestions for future directions to be given. Continuity to occur in future lessons.

Summary

The fears I had about the class not working were ill-founded. The whole class continued to work throughout the lesson except for the occasional disturbance caused by the editorial boards.

More resources would be an advantage.

Pressure must be applied if the first editions are to hit the 'deadline'.

Investigate the production costs of the newspaper — duplicated copies for how many required?

Newspaper unit in greater difficulty than radio at present.

Evaluation of Environmental Studies Lessons — Week 3

I have decided to evaluate the two environmental studies lessons undertaken this week together because in actuality the content of both really could be one. Equally the evaluation of either independently would be pointless due to the entwined nature of them.

The topic of 'communications', as has been said in the overall planning, is one recommended in the curriculum guidelines of the school, although the actual approach is open to individual teacher's desires. Consequently the design of my programme of work deliberately concentrated on not only the factual discovery of forms of communication such as the invention of the radio, or the production of a television programme, but also on the development of the oral abilities of the class. To this end much stress has been placed on each child asking questions of fellow pupils and staff, and also on discussing the group folders within their groups to formulate their work. In this way it is advantageous in two ways. Firstly, it allows the child the opportunity to formulate questions which are aimed specifically at gaining particular types of answers, for example, those of the newspaper groups who decided to investigate the curricula of other classes have to decide on a standard style of precise questioning to gain the types of answer required for the eventual article. Secondly, it means that in the folder work there is no 'wrong' answer in content terms. It appears that the use of the broad headings of past, present and future are sufficient to stimulate the class into work of a self-directed nature and, at present, the ideas forwarded by the class in their brief contents pages suggest that the topic is sufficiently stimulating. From the reactions of the class thus far it would seem that the content (and likewise the design) of the project is appropriate to the learners.

How educationally significant the work is can again be judged by reference to the advantages discussed above. I believe that it is important that children develop their personal communicative skills whilst at school, and that both written and oral skills are given equal attention. This belief I have tried to build into the course, placing great stress on the oral skills of the class. From Thursday's lesson it became apparent that for some children, especially Lynsey, who have difficulties with written work, oral work is highly appropriate, Lynsey is a member of the editorial board currently responsible for producing the *Redgate Express* newspaper. Normally Lynsey shows signs of disinterest when undertaking written work, but in these sessions she showed great interest, in fact becoming the leading member of the 'board'. She contributed several ideas for articles and was largely responsible for the outline layout of the newspaper. It would appear that for Lynsey and her editorial board the exercise was valuable.

The second editorial board made up of girls was able to produce a series of ideas without any prompting which should translate into a workable radio show. The discussion which produced this plan was obviously constructive, although occasionally heated, and suggests that the group as a whole shared a higher ability in discussion techniques than some members of the other board. It will be necessary, I feel, to spend more time with the newspaper board to ensure that Estelle and Martin play a full part in the discussions. At present this part of the project appears to be working adequately.

What then of the individual folder work? At this stage it is not really possible to assess in great detail the work being undertaken, but it is noticeable that some of the class are prepared to do as little work as possible with little attention to grammar, spelling etc. and with only a few lines being written. This must be the major area of concern in the written work of this project.

My own performance was, I feel, rewarding from the relationship point-of-view, with the class appearing to accept me in my role as teacher, but also being prepared to discuss things on a personal level. The major reason for this I believe was the absence of Mrs. Darby which made me a kind of surrogate class teacher — a fact which had both advantages and disadvantages. In lesson times the former far outweighed the latter as it meant that I felt I had the freedom to operate in my own way without needing to consider the usual approach adopted to the class. Of course, this also had the drawback that the class had to adapt to a new set of demands which must have unsettled them to a certain extent, but hopefully this situation will soon settle down.

From a more general performance point-of-view I feel reasonably happy that I had provided sufficient resources or that they were available in the library area, and that the class were made aware of their location and were able to use them when required. The second consideration in this area, namely the questioning and explanatory skills, also seemed to be working fairly well although I must take care not to over-direct or explain things which would be counter to the overall aim of the course.

The above seems rather self-congratulatory, and must now be tempered with some criticism. Strangely this relates to my enthusiasm. My biggest worry is that in my enthusiasm for the production of media it may be that I am over-expecting of the class. By this I mean that I may be expecting the final production to be too 'polished' for such a short length of time — consequently I must make certain that I do not over-demand of any child which might deaden the prevailing enthusiasm they feel. My second major problem was that I spent too much time with one editorial board at the expense of the rest of the class. This had two effects: firstly the rest of the class had to work alone (which in its way is no bad thing) and may have felt unable to ask about problems, and secondly those that did only disrupted the editorial board. It became obvious that this board needed help with their discussion, but my major worry must be to assess the right moment to leave such a group for elsewhere — this must be worked on.

In conclusion it seems that the class are gaining experience in the skills I had intended them to, albeit at a varying pace. It is at this time too early to assess in detail the development within the folder groups although Matthew Page and Tim. Little are starting to produce a series of ideas for their topic which show that thought has gone into it concerning methods of enquiring into the types, costs, usage etc. of telephones. It will be particularly interesting to see how they present this information.

Hopefully, therefore, the course has been adequately initiated and the class will gain greatly from it.

UNIVERSITY OF EAST ANGLIA SCHOOL OF EDUCATION RECORD OF TEACHING SUPERVISION

Student's Name	Year	School	Supervisor/Teacher

Date	Time Seen	Class/Group	Age	Activity
4.6.85	From 9.15 To 10.30	5	10–11	Environmental Studies

Comments

The series of lessons recorded in the log book, of which the lesson observed is one, is complex and adventurous in intention, in the demands upon class management, use of space / resources, and your own transmission skills. Your notes show that you are acutely hesitant, i.e. lacking in confidence. You need not be. This represents the kind of planning and practice which many experienced teachers shy away from because it is so difficult and demanding. The learning intentions are varied — they take account of group and individual needs. Activities devised for achieving them are meaningful to the children, within their grasp but also extending experience through first-hand involvement Organization involved the children in responsibility for their own learning and in cooperation with others, yet it shows your own responsibility for guiding the work of individuals. Your evaluations are detailed and extensive, with accounts of pupils work and your own actions. They show your awareness of events, and a sense of flexibility. You are honest and realistic in handling the dilemmas of teaching. If you can accept that we all face such dilemmas you may gain some confidence. Some of those dilemmas were evident in this particular lesson — 'self-initiated' activities stated as your intention (a laudable and admirable one which you should continue) do not come easily to some children (your notes say '. . . needs pushing'). Your actions in relation to individuals, i.e. as consultant, do constitute 'teaching' but of a different kind which needs balancing with a system of class pacing. Individuality has to be fitted to group production — and so on.

It seems that the major need you have is to devise a monitoring/pacing sytem whereby the various activities and individuals/groups can be *seen* to be progressing by the class as a whole. Overall this work represents commendable progress and incorporates many features of good classroom technique which I have not mentioned above, but which now constitute your demonstrated classroom competence.

Part Four

Recasting Partnership for
Learning Teaching

Implementing Research-based Initial Teacher Education

In 1982 HMI identified 'a number of factors most frequently associated with good practice' among new teachers in a sample of 294 schools in England and Wales (DES, 1982). Three-quarters of the teachers were said to be adequately trained. The factors were:

pupils' participation, interest and involvement;

good organization with a balance and variety of objectives;

efficient use of materials and equipment;

good relationships often characterized by a shared sense of purpose and mutual respect;

productive and lively discussion usually associated with varied questioning techniques;

good planning and preparation and a choice of content appropriate to the ages and abilities of pupils;

The factors were seen as interdependant; that is, teaching is recognized as an holistic and complex activity demanding a high order of affective, intellectual and practical capability. What seems surprising is that after more than a century of compulsory schooling the characteristics of good practice among new entrants to the profession have only so recently been the subject of analysis. There would probably be little disagreement among professional teachers about the importance of the factors identified, though they were not listed as a definitive set of criteria by which good teaching could be judged. Nor did the study offer clear means by which such criteria might be applied, nor principles about how good practice could be acquired, by the teachers themselves and particularly by those who were deemed to be performing inadequately. For all of the sample the factors considered were associated with individual teacher-pupils activities within classroom instruction. They do not extend to the wider role of teaching — relationships with parents, participation in the community, and curriculum evaluation and development, which are clearly regarded as part of teachers' professional responsibilities. The implications are that, based on that sample and the judgment of HMI, a quarter of new entrants are not adequately equipped for good classroom practice nor the means to improve their practice. Perhaps none are prepared for the role of self-improvement of practice and their wider professional responsibilities.

Within the learning of instructional techniques, the micro-teaching movement in initial training set down hundreds of mechanical acts for the student teacher to learn to perform. (for example, Brown, 1975) The method of micro-teaching, which often assumed clinical and sterilized learning conditions far removed from classroom realities and often associated with a particular kind of instructional teaching, has largely been submerged within more dominant conventions of teaching practice. Those conventions have involved the observation and testing of holistic acts of teaching. Between micro-teaching and the holistic view of good practice conducted by experienced teachers for students to model there have been numerous attempts to define the essential elements of the tasks of teaching and to develop 'effective' training programmes. (The Teacher Education Project discussed earlier is one extensive systematic approach to the problem.) There have also been moves to systematize 'partnership' between students, teachers and tutors in order to improve the experience of students learning classroom technique, to establish school-based in-service education for teachers, and to keep tutors in touch with classroom practice. Models of 'IT-INSET', which were also discussed earlier have been said to offer the potential for effective partnership which would serve the needs of the partners, at least within the conventions of professional or 'methods' courses. Those needs, however, are being radically altered by the increasing complexity of the teacher's role, including those aspects of it conducted outside of classrooms. I have argued therefore that new conceptions of teacher education and professional development, and especially a new conception of partnership, are needed. In this section I will discuss in detail the programme of *Student Attachment to Schools* at the University of East Anglia as an example of the practical implementation of a reconceptualization of partnership.

In the earlier sections I have argued that the acquisition and extension of practical knowledge is the key to professional credibility and the heart of the professional enterprise, and that research is the key to practical knowledge. Research-based teacher education seeks commitment to the construction and reconstruction of teaching beyond competence, through proficiency, to the point of excellence for individual teachers. In the case of partnership for initial teacher education I have contended that this can be achieved by involving students, teachers, and teacher educators in systematic questioning, the development of research skills, and a concern to generate and test theory in practice. A commitment to systematic classroom research provides the essential characteristics of autonomous professional self-development through educative experience. It offers the means by which good practice may be acquired by individual teachers, and also offers one avenue of potential reform in schools. Through this unifying view of classroom practice and educational research, literature generated in the wider professional community on substantive, methodological and theoretical issues can become more accessible and more valuable to students, teachers and teacher educators by being grounded in educational experience and practice. To achieve recognition of this unity between practice and theory in partnership means working for an understanding of the apparently disparate overt interests of and demands upon students, teachers and tutors in order to establish dialogue in a framework of community interest. That means establishing relationships which will enable benefits to be seen to accrue to schools and their pupils through the professional commitments described in Part Two. Central to the whole purpose of those relationships and the benefits to pupils is the student teacher, the experiences s/he gets, and the consequences of those experiences in the kinds of teachers who enter the profession.

In Part Three I discussed what the practice of research-based initial teacher education begins to look like in the treatment of the early experience of student teachers, and the formal place of practical professional preparation within an undergraduate programme. There were also illustrations of the ways in which practical teaching is developed to a stage of proficiency for recommendation to certification, through a dialogue in partnership centred around the *Professional Preparation: Discussion and Assessment Document*. Those illustrations, like the description and analysis of aspects of *Student Attachment to Schools* which follow, represent a very small part of the evidence available from the conduct and evaluation of the programme since 1982. The degree programme, which I will describe briefly, has a formal structure with defined areas of curriculum content and aspects of teaching competence to be learned. A compulsory range of classroom methods courses reflect the basic demands of preparation for teaching the conventional range of primary/middle school curriculum subjects: language, mathematics and science, humanities, creative arts and physical education. Cross-discipline issues such as those related to children with special educational needs in the ordinary school, and the study of psychological, philosophical and sociological foundations of education are also compulsory. A required proportion of 'elective' courses to complement 'core' units allows students to accumulate particular strengths or to broaden the range of curriculum expertise, in accordance with intending career routes and individual interests. Classroom experience is provided for in four courses of *practical professional preparation*, in each of which 'blocks' of teaching are complemented by seminar group preparation for, and analysis of, practice. Subject options are studied alongside mainstream subject students within the University; education students may specialize in one subject or gain a broader spread of subject study experience.

The content and formal administrative structure of the degree is underpinned by a curriculum structure in which the aspiration towards the active participation of students, teachers, and tutors within a concept of partnership for research-based teacher education has played an important part. That has been sought by defining the curriculum process according to a set of *principles of procedure*. The *principles* were devised to guide and inform the conduct of the teaching and learning experiences of the students, teachers and tutors. Set out in a formal statement the *principles* read:

(i)   the content and pedagogy of courses should be designed to promote students' acquisition of classroom skills and capacity for reflective thinking about their own action;

(ii)   the role of the teacher will be explored through the explicit acceptance of the reality of the student's situation as a *student-teacher*;

(iii) tutors should consciously present themselves in a variety of teacher-roles (for example, teacher as enquirer, master practitioner, consultant etc.) and discussion of these roles should be incorporated into courses;

(iv)   the pedagogy of a course should be open to examination with students and should be expected either to reflect the content of the course or should be capable of explicit justification;

(v)   the Principles of Procedure should be discussed with students and among working teams of tutors and should be seen as representing a commitment to debating professional issues and approaches.

The aims or goals of the programme are defined as the acquisition of professional skills, understanding of professional responsibilities, and the development of a capacity for reflective thinking. The procedures for this acquisition and development are to include enquiry and dialogue among the members of the partnership, with the responsibilities for defining specific classroom skills and understanding, and the methods of acquiring them, led by tutors and teachers in an accepted framework of critique and evaluation. A strategy for evaluation based on cooperative investigation by students, tutors and teachers was also implemented through a system of enquiry teams. The evaluation is intended to inform and change the teacher education process itself in a way consistent with what is expected of students and teachers in their teaching.

Experience-based exploration of the nature of teaching and learning through enquiry and analysis sets the tone for developing professional practice beyond competency-based 'skills', beyond entry into the profession for inductees, and into the realm of research by practising teachers and teacher-educators and *their* continuous professional development. It is that range of research which has been generated since the degree began which provides the background to this report. The research has involved a large number of people, studying different aspects of the work, including for example, the history of the degree; the socialization of students into the University; staff and student perceptions of the *principles of procedure*; the conduct of practical professional preparation courses; the evaluation of teaching and learning within educational studies courses; and the perceptions of headteachers, teachers, tutors and students in the development of partnership. Most of the research has been conducted by students and lecturers, with participation by research associates from the Centre for Applied Research in Education. It has been pursued within a research and development framework of educational evaluation consistent with the curriculum design of the degree.

The research has mostly been participant and participant-observational in its methods, utilizing documentary evidence and adopting techniques of classroom observation, interview, discussion and reflective accounts of practice. As well as extensive documentary data, other data includes field notes and audio-tape recordings. The work which follows represents one element of the BA experience, the development of partnership between the School of Education and local schools through *Student Attachment to Schools*.

Student Attachment to Schools

The criticism that teacher education contains insufficient experience of schools for students; the fragmentation of courses into subject, professional and practical elements; and too many over-theoretical courses, can be levelled at almost any conventional unit structure in teacher education programmes. While the coherence across units in the BA degree is anticipated through the principles of procedure, the principles imply that coherence has to be facilitated through access for students to the source of practical knowledge in schools, and through a commitment to research practice by tutors and teachers. Schools are also the base for the improvement of practice through curriculum development by practising teachers and the centre for the educational research enterprise. I want to claim that *Student Attachment* has provided for integration between theory and practice, coherence across courses in the central concern for the students' acquisition of classroom skills, and partnership in curriculum development and research. These have enhanced the potential of professional development well beyond that which is possible through conventional 'teaching practice'. The intention and essence of *Student Attachment*, which came about as a responsive idea of students, teachers and tutors seeking ways to get beyond teaching practice conventions, was initially defined as:

> The development of collaborative ventures in teaching practice which might stimulate more open questioning in the profession about teaching;
>
> Closer relationships between students and schools in a period of static staffing and declining provision, as a means of introducing innovations in schools' curricula;
>
> Greater amounts and more flexible time for students in schools, over longer periods, so that students can experience wider aspects of teaching and learning in addition to classroom practice;

Involvement of tutors, students and teachers in consultancy, curriculum development and enquiry in schools;

Development of dialogue in the partnership, for professional development of those involved. (Internal discussion document February 1982)

The project was started in 1982. After a one-year pilot project with sixteen students (the final intake to the 'middle years' sector of an existing B.Ed. (Hons) Degree programme) in eight schools, it was extended by October 1984 to involve 160 early years and middle years BA students in fifty-five schools. The model of *Student Attachment* has since been incorporated in modified forms into PGCE courses for early years, middle years, and secondary students — a further 125 students in some sixty additional schools each year. For most students attachment is compulsory, providing long-term access to schools for professional induction from the beginning of their course. (Students in the middle years sector of the BA are offered the option of being attached after compulsory attachment in year one, with a large majority taking up that option.)

In the pilot project the negotiation of time commitments by students and of activities undertaken by them or experiences made available to them was initially left to individual students and schools. Many of the perceived benefits to both were seen in the pilot project to accrue from an individual and flexible approach which enabled student and teacher choice, responsibility and decision making. The facility established without tight routine and prescription was seen to enhance experience, but with associated problems. Some students and teachers found it difficult to work without direction from the University, and to enter into negotiations. The balance between facilitating initiative, individuality and flexibility and the expectations from both students and teachers that they should be directed in their activities by teacher educators became an issue for partnership. This issue is central to the initial statement of intent for *Student Attachment*, which had been devised collaboratively by teachers, students, and tutors, and which was reiterated in the principles for the extension of the project:

UNIVERSITY OF EAST ANGLIA
SCHOOL OF EDUCATION

Student Attachment to Schools
PRINCIPLES
Year 1
All first year students, would be allocated to a school soon after arrival at UEA. Attachment would provide for professional induction through contact with teachers and children; it would enable contact with students from other year groups; and it would provide opportunities to relate education studies to experience in schools. Individual arrangements for contact times and commitment would be negotiated between students and school on a contract basis.

Year 2 and 3

Second and third year students would be offered the *option* of attachment for a year. Those who took the option would be allocated to a school at the start of the academic year. Commitment would be negotiated on a contract basis, i.e. it would be open to students themselves, in consultation with their tutors and schools, to determine in relation to coursework demands, how much time they could give to their school. (See note below — Negotiating Commitments).

Students who opt for PPP only would be allocated to schools for PPP for one term.

A Link tutor would be named for contact in the School of Education for particular schools/students.

A Link teacher would be named in each school to enable a single contact through whom students would initially be introduced to the school, and with whom tutors could discuss the development of attachment in each school.

Attachment would not be assessed and would not be part of any PPP course.

A complete list of personnel would be published and circulated so that 'contact points' are known to each person.

Negotiating Commitments

The problems involved in negotiating a contract between students and teachers are considerable, yet the benefits from the experience are valued highly by those who were involved previously. However, several points need stressing:

Undergraduate students may be highly constrained by coursework timetables. This will vary. BA students in science schools, for example, have extremely heavy commitments in some terms.

Most students will have limited experience on which to base negotiations. Adjustments may prove necessary. First year students in particular will need time to adjust to their commitments after arrival at UEA.

The nature of possible activities will vary between students and schools and the demands of different kinds of activities also varies.

Activities

The actual activities in which students might become involved are numerous. It is assumed that Attachment offers opportunity beyond classroom teaching, to be involved in wider aspects of school life.

Individuality and Flexibility

Many of the perceived benefits have arisen because there has not been tight prescription. The qualities of experiences for individual students and schools have been enhanced because the attachment *facility* was established without routine. Although large numbers will be involved, these qualities (identified in evaluation comments) can be maintained if there is room for initiative, individuality and flexibility.

With the extension to large numbers of students, tutors, and schools and the associated logistics for administering, developing, and evaluating the arrangements the principles of *Student Attachment* and other aspects of communication had to be formalized through a network of link tutors and link teachers. Each link tutor has responsibility for working with several schools and contact with those schools is made through the link teacher. Where several students are attached to a school the link teacher coordinates activities within the school, liaising with supervising teachers and students internally. The team of link teachers are thus key personnel, representing the perspectives of the schools at policy meetings held regularly by the School of Education. Supervising teachers meet and are consulted within schools, though this is predominantly with regard to *Practical Professional Preparation* courses, which are conducted within the schools to which students are attached. The longer-term contact with the teachers enables their involvement in the conduct of professional courses in activities both in the schools where research-based assignments are negotiated and carried out, and in seminars in the School of Education. Partnership arrangements are co-ordinated and administered within the School of Education, separately for 'early years', 'middle years' and 'secondary' sectors. In each sector the network of schools is sub-divided between link tutors:

School of Education Sector Administration

Link Tutor

Students	Students	Students	Students
School	School	School	School
Link teacher	Link teacher	Link teacher	Link teacher
Supervising	Supervising	Supervising	Supervising
teachers	teachers	teachers	teachers

Administrative coordination ensures that written requests to schools for student placements, information about meetings, details of changes in placements, documentation related to *Practical Professional Preparation* courses, and other similar details are centrally controlled. Individual commitments of link tutors and internal discussions among them are negotiated and held within sectors.

In the idea of closer partnership a central concern was to overcome the inadequacies of conventional 'detached' teaching practice, its short time-span, and the gap between education studies and 'real' school life. Students and teachers have regarded *Attachment* as a step towards better preparation for developing classroom competence (which is formally dealt with in courses of practical professional preparation); providing broader experience of school life and the social context of school communities; enabling the establishment of relationships between those involved; and permitting teachers to participate in students' development over longer periods. But attachment can only be innovative if the nature of activities undertaken moves beyond the concern for basic classroom competence, to involve students and teachers in investigating and understanding learning/teaching for the promotion of excellence. To be seen to be different from the conventions of teaching practice it needs to be judged against the conceptions and promise of research-based teacher education outlined earlier. The students' acquisition of classroom competence and its development to proficiency was considered in Part Three. Here I want to consider the wider relevance of *Attachment* for the professional development of students, and the effects of that on the work of the teachers in terms of professional development and school-based curriculum evaluation and development.

In the pilot project research-based activities included, for example, commissions from schools to:

evaluate mathematics teaching in a school programme;

develop 'Man: A Course of Study' provision in four schools;

undertake social studies curriculum development in isolated rural schools;

establish ceramics teaching;

cooperate in establishing a team-teaching approach to art education;

mount week-long field work expeditions with teachers and pupils.

Subsumed within each of these sorts of activities students worked on acquiring a range of competences in classroom and school 'techniques'. They went further in developing collegial and management expertise in innovation and evaluation, together with the handling of the tools of enquiry and the development of critical awareness. Individual student initiatives included matters such as:

the diagnosis of difficulties in individual pupils' spelling, and devising ways of teaching spelling;

a study of changes in pupil grouping within a classroom organization, and the consequences for pupil interaction and learning;

development of assessment and record keeping as a means of monitoring individual pupils' progress and maintaining continuity in learning;

introducing an innovation in pupils' learning through problem-solving in mathematics;

an analysis of sex stereotyping in curriculum practice in first schools.

In these kinds of activities too the types of skills and competences developed through a research approach to practice subsumed the practice itself. Those skills involve judgement, analysis and further application of understanding in practice, conducted in cooperation with teachers. In the example illustrated below, the student is learning teaching technique within the mode of 'real problem solving' by working with the teacher. Concurrently both cooperated in evaluating the particular mathematical experiences of the pupils, while the student was also able to analyze his own learning during the project.

Real problem solving — mathematics?

If your aims for mathematics do not include that mathematics can be *fun* and that the mathematics the children engage in should be *relevant* then it is unlikely you would wish to involve your pupils in Mathematics: Real Problem Solving. The notion that children develop problem solving skills when they are given the opportunity to solve, through mathematics, a problem THEY have, was suggested by the Open University Mathematics Course. I first heard of this during my INSET BEd Course. Since then I have used Real Problem Solving each year. When Toby Salt, my student, heard he was to teach the top set of twelve year olds for mathematics, he almost panicked! Unlike myself he had never found that mathematics was 'fun'. (Although no great mathematician I have always enjoyed mathematics and try to show children that it is *fun* but also relevant to their everyday lives.)

And now a word from the student — yes, I nearly panicked! I was asked to teach thirty-four 4th Year top set mathematicians at Catton Grove Middle School. There was a 'real problem' of how I was going to generate enough enthusiasm to motivate the children. I had the advantage that I was going to be attached to the school for the whole year which meant that it was possible for us to embark on a long term problem solving project. It was agreed that such a project would extinguish many of my worries. The problem if relevant and real enough to the children would motivate them itself. My role would also change from being an unconvincing expert to an informed advisor — the emphasis would shift from my shoulders onto the children's, as they found solutions to a problem that affected them.

Faced with this we decided to ask the children if there was a problem they wanted to solve. At the time they were deciding which secondary school they would attend. The problem became 'Which Secondary School?' Is there a *best* secondary school in the Norwich area?

Too often we are satisfied with 'our' children using the lower-level mental skills, but for Real Problem Solving they are required to use:

Formulation and interpretation
Existing skills in a wide variety of situations which are often
    unexpected and both social and mathematical skills in
    relevant situations

From their viewpoint they can see that what is involved is part of adult life, provides a flavour of adult experience and requires that the problem is solved to the satisfaction of the problem solver and does not depend on a 'right' answer.

As the 'leaders' we became aware that with the number of children involved, thirty-four, and the breadth of this Problem a certain amount of structure would need to be imposed. The acronym PROBLEMS provide this.

P: Posed the Problem — 'Which Secondary School?'

R: Refine the areas to be investigated — The set divided into eight groups, six to investigate Comprehensive Schools, one for Norwich School, and a 'Questionnaire Group' to collect internal data.

O: Outline the question to ask. This involved producing a questionnaire on which aspects of school life the group (they were sometimes different) considered to be important in the choice of school.

B: Bring home the data — Each group wrote a letter to their school and letters were also sent to the Police and Eastern Counties Bus Company. The Questionnaire Group interviewed each child in the year group.

As a result of the letters information was obtained, sometimes by letter but, more often, by an invitation to visit the school for part of a day and conduct interviews.

L: Look for solutions — Having receivd the information then decisions had to be made about how best it could be presented in order to answer the following questions:

'Can we find a clear result?'

'Does it answer our questions?'

'So what is the solution?'

This required the groups to re-form so that the statistics from each group could be examined and interpreted.

E: Establish recommendations — 'How can we fit the solutions together?'. At all stages of the Mathematics Real Problem solving the children report back. This involves a considerable amount of group discussion and decision making. Each member of the group presents a resume in turn.

Is there *a best* secondary school? Not according to our findings. We have, however, decided that there are certain conditions which will influence the choice:

1   How far you are prepared to travel.
2   How long you are prepared to be away from home each day.
3   If your brother/sister attends the school.
4   How much your parents can afford to pay for uniform and travel.

   M: Make it happen — We leave the choice of school to the individual, bearing in mind the previous findings. All the schools have excellent facilities for games, physical education and computer studies. Comparison of CSE and 'O' level results helped identify the major 'success' areas, which may vary from subject to subject, but are really very similar. Every school visited has shown the 'caring' attitude children need on transferring from the 'homely' atmosphere of a middle school to, what appears on the surface an enormous, overwhelming institution. We would like to extend our gratitude to the schools for their invaluable assistance.

         Something we are both agreed upon is that much of the success of this project can be attributed to the following:

         (a) that we were joint facilitators prepared at all times to both teach and *learn.*

         (b) the problem was REAL and

         (c) *All* of us enjoyed the experience and were prepared to make mistakes as well as 'glory' in our successes.

   S: So what next? Have your children a problem they can solve through Real Problem Solving? Why not ask them and maybe they (and you) will find that mathematics *is* relevant and is fun.

The range of experiences and activities described are representative of work carried out during the pilot project which was monitored by students, teachers and tutors. The benefits of *Student Attachment* which accrued to the schools were seen in the eyes of headteachers and teachers to be in the ways in which staff development occurred through working with the students. It was said that the teachers became more consciously analytical of their own teaching and developed higher expectations for that teaching. That arose as teachers became more involved in the professional development of individual students over a whole year, and in the research-based activities which were said to bring qualitatively different expectations about the job of teaching. Students were seen as a significant asset in terms of skills, ideas, and manpower, and were seen to gain from experiencing 'what school is really like'. Closer contact with academic staff and increased dialogue about teaching had also become possible. Pupils were seen to gain from continuity in content and teaching strategies, and from students' familiarity with the school and their knowledge of the pupils. Overall students were seen as being better prepared for entry into the profession through more extensive and wider ranging practical experience of school life.

    Students' perceptions of their gains recognized the value of opportunities to work with children in a variety of situations and a range of activities, including extra-curricular and field-work programmes. They also valued being able to initiate activities and carry them through because there was time to do so, but also because they felt more fully accepted within the schools as relationships became established. Those activities and relationships brought increased confidence in the light of developed competence, with opportunities to analyze problems in practical teaching and effect action to improve it. The opportunities to work with others, engaging in co-operative learning ventures, were also seen to bring considerable advantages over the more isolated classroom teaching practice. A less tangible benefit, perceived impressionistically by academic staff and students, was the quality of experiences in related academic course work and seminar participation. The development of a school experience enquiry base, with opportunities for investigative/curriculum development studies related to theoretical issues, was reflected in seminar and written coursework assignments, including public presentations of 'findings' for academic staff and students.

The practicalities of implementing the degree programme and *Student Attachment* are complex and problematic. The initial evaluation provided an image like Janus, facing the optimism of educational renewal in the benefits such as those described above, and viewing the pessimism of a wintry conservatism in the difficulties of innovation. Some features of the wintry face of Janus will be discussed later, in a consideration of constraints on authentic partnership. For the moment I want to take the optimistic face defined in the initial evaluation of the pilot project. The dissemination of *Attachment* was based on that more optimistic image and was achieved through a range of activities. A conference for teachers, students, tutors and LEA officers was hosted in cooperation with the local teachers' centre, where evaluations, issues and revised proposals were considered. Discussions were led by teachers and students involved in the pilot project, and involved representatives from all the schools which would be involved in the extension programme. Negotiations with those schools had been conducted through discussions with headteachers and teachers about the concept and practical arrangements of *Attachment*. Briefing sessions with students and tutors within the Sector were arranged, and a 'forum' for supervising and link teachers was planned. These discussions allowed issues and policy to be considered and reformulated over several meetings. Formalization of the link tutor and link teacher contact, to enable more regular and more frequent meetings within schools, also occurred though the role of the tutor did not become that of supervisor of individual students. The implementation of teaching, curriculum development and research involving tutors directly in the schools through work with teachers began to redefine the relationships in the partnership, in complex ways. Through these means participation in the partnership led to reformulation of the principles and policies for the conduct of activities in *Attachment*. A set of 'guidelines' was devised so that conduct by students, teachers, and tutors could be seen within an agreed code of practice. The aspirations for individuality and flexibility with opportunities for initiative and decision making, together with the difficulties which they presented in negotiating activities and roles, underly the content of the 'guidelines'. They were explicitly devised to inform the conduct of all members of the partnership, incorporating their *apparently* diverse interests in learning teaching; improving teaching through reflection, evaluation and curriculum development; and reforming teaching through research. The concurrent routes of student development, curriculum development, and research development, which emerged as *Attachment* was reformed are clearly indicated in the 'guidelines'.

MIDDLE YEARS SECTOR: Forum for Link and Supervising Teachers

Recommendations for the Improvement of Student Attachment

From the 'operational' point of view of link and supervising teachers, the development of partnership between EDU/schools as a basis for the professional development of student teachers was seen as needing three main improvements:

1   Information for schools — in addition to the booklet about the BA, and the student profile of experience, teachers would welcome information about which other schools/link teachers are involved; which schools share the link tutor. It was suggested that a booklet of experiences be compiled for reference/sharing between schools.

2   Guidelines for students/teachers/tutors for the conduct of attachment especially at the stage of negotiation. These represent an immediate need to establish 'minimum practice levels', so as to clarify expectations and remove misunderstanding. (Guidelines 1)

3   Guidelines for students/teachers/tutors for the conduct of 'attachment related activities'. This arose from three sources:

    (a)   concern about research-based assignments, for instance about the student beginning research, and issues of access, anonymity, confidentiality, and potential audience. Such issues are important, given the political context of teachers' work, and the development of student expertise in enquiry methods;

    (b)   recognition that attachment in its conception set out to offer professional development for teachers/curriculum development for schools;

    (c)   aspirations for the development of research activities by teachers and tutors as a basis for *their* professional development. (Guidelines 2)

February 1985

Student Attachment to Schools — BA degree

The following guidelines for *conduct at the start of an attachment period* are proposed following discussions in the forum:

During Weeks 1, 2 and 3 of the University term:

1 Students should initiate the first meeting with the link teacher in
2 Where several students are attached to the same school, they should *jointly* arrange the first meeting (by getting together first and arranging with the headteacher/link teacher a mutually suitable time to visit the school)
3 Each student should provide a copy of their University time-table for the term, to complement the 'profile' of experience/qualifications, and a planned proposal for attachment activities which could form the basis of negotiations.
4 A minimum weekly commitment which the student knows s/he can fulfil should be agreed with the link teacher. (less than half a day a week is unlikely to be worthwhile).
5 Assignment tasks set for coursework should be copied by the student to the link teacher (and where necessary to a class teacher) as soon as available (usually week 1 of each term).
6 Link teacher should construct a mutually agreeable programme for the term, which would include defined responsibilities for the student.
7 Each student should meet with the link tutor at this point to discuss the programme of responsibilities.
8 The link tutor should visit the school, to ensure mutual under-standing of progress.

During weeks 4 onwards, conduct should be guided by the following:

9 Students' commitment should be maintained.
10 Students should meet the link tutor at least once more during the term.
11 Link tutors should visit the school at least once more during the term.
    Where possible, such meetings should occur as an arranged meeting between students, teachers and tutors.
12 For Year 1 and Year 2 students, meetings should occur twice at least in following attachment terms. For Year 3 and Year 4, contact in following terms will occur within PPP courses.

Student Attachment to Schools — BA degree

The following guidelines for *the conduct of attachment related activities*
have been developed following discussions with teachers:

1 These guidelines presume that those for conduct at the start of an
   attachment period will be followed.
2 Students should seek and be given guidance by course tutors and
   link tutors, as well as teachers, in the conduct of enquiry-based
   assignments.
3 Early opportunities for students to take on responsibilities.
4 Responsibilities to be those of real teaching — not a gentle
   immersion.
5 Students to identify and develop, through discussion, specific
   learning needs.
6 Contact between EDU students to be facilitated.
7 The prerogatives for permission to conduct assignments lies with
   the teachers/headteachers.
8 Conventions of research-based study should be followed by all
   involved.
9 The development of individual students' professional expertise
   should be considered as central to the attachment venture.
10 Where possible, the benefits of in-service and curriculum development, for teachers and tutors, for schools and EDU courses,
   should be developed through the attachment partnership.
11 Partners within attachment schools should explore opportunities
   for linking students' professional development, school/teachers'
   professional development and EDU/Tutors' professional development, through research.
12 Activities should be developed in a climate of negotiation,
   bearing in mind principle of individuality and the likelihood of
   diversity.

It was the definition of the seemingly disparate concerns which took some
time to emerge. As the data will show, the central and dominant *shared*
concern is with the students' acquisition of teaching skills, and the gaining of
classroom competence in the conventional sense. Even though *Student Attachment* is additional to the time allocated for learning teaching in that prescribed
sense, its focus first and foremost has been on the development of classroom
skills by individual students, to the extent that it has been difficult to
distinguish between *Attachment* and *PPP* activities in many respects. It has been
regarded as preparatory for *PPP*; students regarded themselves as subject to
assessment even though their work was not formally assessed; and the demand
that the School of Education should prescribe 'teaching practice' requirements
has persisted. The greatest difficulty arose in breaking the conventions of

teaching practice and recognizing the potentially innovative and qualitatively different nature of partnership within *Student Attachment*:

> School of Education was shedding its responsibility to the student and putting the burden of 'supervision' on schools. It was mentioned that perhaps the School of Education could present students with pre-scribed tasks. I do believe that the teacher accepted my explanation that negotiation between student and teacher was an essential part of attachment. (Tutor report of meeting in school)

> The lack of guidance given to both students and the school at the beginning. Everyone feels that both the school and the students should be given guidelines as to what the concept of school attach-ment involves. Some teachers are very poorly informed as far as this is concerned and seem to think that we are doing some form of teaching practice and therefore expect far too much commitment from the students. (Summary by student evaluation group)

> There was a feeling from some quarters that the teachers in schools are taking on the work of the School of Education and that the latter is abdicating its role. (Report from teacher discussions)

The perception that the major benefit of the activities was in the students' acquisition of classroom skills explains the concern about the 'abdication' of the supervisor role. Those benefits were measured against the inadequacies of teaching practice in its conventional format, but remained focussed on the same purposes of teaching practice:

> Teachers and heads applauded the notion of the attachment; they contrasted it to the old TP system in which students visited the school only a couple of times before starting their practice. The feeling is that the attachment exercise is most useful in enabling students to gather information about the school and the pupils over an extended period thus better preparing them for PPP. Secondly, it also allowed for more careful planning of schemes of work for the block practice. What was particularly heartening was the teachers' view that a real *quid-pro-quo* was in operation where schools were deriving some benefit from attachment. (Report of evaluation meeting in a school)

The advantages toward the establishment of classroom competence in teaching skills were seen as particularly pertinent by first year students, for whom subject studies appears to curtail the acquisition of classroom skills:

> It was thought, generally, that the first term would be relevant as an introduction to the rest of the four-year course and that the emphasis would be on preparing us to be capable of taking a class. When 'School Attachment' is considered this seems a particularly logical thought.

As far as the time allocation for education (as opposed to the subject study) is concerned, it seems that the unanimous expectation was more, or at least an equal time allocation with the subject study. In actual fact most students have far more hours to put in both in lectures/seminars and essays/exercises in their subject study. (Student evaluation group report)

A different group, also involved in the evaluation of the whole programme, had little doubt about the centrality of practical knowledge and its acquisition in their professional intentions:

It was felt that sometimes the 'School Attachment' scheme and the experience gained from this was the only factor to remind students that they are actually being professionally trained to 'teach'.

A number of other recommendations emerged from the questionnaire:

1 More practical emphasis on teaching and less theory in the first year. The theory would probably be more relevant later.
2 A greater proportion of time should be allotted to educational studies as opposed to subject studies, (we did come to UEA partly because we believe we were MAJORING in education). (Student evaluation group report)

Other reports from students, teachers and tutors described benefits such as the building of students' confidence through early, extensive and extended access to classrooms; the establishment of longer-term relationships with children and teachers; opportunities for 'insight into the whole running of the school'; and the sense that students were participating in and contributing to the successes of curriculum activities.

The focus on teaching competence, while recognized as a dominant concern by students, teachers and tutors needs to be seen in the context of the initial intentions and essence of the project. These include wider aspects of teaching and involvement in curriculum development. In the definitions of teaching practice, prescription, and supervision implied in some of the judgments by teachers there are a number of underlying problems which it is necessary to engage. It had been envisaged that the benefits accruing to students and schools would be mutual and equitable. Yet the commitment by teachers of time, energy and expertise for the sake of student development was considerable. In cases where students displayed weaknesses in classroom practice the demands seemed more acute, though developing cooperative activities with competent and committed students who also recognized that excellent teaching could enhance the classification of their degree award was equally challenging. The teachers faced those challenges without remuneration. with no time allotted for the work, and without recognition for it by their employers. Whereas the requirements of *PPP* placed students in schools for set periods, *Attachment* effectively doubled that time.

Days in school for PPP	1	20
	2	25
	3	30
	4	Negotiable (average 20)
Total		95

The amounts of time spent in schools for *Attachment* was approximately one day each week during the terms when no PPP course occurred, with the exception of the final examination term. In all, the commitment amounted to an additional seventy days of school experience for most students, spread throughout their programme of study.

The pressures which this placed on students was acute at times. It created major dilemmas for them about where to direct their commitments and loyalties. For example, the tension between going into school and attending seminars; the completion of coursework assignments or preparation of teaching plans; and a focus on personal classroom performance or a commissioned study for the school, recurred in the decisions which students consistently had to make. Though these may seem trite and readily resolvable, these kinds of pressures were faced in addition to the formal requirements of the course and were largely self-imposed out of the professional commitment of the students. Their desire to be in schools and to perform with proficiency in all aspects of their commitments there, while maintaining related academic coursework of a high standard, showed the difficulties of 'redistributing' the time allocated to particular activities in learning teaching. Perhaps these less tangible elements of the project provide a true induction into the management skills of professional practice by involving students in analyzing teaching, making judgments about priorities in their professional development and that of schools, and drawing on the resources of practical teaching expertise and theoretical understanding in solving educational problems. Those 'secrets of the trade' would seem to be of a much higher order than the specific techniques of classroom performance.

A commitment by tutors to supervise the additional time in a formal way would double the demand on supervision resources. It was recognized from the outset that such a demand could not be met in a context of reducing resources. In any case there was a conscious intention not to supervise the students' activities, recognizing that the supervisor role is seen by students as a predominantly assessment role. The intention was therefore that tutors would act as consultants to the students, to engage the dialogue for their development without intervention during the *Attachment* periods. The consultancy role was extended to working with teachers in facilitating school-based curriculum development. That was an expressed wish of teachers who participated in devising the project — a way as they saw it of counteracting the reducing size of school staffs, the lack of professional mobility, the lack of specific expertise in schools, and the isolation of teachers from their professional colleagues in other institutions. The involvement of students and tutors was also a way of meeting the increasing demands of accountability, school self-evaluation and curriculum development. Those concerns for curriculum development were matched by academic staff concerns to develop research opportunities in fulfilment of their contractual and professional commitments. Extensive additional supervision of students would diminish rather than enhance such opportunities. On the other hand, research and development activities could potentially be meshed with the needs of teachers and the learning of students. The range of activities being conducted by researchers in the School of Education included such topics as:

the matching of tasks to individual pupils in mathematics in primary schools;
information technology in primary schools;
the development of discourse in language;
using creativity in mathematics;
problems of children with special educational needs;
information handling in classrooms;
the curriculum of rural primary schools;
language use in science education;
development of children's writing.

This range of interests provides explicit recognition that there is much to be learned about teaching and learning, and that active research which is directly relevant to teachers' and students' classroom activities is in a fluid state. Acknowledgement of the uncertain and fluid 'state of the art' of teaching by teachers concerned to engage in their own professional development by way of curriculum research and the analysis of their own teaching has been demonstrably clear within the *Attachment* project. The intentionality of students to improve their practical competence through action and understanding is also apparent. Where *Attachment* was pursued to its limits for the mutual benefit of the partnership, it was possible to see these at first seemingly distinct concerns as reciprocal guiding directions towards the practice of research based teacher education. Incidentally the requirements of CATE for recent, relevant experience by lecturers and the close involvement of teachers in initial teacher education arose as an inherent feature of *Student Attachment to Schools* where the project was pursued to those limits.

Another underlying problem which was exposed was that of developing closer partnership with the kinds of practices and conditions which have been subject to substantial criticism. In particular the potential difficulty of student teachers spending more time being initiated into outdated practices and outmoded and deteriorating school conditions is a concern which has to be faced. That tutors might be expected to do more of what their research critiques, in pursuit of compliance with CATE, compounds that problem.

The resolution of this problem can be achieved by the adoption of a critical perspective within the framework of research-based teacher education, in which the substantive focus may be individual practice by *any* of the partners, institutional arrangements at *any* level (i.e. in schools, teacher education establishments, LEAs, or the DES), or social/cultural phenomena. That is not easy to achieve within teaching, when teachers are subject to complex expectations which are often personally threatening. During *Attachment* the adoption of critical perspectives has been attempted with some encouraging responses, in a manner which meets the unified needs within the partnership:

Link tutor: Can we start with the way you see the link tutor role from within school? (refers to note of 5 November 1984 and reference to link tutor teaching in classroom, as 'excellent', etc.)

Link teacher: I think a lot of that is to do with how people see each other ... it's excellent from the confidence it gives both teachers and particularly students to see a tutor from the University actually teaching.

Tutor: Why?

Teacher: That's the really good side of someone like yourself actually doing something practical like that.

Tutor: Is that a symbolic gesture?

Teacher: It can be but I think that's a starting point. The spin-offs ought to be far greater than that. I think those kinds of starting points are so important ... for getting away from categorizing people; for building a positive view of people ...

Tutor: Are you referring to the stereotype of a college lecturer?

Teacher: Yes. Well put it this way, in my course I never ever saw anyone teach who was supposed to be teaching me how to teach ... I never saw anyone stand up and teach. I think that's sad ... students should get the opportunity to see all the people they are talking to and learning from and working with teaching. All the people involved should see each other in every situation ...

There's no point you coming in and doing something if that means going back in time and doing a bit of teaching, or child minding or something. There's no point, no point. Everyone has to have something positive out of it ...

I would welcome closer contact with anyone doing some kind of research because — it (research) is so far away from you, the things that you read about, for instance, that people have done ... you might read about it and think what a load of tripe, what on earth were they doing, where were they ... anything that brings it closer and brings more involvement is a good thing. I certainly wouldn't feel vulnerable ...

... the main thing ... it widens your own view of what you're doing, I ... it's purely your (one's) own interest.

(Tutor talks about anxiety/uncertainty associated with learning ('changing states of mind') as an inherent part of dealing with the 'new learning'; and of the counter-productive over-anxiety which can occur.)

Teacher: But it depends how you see yourself. I work *better* with a bit of that, whatever you call it, around. That's why I like working with other people ... Being on your own in a classroom doesn't bring out the best in me as a teacher anyway ...

It depends on what you (tutor) want to do which is useful to you and useful to the school.

(Seeking a way which is beneficial equally to *all* parties, teacher is convinced that tutor presence in the classroom would do that. The teacher reiterates 'people often have fairly negative views of university lecturers in a classroom situation' — a hurdle to be got over to change perceptions of the staff in the school, and students. Such a partnership would be beneficial to the students and could overcome the dominant pressure of assessment for students.)

Teacher: The way I would see it for Attachment is that it should be very strongly grounded in a mutual assessment so that it's not a position of one person being an assessor and the other person being on the receiving end, but that we are taking it in turns to do assessment — in other words to sharpen up our critical faculties.
(Interview and notes, 18 December 1984)

The translation of the conceptions of teaching practice into the innovation of *Attachment* provides a link with the development of research perspectives enshrined in the principles of procedure of the degree programme and the aspiration for partnership towards research-based teacher education. It is in the penetration of professional proficiency that that link exists. Craftsmanship in teaching is enhanced by the longer-term practice-reflection relationship, improving the craft competence and professional credibility which practical knowledge brings, with elucidation, examination and extension of that knowledge becoming possible. It is by the way of changing the structure of the programme that access to that knowledge was provided. But within that, its treatment in developing research perspectives and the capacity for enquiry provided the key to moving even beyond proficiency and into the foundations for excellence. Something of that potential has begun to show among a substantial body of students, whose dispositions are clearly towards exploiting their own potential:

Within the undergraduate section of this School there is forming a large body of students who are beginning to question, evaluate, and research practice. They are, in effect, moving away from the notion of education as the formation of a plan followed by simple translation into practice, but are understanding that there is a serious gap between intention and realization that is contextually caused, and that many other factors fall out from this ... the body of students concerned are not an academic elite group, but come from all directions and have identified real problems to which no forum existed for them to be followed up ... With the introduction of evaluation sessions in the earliest stages of the BA Degree this body of students is likely to increase and encompass the whole of the undergraduate population. (Student letter, March 1984)

Similar potential among participant teachers has already been illustrated. It would be possible to cite many examples which have emerged from the kind of dialogue and negotiation represented in those illustrations. In most cases it has been the work of students adopting the dispositions and attitudes expressed in the letter above which has been the catalyst to school-based research.

This professional disposition to improve practice through research became a marked characteristic of *Attachment* activities, as the extracts below from interviews with fourth year students show. In some cases individual students pursuing their own enquiries, often related to practical teaching or course-work assignments (which became increasingly classroom-enquiry-based), used teachers and tutors as consultants. The case of Guy is of that type. In other cases cooperative activities instigated by schools were undertaken by teams in which head teachers pursued their own research with fieldwork contributions, data collection, analysis and reports commissioned from students. The case of Amanda is in that category. Additionally some projects involved tutors, teachers and students undertaking joint activities in innovation, practice, and evaluation. The case of Johanna is of that type.

To summarize the learning accruing from these activities for members of the partnership is impossible. In most cases extensive data and lengthy reports or exchanges of experience resulted, each with their own worth to the persons involved for informing their own practice. Within them consultancies became reciprocal, perhaps with subject expertise contributed by a student, knowledge of children and teaching coming from teachers, and of research design and methods from tutors. Sometimes the contributions were reversed. In the extracts below, the accounts also illustrate the ways in which particular substantive topics for investigation arose, and ways in which methodological expertise was developed (including recognition of limitations by Toby).

The examples also illustrate those studies which were situated within the confines of classroom practice (Guy); in broader institutional contexts of schools (Johanna); and within perspectives of social, political and cultural contexts (Amanda and Kaushika).

Guy

The proposal

Guy's plan was to devise a set of lessons about underwater diving, a personal interest and expertise. He had assisted in the *Mary Rose* archeological project, has dived in numerous locations in Britain and Ireland, and is Secretary of the University sub-aqua club. A teaching package was devised to use in schools, and sent to several schools with the offer to visit and teach the sessions, supported by his own first-hand experience, equipment, and visual materials. The first session, with twenty-five children in an urban middle school, had been conducted as an after-school activity. That was to be followed up by a visit to a first school, for which the material had been suitably modified.

Description of the activity

The thing I wanted to do was to see how much understanding children can get in just forty minutes of me leading their work. So really I'm a type of television programme but with the ability to question and answer, with flexibility of time. Say, the second session, on habitat and the marine environment, that is putting into forty minutes what first-year undergraduates learn really. Some of it comes from an introduction to a book and one third year undergrad. said 'I wish they'd put it as easily as that in our first year'. So it's putting over quite complicated ideas and a lot of content-oriented stuff but with the understanding behind it, and I just want to see how much they (children) can take in. I'm going into a first school, so with seven-year-olds, if they can reap as much benefit as (middle school children) did it shows how much can be understood in just a short space of time. Because the physics of water is something that is done over a whole term in lots of schools, and they did the physics of water in four to five minute experiments and understood it — or as far as I can tell. The assessment part is very much with the teachers. I have to build in more assessment, but I think it's up to the teachers to expand on that, and hopefully the teachers will come back to me and say they've learnt a lot. With (first school) I'm chopping it into six small sessions of twenty minutes, and if six and seven-year-olds can understand the habitat item, getting on to issues like conservation, I think that's really good.

Slides, experiments, equipment, and underwater video are seen as key means of developing understanding — 'the knowledge isn't just being ploughed at them'. The intention is to trial the material and evaluate it, including the children's learning and the different responses of different age-ranges. That is being done entirely from personal interest, and not connected with course-work. A later phase will look at the way the material can be developed to fit the language curriculum and other areas. The possibilities of constructing a large curriculum package have been considered because the available packs on the sea are 'very, very poor'.

Responses to student attachment

It makes a lot of difference going into the schools as an authority. You're not the student being assessed, you're the person going in helping out the teacher and that teacher doesn't think of you as a student, but you're there as another working teacher who's come round talking about it. Knowing the subject I've got a lot of confidence and conviction in what I'm doing and I think it's got a lot of worthwhile things. A lot of things in the past on *attachment* were done just to fit in with the teacher. (as a fourth year) It gives you more chance to choose what you're going to teach ... confidence and assurance that what you're doing is educationally worthwhile.

The difference was noticeable as a fourth-year student, with assessment for recommendation for qualified teacher status completed. The sense of making contributions was previously not the case, since a student was required to 'fit in' to what the teacher had decided, in a prescribed, routine curriculum.

The more you go in the more they get the feeling that they can depend on you to take over. And it's a really good feeling that the teacher is actually asking you to take over her class while she goes off and teaches another class or whatever, because it gets rid of that feeling that the teacher's always watching.

With this package it gives teachers a new stimulus.

Amanda (and Anne)

The proposal

Amanda's intention was to link a course-work requirement for a school-focussed study with a project undertaken on behalf of a school (or, as it turned out, two schools). She approached the school to seek a 'commission', to offer her services and to negotiate an activity which would be beneficial to the school as well as herself. The outcome of the negotiation is a description of the activity in her own account.

Description of the activity

I've been going into two schools, (A) and (B) middle because they are in the process of amalgamation, and for one of my (course-work) units I've got to do some research. I thought it would be a good idea to use the two schools' amalgamation as a format for some research. But I didn't really know what research, so after approaching (A)'s head because I know him, I had a meeting with both heads and decided on an area that the heads would find useful, for me to do some research on, which is an analysis and comparison of the two schools' curriculum in three areas — maths., language and art, craft and design, — and to produce a working paper for them. It will be the same document I present for assessment. Since that's been arranged I've spent a large percentage of the time this term in (B) because I don't know the school very well at all. So I've been wandering in and out of the classrooms, attending assemblies and anything else like that; helping out; just to get the feel of the school and the children; to get the staff on my side in a way so that they don't feel I'm out to criticize them or evaluate completely everything they do. Now it's become more structured and I go into (A) one day a week and (B) one morning a week. I go into specific lessons like the maths, language or art/craft and talk to the teachers; talk to the children; observe what the children are doing; find out about those curriculum areas — that's how far it's gone.

Responses to student attachment

The point is that this amalgamation, as far as I know no work has been done in the field, actually on paper, not in middle schools. And the two heads haven't got enough time and enough staff time to do everything they'd like to do. So really I'm doing something that I consider useful from ... (pause) ... I'll get something out of it and so will the heads.... You feel as if you've had years of experience even though you've only done sort of three years of bits and pieces if you like, although it's been on a regular basis.

Anne has been in six different schools, working with nine headteachers in the course of her degree programme. Amanda has worked in five schools, in each case for extended periods of time.

Practising teachers don't get that diversity of experience, of a wide range of schools.

Discussion compared previous *Attachments*, directly related to practical teaching courses, with the fourth-year experience. Amanda saw similarities in the need to demonstrate one's competence in research, as much as in classroom practice; of adhering to the contract between student and headteacher; of being adaptable and willing to fit in if timetables are changed or teachers absent; of being 'part of the school' and engaging in the 'give and take' of the relationship with the school. In the earlier experiences and the present one, the major value was in the practical experience of teaching in its various forms, conducted within schools: 'it's experience, you're learning, you're in touch with things'. That had not been Anne's perception of earlier experiences:

Anne: My thought *was*, you go into teaching practice to be assessed on performance.

Amanda: Not on how to learn to teach.

Anne: Did you feel you were assessed on performance?

Amanda: I suppose in the last one slightly because you know it was going to come anyway. I suppose the stress was there. Teaching practice was learning for me, 'cos I was constantly changing my ideas all the way through. By the end I was hoping that some of my performance was getting to where I wanted it to be, and I suppose in a sense where an assessor wants me to be.

Johanna

The proposal

Johanna worked with a tutor who was asked by a senior LEA adviser to run an in-service course for teachers currently using 'Man: A Course of Study' in their schools. Rather than 'taught' sessions, the tutor's response was to try to involve teachers in action research themselves, and to act as consultant as they researched what they were doing. Johanna was invited to act as a research assistant to the teachers so that as they pinpointed particular issues she was commissioned to conduct investigations on their behalf. Teachers from four schools were involved. The student acted as an information link between them, being the only one with access to and experience of all four schools.

Description of the activity

They want to look at discussion and how effective they are and what the children are getting out of it. So some of them are monitoring their own discussions in the sense of the 'Curriculum in Action' type of monitoring, while I am also going in to watch them take a discussion and then remove from that same discussion four or five children to interview about what they felt they were doing, the way they felt they were doing it, and what they've got out of it. That's just one of the issues that we're going to look at.

Johanna has also looked at how the schools organize themselves and how MACOS is presently run within each system, with a report presented to all the teachers. She has also provided the capacity to 'free' teachers to observe others. Her own intentions had been to study the teaching of MACOS in one school. This project had extended her own opportunities to other schools, and provided varied insights into teaching, as well as contributing to the teachers' work.

Responses to student attachment

Having done *Attachment* and knowing what it feels like to have something to offer, rather than being passive, I was very keen to have that much more defined role that (the tutor) gave me than the one where I said to Mr. J. (a headteacher) 'I'd like to come in, you know, and you know, and I didn't know . . . emmm.' Whereas now Mr. J. knows when I'm coming and he's going to give me some time, and he's going to sit down in his office with me, and I'm going to do X, Y, and Z, and it's lovely from that point of view — much better from my point of view.

That arises from Johanna's confidence. She receives the teachers' commissions and is then left with the responsibility to 'set it up' and conduct the work. The confidence would not have existed, she feels, if she had asked the school for help:

because I wouldn't have felt I was giving him anything I suppose, whereas now I feel I am. So he's jolly well got to give me something and I don't feel embarrassed about asking for it.

It was felt that going in to the school to teach would not be offering the headteacher something. The contribution would be to the children, whereas 'Now I feel it's actually him'. The difference between the two kinds of activity, teaching and curriculum development, was seen to lie in the learning benefits which were derived for the participants:

It's very different. What I'm doing with MACOS is not just to do with my learning. It's helping them learn too, about what they're doing. And so it changes the emphasis for me. And I think that's a very good thing as far as the teachers and heads are concerned too. I got talking to Mr. J. about my assessment course and his immediate reaction was 'Oh I've been trying to do something on that myself for years, can you come in and talk to me about it, and about making up some sort of profile for the children in the school' . . . *He* had the freedom to say can you do anything for me. . . . Do you see what I mean? It has freed *them* as well to say I need you as much as you need me.

Toby

The proposal

During school experience within the degree programme in urban schools, and through voluntary vacation work in inner London with socially disadvantaged children, Toby developed an interest in the special educational needs of such children. *Attachment* activities had, in addition to classroom practice and the timetabled school day, been conducted through after-school activities and involvement in community youth clubs. During the fourth year, contacts with pupils in the communities were maintained and youth club responsibilities adopted. In order to further his learning about provision for pupils, he had also become attached to a school catering for pupils removed from mainstream schools because of disruptive behaviour.

> I want to look at using music in special education with maladjusted children. There's very little written on it since the 1950s and 1960s; much of it is irrelevant now because the problems are so much more obvious.

Description of the activity

At this stage the proposal has not been implemented.

Responses to student attachment

> It means that because I've been attached to the schools I feel free . . . (pause) . . . that they want me to go in, and I don't feel in the way. I feel I'm actually giving something to the schools . . . whereas other attachments are clouded by teaching practice, there's no doubt about it. There's the final assessment at the end and they're making way for you. This time you have a chance to do something they're asking you to do . . . to do something for them, so it makes the relationship better . . . We're qualified now, they (teachers) don't feel responsible for our initial training . . . They're concerned with first, second and third years in the school.

Toby's considerations of the nature and value of *Attachment* were also reflective, reporting the views of other students, and comparing the activities of education students with those studying other subjects. The reflective view is summarized in note form:

> T. refers to second year, observing in classrooms in ways which are not purposeful. Yet the techniques lead to heightened awareness during other activities — observing children in the youth club; in ones own formal teaching; leading to reflective thinking and planning in response. 'Opportunity' is the key theme in the value of *Attachment* for

research. For coursework selecting research topics presents a problem of sorting priorities. There are so many possibilities. Selection leads to a desire to study specific topics in depth, with teachers who are 'interested in doing it with you'. The chance to pursue issues in greater depth is valued — one student is reported as saying 'if I could have another year, to go into schools just looking at things, at one thing'. There is a recognition that what *is* possible in the time available 'is bound to be amateur, short lived, but useful for when we do get involved properly'.

Even recognizing the limitations, students in other schools of the University are said to be envious of the practical opportunities which education students have, and of the relationships which are built with tutors, teachers and children — 'the whole side of professional development which comes with teaching'. It is also in the perceived relationship between theory and practical activity that education students are thought to benefit:

> When you talk about an essay, or in a seminar with non-education students the anecdotes (from school experience) come in. And that's something that they grapple for in trying to relate their theory. So many students say 'this is totally irrelevant'. I've heard it so many times from students: 'It's all very nice, it's all very intellectual and stimulating, it's just not practical.' Whereas they can see from us we've got the hooks, we've got the experience to be able to say 'Like when ... so and so.' That's what they're jealous of, having the hooks to hang on. I've struggled for three years to get theory and practice related. In the first year I couldn't see any relationship between theory and practice and now it becomes more and more clear as I go into schools. And to that extent I can talk on an equal level with teachers if not slightly above, because some of the new research they can't expect to keep in touch with, but I can, you know?

Kaushika

The proposal

Kaushika's major interest is in multicultural education and she has a clear intention to teach in a multicultural school and to build her career around a commitment to improving education in such schools. Links with schools in Birmingham and Ipswich have been negotiated in order to study policy and provision in those schools, through a comparative study of multi-ethnic curricula. Contact with LEA advisers has also been made, with negotiations to study policy for all schools within each authority.

Description of the activity

In the schools a pilot study is being undertaken, looking at language and religious education. Research methods are being tested, including observations of class teachers and close-focus observations of four pupils in each class. The specific focus for further study and the methods to be used are to be negotiated in detail during a week's field work at the end of the first term.

Responses to student attachment

The benefits of this study as part of coursework are related to the development of expertise and the ability to follow a long-standing career interest. The opportunity to study in Birmingham was important because it (the LEA) has 'gone through the multicultural tunnel' and has the expertise. Ipswich allows the consideration of recently devised policy. The instrumental purpose of the study, as well as that of working in a Middlesex school during the previous year, is also made explicit: 'I'd like to have something on my CV that I've done a study.' But the intrinsic value and the opportunity to pursue personal choice is also clear : 'It's nice to be doing something I'm interested in as part of a course ... we're given a lot more choice.' That relationship between choice and professional commitment is an important element:

All the reading I've done for personal interest, the odd pieces of assessment work, they don't count. They don't count as much as something like this. This is one piece of coursework, *the* piece of coursework for one of my units ... (previously) I fell in if you like to the whole ethics of the school. I fell into teaching styles, and I fell in to a lot of things for convenience. And I don't think I got as much out of it as I would have if I'd tried to explore my own ways.

Exploring ways in the present year has resulted from a sense of confidence which Kaushika illustrated by referring to

the ease with which I've negotiated with the schools, the adviser, I now go into schools in Birmingham and I know exactly how to deal with the situation. I suppose I know my limits; I'm able to sit down and say now this is the sort of thing I'd like to do. I don't know whether it's because of my reasons for being there. Maybe with *Attachment* it's not easy to be clear what your role is, and having had contact with so many different schools, different attitudes within schools, you get better at it, at liaising with schools.

These examples provide a marked contrast with the characteristics of first year students discussed in Part Three. The further acquisition and development of technical competence in classroom instruction through personal research into new elements of his own teaching is the central intention of Guy.

That teaching would, by virtue of the understanding gained from the research, be modified and adapted to the point of proficiency. The application of enquiry techniques, and the use of instruction in a variety of contexts would in turn enhance his capability to research his own practice, not only in new elements of teaching, but also in those which were already technically proficient. A professional attitude towards self-analysis and reflection upon classroom teaching, with an intention towards appropriate modification and adaptation is well established. The direction of further learning, in cooperation and partnership with colleagues, becomes a matter for self-directed professional development. The development of professional commitments and qualities in relation to the wider teacher's role, beyond classroom instruction, is also evident in the work of Amanda, Johanna, Kaushika and Toby. Confidence, having proved practical competence for purposes of certification, reinforces the approach to research-based teaching which began earlier in the course. Professional relationships with headteachers and teachers as well as tutors, the desire to contribute to the curriculum development of schools, a will to understand better the complexities of controversial aspects of education, tempered by a recognition of their own limitations which underlies the desire to improve their professional capabilities, are characteristics of these students and their peers. Within those personal qualities and professional commitments the enhancement of their knowledge of subject matter — in direct relation to the schools' curricula and the ways it is taught — is an important feature. Understanding the characteristics of children's learning processes is also a major feature of their work. These elements of practical knowledge are complemented by a different order of activity: curriculum development which involves other teachers in their own settings. The expertise in curriculum understanding and leadership which accrues from activities such as these is considerable. It is expertise which, it might be argued, should not enter the province of initial teacher education. Yet the development of professional dispositions, as an aspiration of research based teacher education towards self-regulated professional and curriculum development, requires that such expertise should be a constituent part of the practical knowledge acquired for teaching. That knowledge cannot be left to the vagaries of the induction period. It needs to begin systematically in initial teacher education programmes and be followed up equally systematically through induction into teaching and beyond.

Constraints on Authentic Partnership

The conceptual ideal of research-based initial teacher education, and its practical implementation in *Student Attachment* and the BA degree programme have been discussed at length. Conceptually it would have the development of skill complemented by insight through critical reflection for better practice and understanding of teaching. Partnership towards that ideal would have teaching and learning about teaching conducted cooperatively between students, teachers, and teacher educators. As I pointed out earlier, the discussion so far has focussed on the optimistic aspects of the development of partnership towards that ideal. The empirical work has shown that where implementation has been achieved within a shared conception of professional development, the benefits have been shared in various ways by the partners, irrespective of formal status. Yet the major beneficiaries have, I believe, rightly remained the student teachers. In the 'successful' cases the substantive concerns of each of the partners have not been prescribed. The activities have enabled pursuit of many avenues of enquiry and practice consistent with the complexity of teaching and the situations in which it takes place, as well as the learning needs of students. They have also allowed for the development of methods of enquiry which could be utilized in the working situations of teaching. Dialogue about substantive, methodological and theoretical matters resulting from classroom practice and enquiry into it has also developed. The developments have been possible by virtue of an authentic partnership in which contributions to and participation in the search for effective experiences in teacher education have been equally shared and exploratory. There has been no assumption that the process of teacher education has been predefined.

Understandably, it has been difficult to achieve a shared approach within the partnership which recognizes the attempt to break the mould of teacher training by incorporating competency in classroom skills within a form of professional development which goes well beyond competency. Events show that the processes of learning which have been developed have had to be reconciled with demands for prescribed knowledge of teaching and conflicting views of student teachers' professionalism and the appropriate role of teachers and tutors in relation to them. Reconceptualization of teachers' and tutors' roles towards the incorporation of research in productive relationship with practice has also proved a major challenge. Even where the reconceptualization has occurred, the different conventional needs of students for the acquisition of course content including teaching skills, of teachers for curricular and professional development, and of tutors for the development of subject expertise through research and theory, have had to be reconciled. Constructing an exchange for these apparently different interests has taken up a great deal of time. Together with professional requirements and expectations, the personal involvement of partners in activities which draw extensively on professional commitment, has proved to be very demanding in time and emotional energy. Complex logistics of partnership, which have been subject to the difficulties of fitting within and around existing course structures, schools' timetables, and research programmes, have also inevitably affected developments. It will be valuable to others considering the possibilities of similar arrangements to anticipate the logistical, professional, and conceptual constraints on authentic partnership. In the extension of *Student Attachment* those elements were considered as areas which would need to be developed as central features of the innovation to ensure success.

Logistical constraints affect students, teachers and tutors differently. From the students' perspectives, those with the greatest professional commitments have experienced the most severe constraints on their desire to be in schools and to give of their best in school activities. Timetable structures have often prevented students from spending a whole day in school each week throughout a year. That has been especially so for students with practical laboratory or studio demands. Where a day per week has been spent in school — the large majority of cases — an equivalent day at least has often been required for preparation and follow-up. In particular that has been so where methods of enquiry have used audio- or video-recording, involving transcription, storage, analysis, discussion and reporting of work undertaken in addition to associated library/resources centre use. One day in school used effectively realistically means two days' commitment. Travel to and from school adds considerably to that time in some cases. While the costs of travel have been borne by the institution, the time/financial constraint has meant the use of local schools as far as possible. That has also been necessary because public transport is not available to rural areas. Students' attendance at meetings, usually held after school hours to enable teachers to attend, has sometimes been difficult because their timetable continues into the evening.

Teachers have also found themselves on occasions unable to match their own ideals and commitments in the practice of *Attachment*. Their teaching commitments have made it difficult to discuss matters fully with students and tutors and among themselves. Link teachers have been unable to visit other schools to see different arrangements and practices in operation — a desire expressed consistently by them as they have tried to work out the role in isolation in their schools. Sharing ideas has been achieved in after-school meetings which themselves have made heavy demands on teachers. Negotiations with students have often meant that teachers alter their plans or programmes to accommodate the particular times, assignment work or the wish to teach a particular topic which arises from requirements placed on students. Since contacts extend over a whole year these adjustments, accommodations and involvement in cooperative activities make the commitment of teachers and students both extensive and intensive in ways which are unknown in conventional teaching practice.

Extensive commitment to a group of students over a year is also required of tutors. It was anticipated that teaching, curriculum development and research activities would be conducted in the sets of *Attachment* schools to which a tutor was designated the 'link' tutor. Their perspective shows that it was not possible to give equal commitment to each school. For example, work in one school could involve teaching for half a day for one term, preparation and follow-up for pupils' work and students' seminars, negotiations for research, recording, analyzing and reporting data, and follow-up within the school for staff/curriculum development. A consequence of aborted initiatives easily results if that is attempted in addition to student oversight in several schools. Unfulfilled promises or expectations are likely to prove harmful to the development of partnership. The extent of commitment by individual tutors has also varied where research activities are being conducted in schools other than *'Attachment'* schools. That has often been the case, not least because of the broad geographical region around the University. Teachers throughout the region are involved in research in schools which are inaccessible to students, yet they draw upon University resources through in-service programmes and teacher-research support groups. Bringing together the activities of *Attachment* with some of these other interest groups has been possible in some instances, but often it has not.

Common to all perspectives, the administrative and policy-related written communications have been shown to need particular care. The techniques of using mailed memoranda have been developed to provide information in digestible quantities and formats. Yet responses have ranged from requests for more information to complaints about too much. The device of mailing copies of all documents to headteachers and link teachers in the same schools proved necessary to effect communication within the schools, and even then there were sometimes serious shortcomings in administrative communication and policy discussions.

The extensive commitments which have been experienced from some teachers, tutors, and students in the implementation of *Student Attachment* have been accompanied by some less favourable responses to the development of partnership. Developing relationships in the face of declining resources and low morale, which has been the case in many instances during the period since the project was introduced, has highlighted the features of that other face of Janus which I discussed earlier. Even in stable or expanding educational economics the demands of innovation on time and resources are extensive. Active participation by teachers and the resources to support it at local level are not provided. Participation by teachers and headteachers depends upon professionals who perceive their wider responsibilities as including teacher education and the induction of new entrants into the profession. While their part in the process remains a matter of individual professional commitment, the improvement of that participation is subject to uncertainty amid costs of conducting negotiations between schools and the institution. There has been no recognition of the role of link and supervising teachers by LEA's despite the view of teachers that involvement with students has brought considerable benefits to their own professional development. Their role in relation to students has been developed without formal in-service training. It has also been subverted as teachers' responsibilities have become increasingly disrupted in the face of economic, political and curricular turmoil affecting schools. A resulting response of many schools has been to eschew partnership in any form:

Your plans seem admirable and I believe them to be a big improvement on previous practice.

Unfortunately this school is not yet ready to be part of your scheme. There are two main reasons for this:

1   Until the staff here are given an opportunity to meet and discuss their work with members of the Education Faculty there is no way that they are going to commit themselves to this important work.

2   Unless and until this work is acknowledged to be essentially a part of a teacher's work, by the LEA and/or the DES and appropriate staffing and remuneration is introduced this school will wish to stay outside your scheme.

You will of course be aware that the burdens that teachers carry in their work with children have increased and become more complex in recent years.

The policy of the school will be for its teachers to direct all their time and skill to teaching children. I regret deeply that we have to take such a hard line, especially when I personally believe that school experience which gives students the opportunities to learn the craft of teaching by first-hand interaction with serving teachers is probably the most important part of their teaching course. (Head-teacher's response to *Attachment*, 1984)

The importance of the qualities brought to the task by the link teacher was stressed consistently by teachers, recognizing the need for management expertise in dealing with as many as five students, five supervising teachers, link tutor and headteacher within one school. Those qualities have had to be tried, tested, and developed with relatively little experience or understanding to work from. The role depends upon building relationships, for example, with link tutors who have no rights in schools, with students because the link teacher is effectively the surrogate tutor on the spot, and with teachers as instructors and supervisors of students within a view of research-based teaching in their own classrooms. The demands of the role are considerable. Similar needs occur in the supervising teacher role, which can make or break the students' *Attachment* experience and professional development. The selection of teachers for these roles has remained within the prerogative of headteachers at all times. Motives for being involved, given that there is no remuneration or official recognition, include personal interest stemming from dissatisfaction with one's own training; the satisfaction of seeing students develop; and a sense of sharing professional development *together* on the same level as students and tutors. That is said by teachers to be noticeably different from previous arrangements for conventional teaching practices. It was felt in evaluation of the roles by teachers themselves that:

only teachers who are actively willing to have students attached, recognizing the commitment required, should become link or supervising teachers;

link teachers should be supervising teachers where possible;
roles of link and supervising teachers require clarification, on the basis
of practical experience.

Further information about the network of schools involved, and booklets
of experiences from different schools were requested on many occasions to
enhance the development of those roles. Despite the experiences during
Attachment clarification of the roles and guidance for practice has developed on
the intuitive wisdom of the teachers. There is a need for research evidence on
the conduct of the role of teachers in the education of new entrants to the
profession. While precision would not necessarily help, the variable quality of
contributions by teachers to the educational process of their future colleagues
was of deep concern to many teachers involved in the project. The proposals
above, made by teachers, stem from that concern. Without precision about the
roles, all that is possible at this stage is to pursue partnership based on the
principles that the roles would be undertaken to provide every opportunity for
students to acquire professional proficiency; to develop dialogue about professional practice; and to actively pursue the research of classroom practice for
professional and curricular development.

Evaluation data which helped in the reformulation of *Attachment* indicated
the extent to which tutors were perceived as abdicating their role and handing
it over to teachers. The role of the link tutors was discussed at length in the
context of the problem of defining their role in those aspects relating to
students' professional development which overlap or are shared by link and
supervising teachers. The question of who is responsible for which aspects of
that development remained entangled with the difficulties of moving away
from conceptions of teaching practice and its supervision. The relationship
between *Attachment* and formal courses of practical professional preparation
also created perceptions of the tutors' role as supervisory for *Attachment* where
it was seen as an extension of PPP experience for students. A common theme
in the views of teachers and headteachers is represented in the comment:

> It is felt that their (tutors') contact with schools is much too brief and
> that, if possible, they should become more familiar with particular
> schools. Perhaps they could find time to *teach* in them? In this way
> they may come to appreciate the problems their students face in
> school, get to know members of staff, and, perhaps most importantly,
> get back to the 'chalk face' for a while. (Headteacher's letter, 1986)

A deeper consideration of the issues which this sentiment raises was
rehearsed throughout the development of *Attachment*, in the context of
whether 'real' professional development is possible through the project for
students, teachers and tutors alike. Discussions centred on the aspirations
towards a commitment for professional development by teachers and tutors,
as well as students. Concern with the professional development of tutors was
subject to the catalyst of *Circular 3/84* (annex, paragraphs 3 and 4), underlining

the requirement for tutors to have recent, relevant classroom experience. The recognition, irrespective of that requirement, that partnership implies a 'balanced' working relationship required the active participation of link tutors in schools, in order to develop *Attachment* activities. Whereas the link tutor role had initially been passive/consultative, the need to change practice became clear:

> ... with a stress on *mutual high regard,* based on knowing each other and what each other does. 'There can't be high regard for anyone if you don't know them and what they do.' Getting to know, at the lowest level, is still a question of putting a face to a name as far as teachers were concerned. (Notes from link/supervising teachers, February 1985)

Where a change in policy towards more active involvement by tutors in schools was implemented, it brought about its own demands and problems in the redefinition of the relationships. The difference between the 'minimum practice' needs to facilitate student development, and the longer-term potential for roles which combine student learning, in-service professional development/curriculum development for teachers, tutors and schools, and research opportunities in support of each of those, was particularly notable. It is the minimum practice sentiment which underlies the trivial 'back to the chalk face for a while' approach. The more complex and broader view of how classroom research can in fact fulfil some of the demands being made upon students, teachers and tutors as professional partners, and whether facilitating student learning, in-service and research *could* be combined, remained only partially explored. Problems of logistics in arranging that teachers, tutors and students could meet at the same times are one of the difficulties already discussed. Building relationships around classrooms, and about educational and professional matters, was a further concern. As one teacher put it, being 'thrown into having to get to know each other ... how we feel about things' is demanding in the building of partnership. It is demanding and necessary for the achievement of the aspirations of research-based teacher education, yet it can only be achieved, it was felt, over long periods and in relations between a small number of people. It was fully recognized that this particular partnership represents only one aspect of the work of each of the partners. Students' academic course work, teachers' full teaching timetables, and tutors' teaching and research responsibilities bring their own demands which conflict, sometimes severely, with the demands of partnership. The exploration of the practicability of partnership which seriously addresses professional development beyond the 'minimum practice' view is still necessary. The potential consequences of non-authentic partnership for alienation, compliance and lack of productive participation are considerable. The ways in which authentic partnership can lead to professional participation and commitment need seriously to be taken into account.

The history and institutional contexts of teacher education present a framework of constraints on partnership which is overwhelmingly powerful at times. Institutions of teacher education are part of a bureaucratic and decision–making system in which teachers, let alone students, are not full participants. Nor indeed are tutors in the handling of economic determinants and policy issues on the curriculum of teacher education, as recent events have demonstrated. Events beyond the control of one partner or another can seriously affect the contributions which they may bring to teacher education as individuals. Within that context, relationships between institutions and schools remain asymmetrical. In this particular case, the response of some schools to the attempt to equalize the partnership brought about evidence of an interesting and deep tension between the desire to participate and engage in decision making, and the demand for directives from the institution about the conduct of the school's role. The data below shows the extent to which it was expected that detailed directives would be issued by the School of Education for students and teachers to follow according to prescription. Other teachers in the same school saw that as alienating, seeking active consultation and participation as a means of maintaining commitment. The difference between dissemination in a non-authentic partnership, which might involve teachers as mediators and technicians, and the development of an innovation which was determined by them, is crucial.

AN Other Middle School

Comments on School Attachment

1 A general feeling that (the institution) should have consulted all teachers on the proposed attachment rather than just Head, Deputy or link teacher.
2 (The institution) was not aware of the professionalism of the staff and the responsibilities they would feel, because of this professionalism, to do a good job and, as a consequence, not aware of the extra workload put on to staff by attachment.
3 (   ) should have, regardless of the provision of link teacher, endeavoured to monitor attachment especially from the teacher's point of view.
4 Partly as a result of Point 3 a feeling that (   ) was abdicating responsibility for students' professional training and passing this on to schools.
5 As a consequence of Point 4 there should be some recognition by (   ) of the work done in the school, possibly in the form of financial or promotional reward.
6 (   ) had little prepared the students for attachment, that expectation was hazy and guidance negligible.
7 Linking with Point 2 (   ) was naive in its understanding of the demands of attachment, of the demands of

classroom teaching (and classroom disruption) and displayed a certain irresponsibility in allowing 5 students on attachment.

8 (   ) overestimated the usefulness of students on attachment to schools — although there was one teacher who thought otherwise.

9 (   ) was naive in assuming that there would be no indirect assessment of students; that a weak student could cause problems to the school on attachment; that attachment should be compulsory and assessed; that attachment, if not assessed, should not be followed by PPP which is assessed.

10 That there was real potential in attachment especially if students were committed and that eventual benefits would outweigh extra work especially in the light of school's comments.

11 That the staff should arrange further contact with the school and that they should evaluate attachment, implement changes (in consultation with school staff) and improve the situation.

12 That the above comments were in no way to be seen as reflections on the students currently on attachment but rather as reflecting on the School of Education.

Dear John,

STUDENT ATTACHMENT TO SCHOOL

The enclosed report was given to me by (   ) at a meeting held here on Wednesday 11 January. It is, he said, a collective view of staff who have been involved with students during the past term, and, since it carries the name of the school I presume you are aware of its content.

As you might expect I am very concerned by the comments, for a number of reasons. Firstly, they assume throughout that 'the institution' has acted as definer and implementer of 'Attachment' and appear to misunderstand the basis of partnership on which the idea developed. That partnership was one between practising teachers, heads, students, Teacher's Centre and School of Education staff, with consultation with officers and advisers of the LEA.

Secondly, given the School of Education's part in the development the responsibility lies with myself, and colleagues. To be criticized for lack of awareness of professionalism; abdication of responsibility; naivety about the demands of classroom teaching; irresponsibility in student placement; overestimation of student usefulness; and naivety in assumptions about assessment implications; constitutes a series of charges against my own and my colleagues' professional integrity.

However, those charges are founded on a misunderstanding and a failure in communication about the intentions and purposes of student attachment defined in the discussions in partnership.

For our part, we have seen the development, like any innovation, as exploratory and have not assumed it to be unproblematic. I would welcome the opportunity, if you feel it appropriate, to discuss attachment with the teachers involved and any others who may be interested. Perhaps you would let me know a suitable time if you agree.

Yours sincerely,

The activities and conduct of individual students, teachers and tutors in relation to their professional responsibilities is a difficult and contentious matter to discuss when those activities have been essentially voluntary in nature. It is important to the aspirations and further development of professionalism set out earlier to make a tentative opening of a dialogue about the difficulties encountered by some students, teachers and tutors in the course of *Student Attachment*. These experiences have provided evidence of the need for more open dialogue so that democratic evaluation can lead to reform and refinement. That dialogue has been difficult to pursue in cases where individuals are seen by others to be in some sense failing in their professional commitments. It is possible to envisage, and even to anticipate, a partnership of inequality in which realms of responsibility make the tasks of the partners different in kind. The students' tasks independent of equal partnership are at least to acquire competence in classroom performance for entry into teaching. Teachers' tasks would be to practice that competence as a model for student teachers to follow. Teacher educators' tasks would be to represent teaching expertise and pursue understanding through research in order to educate practising and student teachers. That model of independent roles, conducted without dialogue, is the conventional one which has been found to be inadequate. It is one in which, I have argued, induction into teaching through apprenticeship leaves the activities and conduct of particular teachers and tutors unexamined and offers little hope of reform in schooling or in teacher education. The reconciliation between induction into the conventions of teaching and processes for its reform has to be achieved through dialogue in authentic partnership, where the roles may be interchangeable. More likely, though, will be a partnership where the particular expertise of different individuals may be contributory to reflective dialogue. Breaking through the conceptual barrier to a collective view of research-based teacher education, including the *initial* phase of that education, may prove to be the most difficult task. That, I believe, is in part because the conception is not yet sufficiently located in the practical province of classrooms, nor in the over-theoretical concerns of some tutors. It is also because the opportunity to rethink the processes of teacher education and to build new types of course structure seem to have been missed so far in recent interventions by the agents of central government. The possibilities of building in to accreditation criteria a distinctively new relationship between theory and practice clearly exist. Supporting that new relationship with course structures which in particular direct the resources of student time towards school-based and practice-focussed activities would be an essential pre-requisite to successful partnership. Reconceptualization of the learning processes of students, teachers, and tutors within a framework of reconstruction for professional and curriculum development could be extended through systematic evaluation. For professional development, that reconstruction would lead towards excellence, in Bruner's sense. For the curriculum of schools and the education of pupils, it could also lead to such excellence.

Part Five

Tangible Products

This book itself represents a part of the research into the experiences of student teachers, teachers, and tutors in the development of an aspect of the curriculum of the students. As such it is a tangible product of research-based teaching. Other reports and written accounts have been produced by tutors and presented to colleagues, teachers, and students. In this final section of the book I have included two substantial examples of written accounts which have been produced as a consequence of involvement in *Student Attachment to Schools*. One is from a teacher and reports an aspect of work which was undertaken cooperatively with a tutor, another teacher in the school, and two students. To represent the complexion of all the activities which were undertaken by five people throughout a year of *Student Attachment* would be impossible. I have therefore included this one written account which represents one teacher's participation in the development of one aspect of the curriculum through her own research. The variations in students' activities have also been referred to throughout this book and represented in some brief accounts so far. In selecting one full report of a student project I am bowing to the demands of space. It would be possible to provide volumes of similar pieces of work. Even then the full complex of their work and its benefits for schools could not be represented.

Critical Studies in the Art Curriculum: The Place of Verbal Response to Artwork

Kathryn Batcock

Synopsis

The art curriculum in schools is practically-based. Although curriculum documents may recommend the inclusion of critical studies, little guidance on approaches is given. Evidence suggests that artworks are used primarily to stimulate practical work. This study questions whether there is a place for critical studies in its own right in schools, and how the verbal mode of thought applied to the visual might work out in practice with children in primary school. An investigation was carried out to discover the ways in which children respond verbally to artworks, using a variety of ways of stimulating, eliciting and recording these responses. Hypotheses derived from this investigation are considered in relation to the theoretical explorations by Hargreaves, which seek to develop a view of aesthetic learning based on 'conversive trauma'.

The Place of Critical Studies in the Art Curriculum

Children need to develop critical awareness towards visual material, otherwise they face stagnation in their personal work and an inability to perceive and interpret external visual stimuli. Aesthetic judgment, which develops from this awareness, is, as Meier (1966) points out:

> a basis for art criticism and underlies the appreciative aspect of the aesthetic response. Studies show that it is present in children to some degree but it undoubtedly is subject to considerable development through learning and experience. (p. 114)

Since critical awareness is important, and development possible, why is it that in practice its presence is peripheral rather than central to the art curriculum? Firstly, there is a sense in which it is seen as passive rather than active. Art producers make something tangible; those who appreciate are 'consumers'. But the label of art consumer is misleading, implying little need for response or active participation on the part of the 'audience'. As Gadamer (1975) has indicated, understanding is productive too. Croce (1966) also talks of the active side of appreciation which occurs when the productive association of sensations produces something new — a synthesis, involving intuition. Read (1943) contributes to this understanding of active participation by explaining that a work of art demands the spectator's empathy:

> By 'empathy' we mean a mode of aesthetic perception in which the spectator discovers elements of feeling in the work of art and identifies his own sentiments with these elements. (p. 24)

In establishing the critical realm of the art curriculum as active and creative, it is difficult then to accept that this aspect can be tagged on to the rest of the art curriculum as an optional extra. The reason for its peripheral place may also be due to a lack of understanding of the nature of critical awareness. It has also been suggested that some approaches to aesthetic appreciation, where discussion as a mode of learning common to other areas of curriculum is transferred to the aesthetic, could detract from the immediacy of response for the child, since it involves a translation from the visual and emotional to the verbal mode of thought (Hargreaves, 1983, p. 138). Rowland (1976) goes even further. Whilst stating that artists tend to be very articulate, he also says:

> Apart from simply stating the problem, little verbal reasoning or elaboration of visual processes should be attempted. (p. 60)

Bruner (1962) also queries this approach:

> there is a deep question whether the possible meanings that emerge from an effort to explain the experience of art may not mask the real meaning of a work of art. (p. 59)

These are just some indicators of a considerable lobby against the teaching of critical studies by means involving verbal response. The statements are, though, very contentious. Rowland's problem is concerned with providing the best circumstances in which the child can pursue a practical artistic solution; verbal response may hinder this solution. Bruner's problem rests uneasily on the assumption that a work of art holds an intrinsic real meaning, which must not be tampered with. These are not problems which I intend to address here, since they are dealt with elsewhere (for example, Field, 1970, p. 21 ff; Wolff, 1981 p. 5). In stating them I want to indicate that there are both pedagogical and philosophical arguments which have kept critical studies at bay. In contrast, Field (1970) gives explicit support to the use of verbal response in the development of discrimination and critical awareness:

It is clear that children will begin to think in a more and more conscious way about the things they make as art; the teacher's part must begin by creating a situation in which ideas can be exchanged about art as art, about meanings and about values. (p. 119)

Certainly in the DES and Schools Council documents from 1970 on, a place is recognized for the critical aspect of the art curriculum. There seems, however, a mistrust for an approach which assumes a change in mode of thinking, and therefore the use of verbal response to what is essentially a visual experience. For example, in *Art 7–11* (1978):

Works of art and architecture and designed forms of all kinds can be used to stimulate children's interest to focus their attention upon visual qualities in the environment. With children in this age-range, it is more appropriate to use art and desgined forms in this way rather than as a basis for art criticism or as a means of developing good taste and discrimination. (p. 38)

Field (1970), however, writing about older middle-school children, takes a different view:

At the time when they themselves are naturally becoming self-conscious and critical, at the time when they are developing ways of thinking analytically, everything is surely to be gained by using these characteristics, by asking them to look, not merely at their own work, but at the work of their peers and of adults, analytically and critically. (p. 27)

Field's statement is based on a developmental view of children, coupled with a commitment to his supporting verbal response, seeing its value in the development of informed choice. Others writing on this aspect of the curriculum also give prominence to verbalization. For instance Marcousé (1974) quotes from Gibson:

Perception helps talking, and talking fixes the grains of perception. (p. 21)

He emphasizes the importance of actively promoting visual awareness and supports relating objects and images to verbal concepts. Here also is recognition of the important role which response (including verbal) plays in the development of critical awareness:

Response is important in any teaching situation for it implies personal reaction and individual involvement with ideas and with objects. To encourage a child to have confidence in his personal image or viewpoint is a first step in training him to look, to discuss, to relate and to understand. (p. 31)

Where these arguments are presented, the emphasis is often on channelling the stimulus of visual qualities into the children's own artwork. The whole thrust of 'Using Pictures with Children' (National Association of Art Advisers) is in this direction. The writer notes that the teachers interviewed (who were using loaned artworks with children) were deeply suspicious of making the art curriculum more cerebral, and thus goes on to suggest that the way forward is to relate works of art to the practical art content of the curriculum. Thinking and developing ideas in themselves are not see as central to the art curriculum.

What is apparent is that conflicting perspectives leave teachers who are interested in the aesthetic curriculum with a sense of uncertainty about involving children in critical response. The philosophical and pedagogical arguments are compounded by a lack of evidence from classroom practice which might illuminate the nature of children's responses, and the best means of stimulating, eliciting and developing them.

Investigating the Role of Verbal Response to Artwork

The starting point for investigating the use of artwork with children in my class (9-year-olds in a rural primary school) and their responses to it was my involvement in *Student Attachment to Schools*, and the impetus to engage in curriculum development as part of it. The development of the art curriculum generally was agreed among students, teachers and tutor. Use of critical response enabled me to develop a specific interest. As a self-confessed non-artist with a degree in art history it allowed the use of qualifications and expertise which had lain dormant thus far. A series of lessons were planned and taught, initially by the 'link tutor' and later by myself, and data on the teaching and the children's responses gathered cooperatively by each of us. The lessons in which the material was gathered were planned to provide opportunities for the children to respond to a variety of types of artworks (in terms of style, media and provenance). Verbal responses were stimulated in a variety of ways, and elicited through different means by asking specific questions, requesting selection of preferred pieces to be explained, inviting questions, giving no direction, asking for written descriptions and judgements, and engaging in 'open' group discussion. A balance between spontaneity of response and accuracy of intention in response was sought by using both 'immediate' and 'reflective' responses, which were recorded on audio tape and in written form. The series of lessons included paintings brought into the classroom by the artist and visits to the National Exhibition of Children's Art and to exhibitions of John Davies sculpture, Edward Burra paintings, and paintings of the Norwich School of Artists. The data produced is extensive. I will consider some aspects of it here.

Table 1: Overview of Data

Children's responses affected by:

	Paintings presented by artist	Mixed Media National Exhibition of Children's Art 1	Mixed Media National Exhibition of Children's Art 2	Sculpture John Davies 1	Sculpture John Davies 2	Paintings Edward Burra 1	Paintings Edward Burra 2	Paintings Edward Burra reproduction 3	Paintings Norwich School
Types of artwork									
Ways in which stimulated	Questions directed by artist	Non-prescriptive	Questions directed by teacher post-event	Non-prescriptive	Questions directed by children (pre-planned)	Directed contemplation	Teacher-directed contemplation	Teacher-directed looking at reproduction	Museum lesson
Teacher role	No communication with children; own involvement with paintings	Informal discussion — freewheeling	Informal discussion	Informal discussion	Non-directive but participatory	Own involvement looking at paintings	Informal discussion — freewheeling	Discussion leader	Discussion leader
Means by which response elicited	Oral discussion in pairs	Individual/group discussion with teacher	Group of 4 discussion with teacher	Individual/group discussion with teacher	Class discussion	Written report from draft notes	Group discussion	Class discussion	Dialogue with teacher
Recording method	Audio tape/written	Audio tape	Audio tape	Audio tape	Audio tape	Written	Audio tape	Written — descriptive and poetic	Audio tape
Location	Classroom	Gallery	Classroom	Gallery	Classroom	Classroom	Gallery	Classroom	Classroom

Interpretation of the Data

The interpretation of the data falls into two sections:

   (i)   the effect of the learning/teaching context on the nature of the responses;

   (ii) the categories of verbal response.

The Learning/Teaching Context

An attempt has been made to make explicit in the data presentation the conditions in which they were grounded, and to provide variety in certain aspects of these conditions, so as to aid development of hypotheses. Three strands have been pursued in this section: a comparison between the immediate and reflective concerns of the children; a consideration of the effects of teacher and peer input on an individual's response; a discussion of the problems of introducing written responses, given the skills needed.

In cases where immediate and reflective responses have been obtained following the same stimulus, differing emphases/concerns have been apparent. In the case of the John Davies sculpture, a comparison is made between the spontaneous questions asked by the children in the gallery, and their considered questions in the classroom the next day. Although the data shows extensive use of judgment and speculative interpretation, the predominant verbalisation was in the form of questions. One group of children knew before visiting the exhibition that they would have the opportunity of putting questions to the other group in class at a later date. Those questions were written down for a specific audience, the day after the visit.

Set 1-Questions in the gallery

Is it meant to be up there? (a swallow on the sculpture's nose).
Are they real? (glass eyes).
Can they still see through it? (glass eyes).
What's that stuff round here supposed to be? (the mask on the nose).
Why have they got bird feathers over their noses?
Why is that thing over its eye?
Why has it got a mask thing on it?
What *are* the eyes made of?
How has he made the bird stay on?
Why has he got a ball on his head?

Set 2-Questions in the classroom

How do you think the sculptures were made?
If you were the artist, would you put the masks on the sculptures, or do the faces?

Which sculptures remind you of a real person?
Why did the man with the bucket have a ball on his head?
Which do you think was the best presented? (displayed).
Why do you think the people made the sculpture?
What feeling did you get looking at the man in the checked jacket?
Did you think they were real?
Do you think there should have been any lady sculptures or not?
Do you think the sculptures looked better with clothes on?

In set 1 the questions revolve around 'making sense of' in terms of materials and composition, as well as interpretation. In set 2 the questions encompass a wider range of concerns; for instance, the lack of female representation, the problems of display. These latter two are aspects which indicate a drawing together of information and interpretation — perhaps less possible in the gallery. The reflective questions also show a shift from trying to grapple with what the artist, through his sculpture, is trying to do, to how the sculpture affects us, how we respond. This does not mean that the immediate concern is dissipated; rather that it is overlaid with reflective concerns. The questions about the glass eyes (Are they real? Can they still see through it?) still underlie the question about the same sculpture in set 2 (What feeling did you get looking at the man in the checked jacket?). This question shows a consciousness of audience role not apparent in the gallery data. It is useful at this point to consider the effect of teacher/peer input on response. Although variety of response is evident in set 2, they seemed to attach importance to finding out that others had shared similar feelings. An example which illustrates that interaction with peers develops understanding (Jonathan, Norwich School of Painting) will be discussed in detail later. As Marcouse (1974) notes:

> The process of sharing is indeed a vital part of visual learning. (p. 21)

The following (Burra paintings 2) is an interesting example of spontaneous response in which one child's response triggers off a series of related ones from a group. In this case the teacher's question acts as a starting point, apparently not influencing response!

Teacher: What do you think they're doing?
— What's this bit here?
— A bit like a mask.
— Looks a bit fierce.
— Arguing.
— The shape you know-destruction.
— In cartoons they all have those big eyebrows going down there to make them angry.
— Ghosts, ghosts, ghostly.
— It doesn't frighten me.
— It does me, 'cos of that, and that, and that. (pointing)

Here is exposed a strong vein of 'making sense of' shot through with emotional response involving interpretation and judgement. Interestingly, one child's emotional response does not seem to interfere with another's. The children were also asked to make draft notes in the gallery, providing response in written form. The spontaneous gallery notes were later compared with a draft report made in the classroom later that day. (Burra paintings 1). Although only one example of this comparison of data was obtained, it seems to indicate that some children adopt an editing-out of certain aspects of their gallery notes. In this case, children were asked to contemplate one painting which interested them, make notes, then write about it later. No suggestions were made as to how this might be done, and note-taking in situ was a new experience for this class. Very few children made any notes in detail in the gallery. Reasons for this could include: the imposition of attempting this new skill and contemplating a painting proved too great; constraints of writing without the usual aids of dictionary/teacher; not seeking a need to record. It is also interesting to speculate whether there is a need to assimilate responses before transferring them into words, given the nature of oral response in the gallery. It may be that writing *notes* is not seen by the children as legitimately including the recording of questions, or that note-making as an isolated, individual and essentially private activity does not offer the same social opportunities evident in the spontaneous oral data. However, those who did write notes practised the editing-out to some extent; these are some examples:

The picture looks ghostly.
It has lots of feeling in it.
It looks like a violent picture.
It's a happy picture.
I think this picture is very delightful.

These extracts, which all convey particular emotional responses, lead one to suspect that some of these children are either unsure of the validity of including this kind of response, or they may prefer not to commit their personal feelings to paper. Unlike the more familiar 'creative writing' situation, where the children have many models of personal expression from which to draw, in art criticism that is unavailable. So in addition to the influences of place/time, other people, and particular skills, it could be the lack of suitable models of learning in the school situation which have a bearing on the response children may make. These possible influences provide the setting in which to consider the categories of response deriving from the data.

Categories of Verbal Response

It is appropriate at this point to briefly consider the categories of response which children might make to artwork, proposed by Eisner (1972, p. 106). They are:

     (i)   the experiential (the personal response in terms of feeling);
    (ii)   the compositional (the formal characteristics of the artwork);
   (iii)   the symbolic (the use of associated specific representations);
   (iv)   the thematic;
    (v)   the material (the contribution of media to the form and content of the work);
   (vi)   the contextual (relating to traditions/culture).

All categories except the symbolic are represented in the data derived from the lessons. Prominence of particular categories varies between sets of data (reasons for this will be discussed), but generally, the experiential, the compositional and material dimensions are most frequently used, with a few thematic and contextual references. What emerges clearly is that these children used wide-ranging frames of reference, even though they have received no formal teaching in art criticism. Categories of response deriving directly from the data relate closely to those of Eisner, and I will consider in more detail:

     (i)   the development of conceptual aspects of aesthetic learning;
    (ii)   the effect on response of personal practice in art;
   (iii)   interpreting within a cultural context;
   (iv)   the use of specific personal experiences/understandings in response.

The development of conceptual aspects of aesthetic learning

This is central to aesthetic learning, since it is indicative of children using their perceptions of artwork to develop their ability to relate to and understand what they see. The other categories play a supportive role to this core category.

In the data collected, children sometimes articulated thoughts which indicate that their understanding is developing, without significant intervention by adults. For instance (Sculpture 1):

> If you look at the eyes and walk past, it's as though his eyes keep turning at you and looking. It's as though he's looking at you still, if you keep looking at his eyes. That's only you. He ain't actually looking at you, it's just you looking at him.

This coming to terms with the impact that the sculpture has on the onlooker emotionally, yet ability to explain what is happening physically, shows the delicate balance achieved by both sculptor and onlooker. There is an element of interpretation here, which rests on the child's ability to 'feel' the work emotionally. In other words, this statement has developed from pure description into an understanding of the artwork. Some interesting details are relevant here. Firstly, this is the kind of response which depends on the child's experience with the sculpture; it is inconceivable that by looking at a reproduction in a book or at a slide, this response could have been produced. In this case, the actual physical experience is an essential component to the response. Secondly, the language used by the child does not exhibit a specialist vocabulary; despite this, the meaning is very clear. Thirdly, this kind of artwork (super realism/sculpture) was unfamiliar to the child; this did not prove an obstacle to giving an emotional response and developing a personal interpretation. Fourthly, no expert tutor was needed by the child, although this statement occurred during a conversation with peers and an adult about the realism of the eyes. The implications for the way in which children are taught in responding to artwork are far-reaching. Other examples of this kind of response are not rare. For instance, Heather, when discussing the display of these sculptures (Sculpture 2), shows considerable insight into spatial qualities when she says:

> The one on the rope hanging down from the ceiling (was best presented), because it was the only one that was filling up the whole height of the room, because the rope was coming down and the man was on it . . .

These kinds of response seem to thrive in the open situation allowed. The second example which we shall examine also shows the development of a conceptual aspect of aesthetic learning, deriving from the artwork and also in a free situation: in this case, an attempt at thematic interpretation. This statement was made by Nicola in the gallery, after spending half-an-hour looking at the paintings on her own (Burra 2):

> There's one thing they're all linked together by. They're all sorts of senses of evil and destruction. I like the way they show all their faces and the way they're sort of acting.

As well as being a clear example of thematic interpretation, this response gives some insight into how this child has coped with her experience in the gallery. She felt compelled to make sense of the total impact of these paintings; this was not something that she was asked to do; however, given the freedom to use her time in the gallery, this was her approach. Although a thematic response has been unusual in my data, it is obviously a possibility for even nine-year-olds. It would have been difficult to arrive at this kind of interpretation without entering emotionally into the experience of the paintings. She herself noted: 'It's up to your imagination', when asked whether the pictures were trying to tell her anything. Would she have been able to develop this thematic response without the gallery experience?

In the third example of conceptual development, although occurring in the classroom, the experience of the paintings in the gallery also seems to be crucial. In this extract, Jonathan wrestles with a problem about perception, during an afternoon's discussion (Norwich School). Unlike the two previous examples, the teacher consciously adopted an interventionist teaching role, knowing beforehand that she wished to see how far a discussion about perception could be taken with nine/ten-year-olds. Jonathan has a clear idea how the artist selects and composes:

Well, when people say, through artists' eyes, they mean what they've made up. They draw sometimes what they see, and sometimes they make up things, and sometimes they draw a whole picture or make a world up all itself.

The ensuing discussion provides Jonathan with a setting in which to unravel some of his confusions. Initially, he says that we do not all see the same thing when we look at a picture ('No, it's all imaginative things') then changes this to a 'yes'. But throughout, it is clear that he understands that the artist sees different things and interprets in different ways. Other children make statements about the audience's perception which subsequently seem to have helped Jonathan formulate a clearer idea of what actually happens when we look at a picture.

James says: It depends on what you think.
Emma adds: I like different things from what other people like.
The teacher (trying to clarify): So you take in what appeals to you, is that what you mean?
Emma: Yes.

At this point, Kevin relates to his own experience as an artist saying:

If we had to paint the same thing, what we paint comes out different.

Although this is an ambiguous statement, in that he may actually be referring to the effect that physical skill has on a painting (rather than perception), and that indeed is the way in which some of the children are thinking, Naomi steers the discussion clearly into the realms of perception again:

If we were painting a picture, you'd all have different feelings about how you'd want it to be.

Jonathan joins in the discussion, but at this point his understanding of 'seeing differently' is very much at the physical level since he explains that his friend Mikey sees differently because he is colourblind. Eventually, having worked through a whole range of complex ideas, he is able to recognize that interpretation of perception is as much reality for the audience as for the artist:

When we were talking about whether we see paintings differently, it's like what the artist is trying to do. They're trying to scare you, or make you feel lonely or feel happy. Then one person might feel happy and another might feel lonely, and you see things differently in your minds.

There was a sense of satisfaction in this statement, as though Jonathan had come to an understanding of perception which he was comfortable with, but which, having worked through new ideas experienced that day, was at a different level to that held previously. In this case, the contributions made by the others in discussion had been invaluable to Jonathan. By looking at further data, it can also be shown that he was drawing on his experience with the paintings in the gallery to further his understanding. After the gallery lesson 'Norfolk through Artists' Eyes' in which a museum teacher introduced a variety of interpretations of Norfolk landscape, Jonathan viewed the Burra Exhibition, and chose a painting to contemplate, *Landscape with Red Wheels*. On return to the classroom he wrote:

> The picture was bright but it didn't have much atmosphere it looked a bit lonely. There was something I really liked and that was how Edward Burra put little dots on it and it looked very accurate. I think he was trying to make you feel lonely. I liked it because it was bright and it had an effect in it somewhere.

One other child, Stephen, also chose this painting, but his response was very different. It concentrated on describing the colours in great detail (Burra 1), and ended:

> I liked it because red is a nice colour and it looked as if it was a happy picture.

They came to different conclusions about how the painting made you feel — either lonely or happy. This provides strong evidence that Jonathan's previous statement is rooted in this experience:

> They're trying to scare you or make you feel lonely or happy. Then one person might feel happy and another might feel lonely, and you see things differently in your minds.

He has come to realize an important fact: that there is no one solution to the interpretation of artwork, and that his response is valuable and valid. But this realization is firmly grounded in two experiences: a personal response to paintings in the gallery, and discussion with colleagues.

The effect on response of personal practice in art

Personal experience as artists provides children with a basis for their response, with particular concern for compositional and material aspects, and could be seen, therefore, to influence the nature of the response. These children are experienced as painters but not as sculptors. It is instructive to compare responses to these two media. Responses to paintings show considerable understanding and appreciation of problems and solutions explored by the artist. The compositional/material responses in the sculpture data indicate that the children are still trying to define sculpture for themselves:

> I don't think they made them with moulds and concrete.
> I don't think they used moulds because otherwise they wouldn't be sculpture, because really sculpture means like being carved or chiselled out.

Their lack of experience as sculptors does not prevent a sense of admiration for the sculptor's efforts:

And his eyes, cor, that must have been hard.

The confidence with which children utilize terminology in the responses to paintings may indicate that their productive experience provides them with a firm base from which to articulate these responses:

I was interested in the way it was painted.
— discussion of the range of colours used.
— references to materials such as charcoal and watercolours.
   shading of the sky; colours blend; bright contrast. (Burra 1)

It is clear that although experience as artists adds particular dimensions to response, lack of this productive experience does not inhibit response in other categories, notably the experiential, which draws upon understanding *as* respondents.

The use of specific personal experiences/understandings in response

The children in this study did not apparently need to be taught to delve into their experiences in order to respond to artwork, but as we have seen, certain conditions figure highly. I wish now to consider more closely some of the responses which indicate that the child is drawing on specific personal experiences or understandings.

An understanding of definitions can affect response, as in the example given above in which an attempt is made to define sculpture. Some of these children are already displaying fixed notions of what is art:

A good introduction to real art (describing the artist's paintings). I don't like the ones with clothes. Because all statues everywhere else, you won't hardly see any, there will be some but hardly any, with clothes on. The really ancient ones won't have clothes on. They weren't done up in clothes.

Responses for some are modified to fit in with a learnt definition or an accepted convention. Sometimes experience thus far tells the child that art equals realism, and in the following case (paintings presented by the artist), the desire for realism is prominent:

We think this one is an eye here, and a nose. Or it could be a roundabout, with a house down here and a house there. Or it could be a bridge across here. We don't know what it is. We think it's good, but we thought it might be better if we knew what it was.

Not knowing what a work is meant to be can prove troubling, and occurred most frequently with the sculpture. In addition to the unfamiliarity of the medium, the impossibility of categorizing the subject of this work in

terms of realism may have contributed to the disturbed responses. Nevertheless, the children coped with the ambiguities and uncertainties, within a sense
of puzzlement and curiosity. This was expressed in the desire to understand
the artist's intentions, and the resulting effort to identify with the artist can
deepen understanding (Sculpture 2):

Why do you think people made the sculpture?
— It might have been their hobby.
— He was bored.
— Because he enjoyed doing artwork so he decided to do something
   like model-making.
— I think he does it because he likes doing it, enjoys it and he's very
   artistic and he's making use of his artistic talent.
— Because he's interested in sculpture.
— I think he done it because when he come home from work he didn't
   have nothing to do.

Interestingly, the responses now turn to the sculptor's conscious effort to
affect the audience:

— Perhaps he wanted people to feel things about what he'd made.
— He wants people to enjoy them.
— He might have felt people would get ideas from him.

Although not sculptors themselves, they are drawing on their experience as
both artists and audience to understand the sculptor's intentions.

Interpreting within cultural conventions

Interpretation within cultural conventions, like the example in which clothed
sculpture is discussed (Sculpture 2), occurs fairly frequently. In particular, this
features when an attempt to make sense of an item occurs. In the discussion
about whether sculptures should be clothed, although there is tacit acceptance
of the convention of nude sculpture, the logic of realism conflicts with the
cited convention when one person points out that the 'bucket man' figure
would look out of place without clothes: nudes are not the norm on building
sites.

The bucket man looks good with clothes on because he wouldn't be
walking about with buckets if he didn't have clothes on.

In addition to this making sense approach, the children's awareness of
social issues is evident in their responses. For example, the impact of the John
Davies sculpture was for some the realization that there were no female
figures. Both the basic rivalry between the sexes and some worthwhile
perceptiveness emerge:

Lisa: It's a bit boring looking at men all the time.
Nigel: . . . women aren't interesting.

The discussion then turned on the appropriateness of using, for instance, female figures in the gymnastic positions; some arguing that these would have been more graceful. An appreciation of the interesting qualities of the human form was expressed:

> *Heather:* I think there should have been some (women) because women are different to men, and he could have got all their features in as well.

Although it could be argued that cultural conventions inhibit response, one could also see that they provide a certain richness of interpretation, and that the using and sharing of these is the first step to the conscious recognition of one's own position in relation to the artwork.

Conclusions: a comparison with Hargreaves' theory of 'conversive trauma'

How can this study increase our understanding of the teaching of critical studies in the aesthetic curriculum? First, it has provided experience of new practices in my own school, and insight into my own teaching and the experiences of the pupils on which it will be possible to build. More widely, it is possible to relate this experience and its tentative findings to other practice and to theories already put forward. As indicated in the introduction, evidence from practice is thin on the ground, although the forthcoming book by Taylor (1986) should be illuminating. For the present, I want to consider the investigation in relation to Hargreaves' theory of 'conversive trauma'. Although Hargreaves' fieldwork was carried out in the secondary sector and with adults, his theories provide a rich backcloth against which to work.

Hargreaves' theory provides an exploration of how school teachers, as major consumers of the arts themselves, can use their position to disseminate 'cultural capital' to all the children they teach including working-class children who, it is claimed, are relatively disadvantaged in their access to 'cultural capital'. His observations of art appreciation lessons demonstrated that older working-class pupils find it difficult to talk about works of art in the classroom, and he surmises that, in any case, fluent talk would not be a sure indication of aesthetic experience. He suggests that the impact of a gallery exhibition, giving rise to pleasure from the direct communication of works of art, cannot be replaced by deliberate analysis of a work of art, which serves a different function. His theory of conversive trauma, developed from researching the experiences of adults, is seen as complementary to incremental theories of learning and proposed as an alternative way of initiating pupils into art appreciation. The main thrust of the theory is that direct experience with the work of art must precede talk. That direct experience, he argues, provides the means of access for those who do not appreciate art into the domain of aesthetic experience, because the experience (or set of experiences) is characterized by a sensation of positive, traumatic conversion. The conversion may be by sudden impact or by more gradual immersion in experiences, but Hargreaves identifies four elements in this initiation process:

    (i)   concentration of attention — the experience is totally absorbing;

    (ii)   a sense of revelation — heightened sense of reality and discovery of inner feelings;

    (iii) inarticulateness — an inability to communicate the experience verbally;

    (iv) arousal of appetite/motivation — a desire for the experience to continue.

The latter in particular is said to lead in turn to commitment, exploration, discrimination, and the search for background knowledge in relation to works of art, such that the participation in the realm of aesthetic experience continues in conjunction with the acquisition of 'cultural capital', especially through language. The order of events, from conversive trauma as the first step in the process of initiation, towards a more verbal, analytical and critical approach is presented as potentially a more effective form of teaching than that used in the conventional art appreciation lesson. This is seen as normally conducted from the wrong perspective, demanding the use of language and thought drawn from the 'cultural capital' held by some pupils, rather than initiating all pupils into and developing that asset.

It is not clear from Hargreaves' proposition how and when the conjunction between traumatic initiation/aesthetic experience and 'cultural capital' occurs; except that he sees the relationship as sequential with traumatic conversion necessarily coming first. Among the primary school children in this study, it is possible to see the conjunction as concurrent, rather than consecutive. Of course we cannot say what 'cultural capital' each individual brought to bear *on* the works of art, nor to what extent the language and thought processes had been developed as a result of earlier aesthetic responses to the natural environment, to 'everyday' designed objects, or to their own artwork and that of other children. In that respect Hargreaves' theory is exceptionally difficult to test, since the idea of initiation can only work on a premise of the individual having formerly been excluded or in some sense deprived of access to experience. Working with the spontaneous enthusiasm of these children it is difficult to accept such a premise, even though access to 'high art' had not formally been part of their school experience thus far. Indeed, Hargreaves himself quotes Herbert Read as saying that aesthetic impulses are the normal possession of children. The question therefore seems to be: how can we prevent the atrophy of those impulses, and develop the assets of the pupils? If the relationship is concurrent and dialectical, even *during* engagement with a single work of art, it will be helpful to know what responses are stimulated *by* works of art, and also what thoughts and experiences are brought *to* those works. There seems no need to strive for these children to respond to artworks. They demonstrate that language is conjoined with direct aesthetic experience in a complex dialogue. That dialogue, in its visual, emotional, intellectual and linguistic modes, is informed by many of the children's experiences. But it also informs their experience, as they come to understand the characteristics of the art and their dialogue with it, and the place in their learning of that dialogue. Not only do these children talk about the works of art, they also analyze their responses to that art. That, presumably, is the nature of the cultural capital which Hargreaves seeks to engage pupils in.

It seems, with these pupils, that the cultural gap perceived by Hargreaves has not yet developed. How important, therefore, to learn at this stage as Jonathan was doing, the ability to discern for themselves, from a standpoint of appreciation and understanding. It has often been noted that:

> Students' self-concepts stabilize relatively early (by age 10 or so), and after that point most are unwilling to accept evidence that they are better or worse than that view of self-worth. (Good and Brophy, 1978, p. 84)

The young children in the data displayed a wide range of responses. They had the ability to discern: left to a later age, this situation may be less hopeful. This seems to be borne out by Hargreaves' (1983) findings in the art appreciation class:

> Not only did the pupils seem to find these questions difficult, they also gave indications of their fears that an answer which expressed their true personal reaction to a painting would involve a degree of public exposure they were unhappy to risk. (p. 135)

If we accept the evidence that young children are interested in artworks and respond widely and energetically to them, the need seems to be to provide them with the opportunities to do this. Hargreaves says:

> ... we can interpret the educational task to be this: that the teachers, who are the major consumers of the arts, should transmit their own capacities to appreciate the arts to more and more pupils.

I would judge the capacity to be already there in the pupil; what is needed is the space and freedom in which to utilize it. It is after this point that teaching is perhaps appropriate (for example, Jonathan, Norwich school), within the provision of a range of first-hand experiences rather than the more conventional school use of slides and reproductions. First-hand experience seems to be the well from which further understanding was drawn. As Hargreaves (1983) notes:

> They had little experience of looking at art objects in any serious way; they were not used to forming and then expressing judgements about them and were nervous of so doing; and most of all they lacked a working vocabulary in which to talk openly about their reactions beyond the level of 'I like that' or 'I don't like that'. (p. 135)

It would seem from my data that lack of long experience of looking at art objects has not hindered response, nor has the lack of working vocabulary upon which Hargreaves lays so much emphasis. However, an atmosphere in which the children's views and judgements are accepted and encouraged would seem to be crucial to their ability to articulate a response. This, as he noted, is unlikely to be nurtured in art appreciation lessons in isolation from the aesthetic experience.

References

BRUNER, J., (1962) *On Knowing*, Harvard University Press

CROCE, B., (1966) 'Art as expression' in EISNER, E. and ECKER, D. (Eds), *Readings in Art Education*, Blaisdell

EISNER, E., (1972) *Educating Artistic Vision*, Macmillan

EISNER, E. and ECKER, D. (Eds), (1966) *Readings in Art Education*, Blaisdell

FIELD, D., (1970) *Change in Art Education*, Routledge and Kegan Paul

GADAMER, H-G. in WOLFF, J. (Ed.), (1981) *The Social Production of Art* Macmillan

GIBSON, J. in MARCOUSÉ, R. (Ed.), (1974) *Using Objects*, Schools Council

GOOD, T. and BROPHY, J., (1978) *Looking in Classrooms*, Harper and Row

HARGREAVES, D., (1983) 'The teaching of art and the art of teaching: Towards an alternative view of aesthetic learning' in HAMMERSLEY, M. and HARGREAVES, A. (Eds), *Curriculum Practice*, Falmer Press

MARCOUSÉ, R., (1974) *Using Objects*, Schools Council

MEIER, N., (1966) 'Factors in artistic aptitude' in EISNER, E. and ECKER, D. (Eds), *Readings in Art Education*, Blaisdell

NATIONAL ASSOCIATION OF ART ADVISERS, *Using Pictures with Children*, National Association of Art Advisers

READ, H., (1943) *Education Through Art*, Faber

ROWLAND, K., (1976) *Visual Education and Beyond*, Looking and Seeing

SCHOOLS COUNCIL, (1978) *Art 7–11*, Schools Council

TAYLOR, R., (1986) *Educating for Art*, Longman

WOLFF, J. (Ed.), (1981) *The Social Production of Art*, Macmillan

The Use of Nuffield Mathematics Scheme in a Middle School, with Particular Reference to the School's Pedagogy, Curriculum Document and the Recommendations Made in the Cockcroft Report

Amanda Peirce

Introduction

This report documents the use of the Nuffield Mathematics Scheme in one middle school, with particular reference to the school's pedagogy, curriculum document and the Cockcroft Report. The purpose of the report is to highlight the development of the school's mathematics curriculum in relation to the implementation of the Nuffield Mathematics Scheme.

Innovation in the middle school was the result of an eighteen-month staff review of mathematics teaching in the school. The result was a recognition of the following problems, that needed to be addressed. Improvement should be made in the following areas:

  (a) lack of continuity from year to year;
  (b) no agreed teaching method;
  (c) varied use of text books;
  (d) very little practical work was being done;
  (e) many teachers expressed a lack of confidence in the subject.
       (Mathematics document, December 1984)

It was decided at a staff meeting that a standard scheme and pedagogy should be used throughout the school. The Norfolk Primary Mathematics adviser suggested three schemes which he felt suitable for the children of the school. A framework for analyzing the scheme was also suggested giving a focus to the teachers' scrutiny of the schemes.

The Nuffield Mathematics Scheme was adopted after close examination and discussion of the schemes offered for the following reasons. It offered:

(a)   clear attractive presentation;
(b)   simple instructions;
(c)   suitability for group teaching;
(d)   plenty of opportunities for practical work;
(e)   extension and reinforcement material;
(f)   good revision of work;
(g)   detailed teachers notes (*Ibid*)

Mathematics in the Primary Age Range

This section presents firstly, a view of children's mathematical learning; secondly, a view of mathematical teaching; and thirdly a description of one topic in the Nuffield Mathematics Scheme showing: purpose, content, presentation and highlighting student tasks.

Glenn (1977) outlines four broad stages in a child's learning of a particular mathematical concept or skill. They are:

(i)   preliminary practical investigations;
(ii)   the formation of a mathematical model of the situation;
(iii)   the application of the mathematical model to similar situations;
(iv)   consolidation and practice.

Glenn perceives the above stages as the main framework for planning children's mathematical learning. Stage 1 should provide practical activities in which they can revise ideas and investigate the new topic. For example, finding the area of objects in the environment, cardboard plans of shapes and shapes drawn on paper. This stage can also provide the necessary motivation. Stage 2 can be seen as utilizing the children's findings in stage 1, to discuss and draw out through appropriate questioning, the important mathematical points. For example, squares form regular rows and therefore we can multiply how many squares in each row, by how many rows there are, rather than counting all the individual squares. Stage 3 involves applying the new (to the child) mathematical knowledge to relevant situations; this promotes an understanding of the 'use' of a mathematical concept, rather than the rote learning of a rule. For example, area has a use in calculating the amount of tar required to cover the playground or the amount of carpet to cover a floor; rather than in answer to the question: 'What is area?', reply: 'length times breadth'. Stage 4 involves practice to establish and consolidate the mathematical knowledge otherwise it rapidly disappears. Problems in abstract and concrete terms can be given, to include finding the area of irregular shapes; shapes with dimensions not in the same unit and regions that can be divided into regular shapes.

The Cockcroft Report suggests certain elements and opportunities need to be present when teaching mathematics to children of all ages. Mathematics teaching should be SPICED, in the following ways:

(i)   Solving problems, including application of mathematics to every-day situations.
(ii) Practical work appropriate to the topic.
(iii) Investigational work.
(iv) Consolidation and practice of fundamental skills and routines.
(v)   Exposition by the teacher.
(vi) Discussion between teacher and pupils and between pupils themselves.

Cockcroft's view of mathematics teaching as shown above complements Glenn's view of children's learning, and illustrates how these can be implemented by the class teacher. Cockcroft states that the primary mathematics curriculum should not only create a basic mathematical understanding and give numerical skills but provide enrichment for children's aesthetic and linguistic experience, develop powers of logical thought and provide children with a means of exploring their environment. Plus mathematics should be presented as a subject both to use and to enjoy.

Nuffield Mathematics Scheme

Glenn's and Cockcroft's views have the potential of being implemented in the use of the Nuffield Mathematics Scheme. The Nuffield Mathematics proverb is:

I see and I remember: I do and I understand.

The scheme's proverb can be related through-out the series of text books for the 5–11 years age range. There are six non-expendable text books, spiritmasters for each text book, a teacher's manual for each text book and a series of *Bronto Books*; these are mathematic reading books which introduce mathematical concepts and language. The general aim of the scheme is: 'to promote understanding of the concepts and proficiency in the basic skills'.

In accordance with the Cockcroft Report the scheme's philosophy highlights the importance of language. Whether written or oral, language plays an essential role in the formation of mathematical ideas. The scheme therefore encourages practical work, discussion and explanation, viewing these as essential in developing children's mathematical understanding. Nuffield (1984) advocates a sequential line of development for children learning mathematics; this has the same components as Glenn's stages; activity followed by discussion followed by consolidation of skills through application:

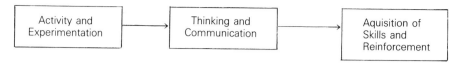

This view of development is supported by the Cockcroft Report. The scheme instructs pupils to copy and complete sentences and gives examples of recording methods in table form. This establishes a good method of presentation and reasonable standards which the authors believe cannot begin too early.

"Learning good habits, such as careful placing of figures, will pay dividends and reduce frustration and inaccuracy later."

Nuffield (1984).

Text book 3 provides an overlap of text book 2; revisiting the concepts presented in text book 2; this is useful for revision both for children who have and those children who have not used the scheme before.

The scheme can be used in a variety of pedagogical methods: individual work, group, class or topic based.

The only prerequisites required of the children are an adequate reading level and some very basic number concepts. Many of the children who have difficulty with the scheme are those that are unable to read or who have an inadequate reading level. Yet the mathematical content is of a suitable standard/level. In the classes of Mr. D and Mr. E the grouping of children has enabled children with a lower reading ability to participate in a text book of the appropriate mathematical level, even though this is above their reading level: this has been achieved by the group of children helping each other in their difficulties. The content of the scheme is organized in a spiral format. The basic concepts are constantly revisited, revised, extended and deepened throughout books 3 to 6. Mathematical understanding is strengthened by examining a variety of methods of calculation and presentation building to a high level of abstraction, application and investigation at book 6, where concepts are brought together. Within each chapter the content is sequentially structured to enable experience through activities and experimentation; to lead into a discussion of ideas, findings and problems which can then be recorded in some format; and to promote the aquisition and reinforcement of skills, giving confidence and enjoyment for the individual.

The teacher's book is a very succinct resource book, which is easy to use. Each chapter is clearly headed, well illustrated highlighting 'correct' verbal use, ideas, concepts, introductory sessions and extensions. It is also time saving for the teacher since it lists resources required, vocabulary and copies of pages from the childrens books.

It is implicit and explicit in the text material that mathematics can be enjoyable and fun. The use of different coloured print, cartoon characters coupled with congenial activities using a variety of equipment adds to the success of the scheme with the children.

Bronto, Bird and Frog are featured throughout the course to help clarify mathematical points, bring a touch of humour and keep the children interested and eager to learn. (*Ibid*)

Each text book is accompanied by a comprehensive teacher's handbook. This is a concise resource which gives ideas and advice on what to teach. Each chapter is formulated in the following way:

(i)   *For the teacher*; this gives a brief outline of the content and aims of the chapter, any revision that might be needed and how the theme is developing.

(ii) *Summary of the stages*; this gives the title of each section in the child's book.

(iii) *Vocabulary*; any words and phrases which are used in the chapter which the child will need to use and understand to explore the chapter's content to its full.

(iv) *Equipment and apparatus*; the quantity and type required in the chapter. This enables the teacher to prepare and ensure resources or alternatives are available.

(v)   *Working with children*; expands on the summary of stages giving introduction ideas, hints, activities and background to subjects, stressing the learning points of the text.

(vi) *Copies of the pages in pupil's books and spiritmasters*; reduced copies, answers are presented at the back of the book.

(vii) *References and resources*; lists of further exercises, texts and equipment to aid or supplement the work and ideas in the chapter. (*Ibid*)

The underlying contentions in the pedagogy are that:

(a)   children learn at different rates and so will not reach the same stage simultaneously;

(b)   young children learn by doing and by discussion;

(c)   as well as finding out and 'discovering' things about mathematics, children need to be told things about mathematics, particularly if new vocabulary is involved. (*Ibid*)

In accordance with this view the 'style' and organization of the material enables the teacher to select an appropriate teaching method to suit particular topics and ones own teaching 'style'. It was however decided amongst the staff that 'group' teaching would prevail throughout the school.

The Topic 'Length' as Presented in the Nuffield Mathematics Scheme

Length has been chosen as an example of a topic presented in the Nuffield Mathematics Scheme. Appendix 1 lists the content of each book on this topic.

The topic is very structured throughout text books 3 to 6. Book 3 introduces the concept of length and measurement through relevant activities and experiments concerned with estimating and measuring parts of the body. By measuring small parts of the body the children recognize the need for arbitrary units. The practical activities encourage the children to discuss and explain their findings; through this the need for a standard unit of measure is recognized. The following exercises familiarize standard measures and goes on to reinforce these concepts and ideas. Length is revisited at a later stage in the book giving a quick but sufficient revision of the work previously completed. From the revision the tasks reinforce and extend the concept of length. In book 4 length is divided into two chapters, dealing with the metre, its parts, the measurement of perimeters and the use of a measuring tape. Book 5 introduces the arithmetical skills of multiplication and division of metres and centimetres. In the second chapter in book 5 measuring in millimetres is introduced, an extension of the accuracy required in measurement. In book 6 the concept of length has been extended to include estimating distances outdoors and the use of conversion graphs.

Group Teaching

The Handbook *Mathematics 5 to 11* (HMI) stresses the role of organization in the classroom and throughout the school in determining the effectiveness of mathematical learning. As the schools mathematics document states: 'mathematics advisers make the observation that the average amount of direct, one-to-one contact between a teacher and a pupil in mathematics is about two minutes per day, i.e. ten minutes per week'. I would suggest that the one-to-one contact time per week using the Nuffield Mathematics scheme is likely to be twenty minutes plus per week in most classes; this, however, has been speculated from observations carried out in classes. The benefits to the children are shown simply through their increased understanding, amount of work covered, reduction of time wasting waiting for the teacher's attention and an understanding as to the class/teacher organization in mathematics lessons. In teacher A's class he responded to individuals waiting at his desk; a queue often formed and the time children spent waiting varied considerably. Some children were seen to leave the queue when friends answered their queries. The amount of teacher-pupil contact time in this class seemed biased towards the children who required frequent help. Does the work of the children who are infrequent visitors to the teacher suffer? I was unable to assess this from my observations; however it was noticeable that these children often worked in pairs and sought help from each other or friends on the same book. In other classes very few children were seen to be waiting; if they were, the time spent waiting for the teacher was a couple of minutes at the most. Teachers B, D and E made available alternative mathematical activities for the children in the class who found themselves 'stuck' or with nothing to do. This reduced the number of interruptions to the teacher when working with groups or individuals. When the mathematical activities of the class are well organized children are able to work with much less direct supervision and teacher support. This allows the teacher to work with groups and individuals within groups. The benefits of increased class organization and increased teacher-pupil contact time were seen in Mr. B and Mr. D's class. Pupils/groups had the teacher's undivided attention for a large percentage of the lesson, this enabled the teacher to discuss the work with the individuals in groups without interruptions from other individuals. However this was clearly only possible because the rest of the class were settled in their own work and knew the teacher's method of work. Questioning the children clarified these thoughts; the children in these classes knew exactly how the group teaching operated and what was expected of them in maintaining this sytem of organization.

The Middle School uses 'vertical grouping' in which children of two-year groups are placed in the same class. The Cockcroft Report presumes that vertical grouping will manufacture a great spread of mathematical attainment in any one class and that consequently this increases the problem of the teacher 'matching' the level of the work to the needs of the individuals. From my experience and observation in this particular school, vertical grouping seems to have decreased the diversity of ability and problem of 'matching', if only by increasing the number of children at each ability level and therefore the size of the ability groups. In teacher E's class the children are placed into four ability groups. The highest ability group has four children; three of these are in the second year, one is in the first year. Now if the children were not vertically grouped there would only be one child at this level (presuming that no other children joined the class) in the first year. This child in the group situation therefore has the benefits of firstly, working as part of a group rather than in isolation; secondly, the child is likely to be 'stretched' working in a group of the same ability and thirdly will receive a greater amount of teacher time as part of a group than on their own.

Organizing children within the class into ability groups for mathematics enables children to work at a pace appropriate to the group in which they are placed. A further advantage is that it enables children to work alongside and discuss the mathematics with children of roughly the same ability, with the advantage of presenting sufficient challenge to the more able in the class and decreasing the isolation of the lower ability. This was clearly seen as the effects in Mr. F's and Mr. C's class; the lower ability groups had work produced for them by the teacher, which is unlikely to happen if there is only one child in the class of lower ability. The children worked in groups as did the rest of the class and this reduced any isolation fears. In Mr. F's class the higher ability worked on their own ideas 'sparked' off by the text book. These sorts of activities are unlikely to occur if the ability level in the class is so diverse that it does not permit grouping by ability. Encouraging discussion within the groups enables children to clarify their ideas and understanding. Explanation by peers can aid children in their learning as language used is of an appropriate nature. In all the classes in which I observed mathematics lessons, discussion between children and with the teacher was encouraged. The noise levels, however, varied according to the teacher's preference, but in all classes still enabled children to talk. It is encouraging to report that I estimate approximately 95 per cent of the talk I overheard or observed was task orientated.

Grouping allows the teacher to work with relatively small groups therefore increasing pupil contact time. If the 'cyclical' approach is adopted each group is at a different stage in the process of a topic. Each topic should include the following elements: introduction (exposition and discussion), practical work, consolidation and extension (investigation and enrichment). If the theme approach is chosen a framework for organization of lessons during a week may look something like this:

	Group 1	Group 2	Group 3	Group 4
Monday	Class lesson:– introduction, discussion, practical work, demonstrations, examples etc.			
Tuesday	Consolidation	Moving on	Extension	Investigation
Wednesday	Moving on	Extension	Investigation	Consolidation
Thursday	Extension	Investigation	Consolidation	Moving on
Friday	Investigation	Consolidation	Moving on	Extension

Source: Haylock, D (1984)

The above model can be adapted to suit class topics or group topics. Using this model the teacher can be concerned with one group at a time knowing that the other groups should be able to cope with the revision, extension and investigational work on their own; this could be extended to give pupils the opportunity to mark their own work. As the school's mathematics curriculum document states: 'group teaching supporters argue that the benefits of teaching one group at a time will outweigh any problems in leaving the other groups to work alone'.

The teacher also has the facility to alter the groups by moving children 'up' and 'down' as and when their performance requires it, this point is revisited later. The schools curriculum document recognizes the following benefits group teaching can offer:

(a)   increases teacher-pupil contact time;
(b)   helps children to work together;
(c)   uses teacher time more effectively;
(d)   stops the teacher from being purely a marking machine;
(e)   increases the actual teaching of mathematics instead of board/book work;
(f)   makes the use of practical apparatus easier;
(g)   aids the operation of a 'cyclic' approach which will provide reinforcement through constant revision;
(h)   increases the amount of mathematical dialogue;

    (i)   increases amount of time available for the less able pupils;

    (j)   assessment-diagnosis-treatment easier through increased contact time with individuals allowing monitoring and continuous assessment. (Mathematics Document, December 1984)

As previously explained the Nuffield Mathematics scheme is structured in a manner which is ideal for topics of pure group teaching. The scheme was developed and based on extensive piloting feedback from teachers, and recommendations made in the HMI Handbook of suggestions *Mathematics 5 to 11*.

Issues

In this section I shall address several issues that have arisen with the implementation of the Nuffield Mathematics Scheme in The Middle School.

Implementation of the Scheme

Innovations in school curriculum development are usually accompanied by 'teething' problems. This middle school has met, and will continue to meet, difficulties at varying levels until the mathematics scheme has progressed through the whole four years of the school. The 'hiccups' that have been encountered have varied in magnitude. Some have been specific to individual teachers; others have been general throughout the school. As Stenhouse (1981) argued:

> the uniqueness of each classroom setting implies that any proposal-even at school level-needs to be tested and verified and adapted by each teacher in his own classroom.

Choosing a scheme and pedagogy to run throughout the school is a hypothesis, actually bringing it into the classroom (the laboratory) is testing that hypothesis in practice. The hypothesis is then open to criticism rather than pure acceptance.

    The 'teething' problems and criticisms have on the whole been overcome either by the individual teacher modifying their own classroom practice, or through discussion with other staff, where possible alternatives are clarified. Each teacher then uses ideas appropriate to their practice.

Text Books

The Nuffield text books are age banded, book 3 is for 7–8-year-olds; book 4 is for 8–9-year-olds; book 5 for 9–10-year-olds; and book 6 is for 10–11-year-olds. Although these age bands can be used as a guide they are not necessarily appropriate in all cases. Three classes found the level of work in book 6 was too high for a large percentage of the children. This was overcome simply by making a greater number of the lower text books available. Even with the wider level of text books available, teacher F still has a small group of children whose poor mathematical and language ability is below the junior texts level. Mr. F found it necessary to structure and prepare the work for these children. Level 2 infant worksheets were found to be below the interest level of the group:

> the trouble with the Infant work is that it's aimed at Infant interest level and they have only got to look around at some of the sophisticated things that the others are doing and they really are made aware that they are at such a lower level. So I try to keep the sort of interest level up with their age but sort of aim the work at their level and bring them up slowly.

There were comments from other teachers that the children had difficulty with the language used in the texts; this related to comprehension rather than the mathematical activities and concepts being presented. The inadequacy in reading comprehension has in some cases been overcome by the grouping of children, allowing for discussion between the group members.

Movement of children between groups in the autumn term seemed a regular occurrence to find the correct level of work for each child. Teacher E comments:

> Last term was very much an experimental term . . . it did take me that long to really get myself going and sorted out . . .

Mr. E carries on talking, this time with reference to the group structure:

> they have more or less stayed the same this term I think I've swapped a couple of people around.

In another class the problem of swapping individuals from group to group still exists, mainly because the text implies that the work is an extension of that covered in an earlier book; it fails to give revision of the mathematics in the earlier book. Teacher C's solution is to withdraw children from one group and place them temporarily in another group:

> the groups are a bit flexible . . . very often because they'll come across something in a book that they don't understand because they haven't done the previous work so they go in a group which is actually doing that the first time round.

In Mr. F's class this group interchange also occurs for the lower ability group. It becomes a:

fluid group because sometimes that remedial group can expand. If
people are having trouble in a certain area I usually take them off the
book.

Equipment in the Classroom

Other problems have been encountered with equipment; either there is not
enough in the school or it is rather dated and 'tatty'. Teachers made the
following remarks regarding the mathematics equipment:

A little bit more in the way of weighing more accurately.

Only one 20 metre tape which got lost ... a lot more things for
measuring ... the money we've got there is fine but I would like
money that looked like money because in the book they talk about the
different things you see on the 10p and the 5p and that isn't on that.

Need some multibase stuff which we haven't got ... a load of
calculators ... and general things, spotty paper.

... Some of it's a bit tatty, I think it's important to have good quality
stuff for them to use especially these children because if it's one thing
school can create: through a bright creative atmosphere.

Some of the above comments were the response to the suggestion of having
extra money available to buy equipment. If the school is to view equipment as
essential in the concrete stage of concept formation and the experimental and
activity process used in the Nuffield Mathematics Scheme, then there does
need to be more equipment in the school, preferably enough for classroom-
based resources. However, teacher F tries to stress to his class to improvise if
they can. Teacher D produces his own games and activities. Teacher C
manages to improvise quite a lot. For example, there is no base three material
in school so Mr. C will either use unifix blocks of similar colours, or cut out
units, threes and sixes from graph paper. I have attached to this report a list of
equipment that was available in the mathematics cupboard in the autumn
term (see appendix 2). A lot of this equipment could be used in conjunction
with the activities in the text books either as consolidation or investigations,
for example, fraction dominoes, visual fraction apparatus, shapes. Teacher F
would like to see a greater supply of card, isometric and dotty paper. I
suggested a workshop session for staff to share ideas, workcards, problems
etc. but this was responded to with mixed feelings. A percentage of the
teachers felt that workcards etc. had to be available in the classroom otherwise
they are forgotten or are unavailable when needed. Mr. D and Mr. E have
produced workcards which are kept in their classrooms, these are used as
extension activities, consolidation — extra examples of work undertaken in
text books, and 'time filling' work. Mr. A finds he writes extra examples in

the children's books where necessary, for example, as extra practice or clarification of the child's understanding.

The use of equipment is a great motivation for children; many reflect on the use of equipment or investigation activities as not mathematics but 'fun'. Equipment as a concrete form aids understanding. The following rather bitty conversation came from two children taught by teacher A:

> enjoy the things in the book ... games in there you can play with
>
> helped understand the fractions ...
>
> everybody wanted to have a go ...

The amount and variety of equipment I observed being used in the classroom varied tremendously. Mr. B introduced 'weight' to a small group of children by using a large 'bucket' balance. The children returned to their desks, after discussing and watching a demonstration of the balance working; to complete an exercise in their book. The children then returned to the 'bucket' balance one by one as they finished their written task. The group of children then experimented weighing a variety of objects around the room against bottle tops and unifix bricks. Other children in the class used abacuses.

In Mr. C's class one child was using a calculator, a small group were making a plumbline from a piece of string and a bulldog clip as a weight. Two other children were using unifix bricks to help them count. One child used counters to check her work, turning to a friend she said: 'checked all mine, got 'em all right'. In Mr. E's class, one child used unifix bricks to count, another child counted on his fingers. A group of children used money to calculate how many 1p, 2p and 5p pieces made 10p and 20p.

How Does the Curriculum Strategy Compare to the Strategies Found in Classrooms?

As mentioned earlier, each classroom and teacher is unique and therefore it would be naive to believe that all teachers would adopt identical strategies in the classroom. Teacher B confirmed this when he stated:

> Individuals teaching in their own individual style to a certain extent even though we agreed that group teaching was what we wanted to do or what we felt was best, you are still going to get people teaching how they feel most comfortable.

I shall present a description of three teachers' mathematics lessons to highlight the variety of teaching methods that are to be found in the school.

Teacher D has arranged the desks into four groups. The equipment is stored on a moveable table. The noise level in the classroom is low and remains low throughout the lesson. The children settle down to work with little 'fuss'. Mr. D uses group topics, that is each group works chapter by chapter through the text books. Mr. D moves to group 1 and crouches at the desk; the balance beam is removed from the table and placed on the floor until it is required. After discussing with the group what they are to do he moves on to group 2. Group 2 has only three children, they have reached an exercise which they cannot solve between themselves. Mr. D, marker pen and large sheet of paper in hand, pulls up a chair. He draws a blank square and adds the numbers shown from the example in the text book. He goes on to discuss the strategies and various procedures for solving a magic square. The rest of the class are busy. On leaving group 2, he confirms to the group that he will return in a few moments. Group 3 are finishing an exercise from the text; one child sits listening to two of the group members talking through their answers. Mr. D calls group 3 to the carpeted area. Sitting on the floor the teacher shows the children some number patterns. Unifix blocks joined together are used as the basis of the discussion. There are two colours joined together. Using a large marker he writes down all the possible sums which can be made from the two colours in the row. This is achieved by appropriate questioning. An example is shown below:

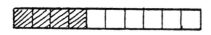

$$6 + 4 = 10$$
$$4 + 6 = 10$$
$$10 - 6 = 4$$
$$10 - 4 = 6$$

Mr. D gives each member of the group a different combination of coloured unifix bricks, in a row. The children return to their desks to write out the number patterns for their 'row' of bricks. Group 4 are playing a game with money, they are not specifically seen throughout the lesson since they have an adult with them, for the whole of this lesson. The teacher returns to group 2 as promised. The lesson continues. The resemblance to the organizational model illustrated in 3.1 is quite clear. Children in their groups are monitored throughout the lesson. Mr. D moves the group onto the next 'stage' of the cycle when applicable, there is no set period of time for each activity and group.

Mr. A has arranged the desks in rows. The class equipment is kept in a cupboard at the back of the class. The noise level varies but never reaches excessive limits, usually being curbed by the teacher, although the class naturally monitor the noise level as well. The children sit next to friends who are not necessarily on the same page, topic or book. Mr. A remains at his desk and the children form a line when they want to be seen. The number of children waiting for assistance at any one time varies. Children were seen to leave the line after being helped by friends already waiting. A child was seen to move seats to sit next to a boy who is on the same page; the two children discuss the problem presented in the text:

B: of course.
G: add 'em up on the calculator.

The girl watches intently and makes another suggestion as the answer 'flashes' up. Another girl joins the pair and standing in front of them says:

G: thirty.

She walks away and returns almost immediately;

G: what did you put for that? 25 and 75 right?
B: yeah

Two girls sit on their own at the front of the class; one works busily, and confidently writes in her book. The other girl sits quietly, dreaming, writing little and very slowly. She gets up and goes to see Mr. A. Three boys are standing at a desk deciding on a plan of action. One goes to get some sellotape, another gets paper from the cupboard. The lesson continues as children wander freely around the room collecting equipment and seeking help when required. Teacher A's method of teaching mathematics does not fit into the model of group teaching shown in a previous section, yet the children tend to form their own groups when necessary. The children who work on their own either prefer it this way, or accept that other children are unlikely to be on the same page as them and therefore only seek help from the teacher.

Mr. F has his class arranged in two large groups and pairs of children interspersed around the room. Mr. F stands at his desk and answers any immediate flood of questions as to resources available. He explains where the paper and other equipment is. One boy is using masking tape to stick cubes together. All the children are working on the same topic but using the relevant chapter in their text book. Mr. F likes to follow the topic across other curriculum subjects. Mr. F moves from group to group marking work, suggesting extension activities to work already being undertaken. Two boys are colouring a large plan of a space shuttle which they have tessellated using hexagons. Two girls are talking about how to stick together the 'plan' of a pyramid they have just drawn. Mr. F demonstrates to another child how to draw a plan of a solid. Two boys are finishing off a worksheet while another two boys are playing a tables game. There is movement around the room to collect resources. The noise level is left to find its own level. Mr. F is shown work finished by one boy, the teacher asks him what the shape is called, the boy responds:

B: A pyramid.
Mr. F: What type of pyramid is it?

Mr. F clarifies that there are two types of pyramid; a square or triangle base. No child is seen to be waiting for Mr. F but he often admits to just standing back watching and listening to what's going on in his class. A boy turns to his friend and demonstrates how to do the breast stroke!

Mr. F's method of class and mathematics organization on the surface seems to bear no resemblance to the model illustrated in a previous section. Analysis of the activities shows firstly that Mr. F uses a class topic approach. Secondly, to do this a class introduction is necessary. Thirdly, the different level text books are worked through by the groups. Fourthly, extension work is suggested to individual groups where applicable. The model therefore applies to sections of the class organization although in no clear-cut format.

As you can see from the descriptions, each teacher has adopted a method that is suitable for themselves. As Mr. B stated:

> ... we might have started off all teaching in groups but gradually it gets adpated because people have preferential ways of doing it ...

What are the difficulties in group teaching? Every teacher uses different methods. For some teaching in groups is no different from usual classroom practice. Teacher E made the following statement:

> I found it difficult to use the books properly. Once I came to grips with the books, well my perception of how it should be taught and sort of finding the right back up ... it doesn't seem too bad.

Mr. B had not used group teaching before and he found he had difficulty in organization and the ability spread in his class. Mr. F on the other hand uses group teaching quite a lot in other curriculum areas. Teacher C found difficulty to begin with keeping the groups together but feels he has solved this problem. In contrast Mr. A finds that the groups have dispersed due to the rate at which individuals work:

> some were working at a much faster rate and so I decided that I want to keep the people who were working quickly going ahead and the others I could take more slowly and gradually. Of course the groups have more or less gone.

So what are the strategies used by the teachers to keep the children in groups? Teacher C solved this problem by constructing his own worksheets:

> to give them to do while waiting, or extension work, revision of basic skills.

Teacher B uses a similar method with a supplementary arithmetic book:

> ... sometimes I'll use it for some children who are moving on a bit quicker than others ... one or two individuals always move on a bit faster than the others and finish sections.

Teacher F uses yet another alternative strategy, he catches onto the children's ideas and suggestions and sets the children off on activities and investigations which will extend the concepts and mathematical understanding. Perhaps teacher F is too much of a risk taker for most teachers, or can we learn something from this? What is the solution to teachers' dilemmas of children working at different rates? The over lying crucial issue is one of organization; of children in groups, desks, equipment, teacher time and 'back up' material. A stock of alternative texts, workcards and investigations which can be used to occupy, and at the same time consolidate, revise or extend the children's mathematical understanding. These activities do not have to be directly related to the topic covered in the text book. An alternative solution is to have two groups on the same book, progressing at a rate applicable to the group members. Teacher E finds this a suitable method in his class. He has four groups, two of which are on the same text book but different pages. The teacher sees the two groups:

> as almost parallel but C have got, um, seem very slow on the uptake but B probably will catch on quite quickly but C group will take a bit longer.

How Do the Children See Group Teaching Working?

There was a mixed response from the children I interviewed. One of the main problems which arose with the younger children was one of group cooperation:

P: . . . others go ahead of you.
S: Them three do.
P: She don't explain.
D: They drop behind because they can't do it.
C: They're too slow.
D: We have to explain.
P: You just go ahead.
S: She explains; they don't.
C: Sometimes I do.
P: No you don't Chrissie.
C: Occasionally.
S: He wants to get his work done.
C: Cause teacher keeps coming up to explain and after a little while they don't know how to do it.

This was obvious, although not present in all groups that I observed in various classes. Children in groups often left one child or perhaps two out of their group by ignoring them or reluctantly helping them. On the occasions when a child in the group was 'able', the group would seek clarification of answers rather than help.

In the older classes group cooperation rested more upon individual's temperaments. One girl remarked:

> . . . sometimes people get in a mood with other people they don't sort of tell you what to do and you're meant to help each other.

Despite the temperaments and lack of cooperation most children enjoyed and found working in a group helpful. The comments collected were very similar. A 9-year-old girl said:

> . . . because if you can't do it other people will show you how to do it.

An older girl commented:

> good thing about having a group is if you get stuck and the teacher's busy you can ask each other.

One boy took great joy and pride in telling me how he helps his friend with his work. A boy of 10 years preferred working on his own and didn't enjoy waiting for other people. In teacher A's class a 'group' was associated with the speed at which children worked. When asked do you like working in a group a girl answered:

> I prefer working with people — but it all depends how fast or how slow they are.

Reflection on Group Teaching

Reflecting on the benefits group teaching has to offer (as stated earlier) from the observations I made during mathematics lessons; if the teacher was well organized in terms of resources, extension or investigational work, this eased the teacher's role during the lesson. This effectively increased the amount of teacher-pupil contact time. In this way the teacher could discuss and monitor an individual's progress. However, the class needed to be 'trained' to work in a group and to take the initiative to take up alternative work. The problem which was highlighted in all classes was the difficulty encountered with the children of very poor mathematical ability. This was eased in some cases where students' and welfare help was available. Although the group teaching aids the amount of time available to these children, their problems, misconceptions and lack of mathematical understanding is highlighted. The type of help required from the teacher is excessive. For the children working in such groups the discussion and help they give to each other is very limited. Also, their problems are idiosyncratic which makes teaching as a group very difficult. All the teachers seemed to be in agreement that additional, rather than alternative, arrangements need to be made for these individuals. The teachers were against ability streaming in mathematics across the years, and believed mixed ability teaching has greater benefits. Having class lessons also gives the teacher flexibility in their timetable. In terms of the Cockcroft Report, I feel more teachers should be prepared to take risks in terms of extending the children's work into different subjects, or purely for increasing the practicality and enjoyment of mathematics for its own sake. As teacher F reflects upon this point:

> if you follow the book rigidly and aren't prepared to experiment ... if you've got ideas you shouldn't let the book stop you from doing them.

Questions to Think and Ponder On

Is there enough mental and oral work in the mathematics lesson?

The Cockcroft Report does not recommend a return to basics but stresses the need for practice to help develop appropriate skills. Written calculations are performed by using standard algorithms; 'doing it in your head' often requires the use of alternative strategies. Since mathematics in daily life is usually mental calculations, practice and discussion of alternative methods used needs to be encouraged. Many children's methods will be highly individualized. Teacher B, at the end of a mathematics lesson, asked the whole class a series of questions requiring a variety of 'mental calculations'; these included the following:

4×4
$17 + 12 + 8$
$54 - 6 + 12$
Make 98 smaller by 16

Many teachers gave tables tests practice but this limits the calculations to one mode of thinking.

Mathematics and its relevance to activities in everyday life

Practical problem solving can be made relevant to individuals if advantage is taken of school activities. As Cockcroft states:

> all children need experience of practical work which is directly related to the activities of everyday life, including shopping, travel, model making and the planning of school activities.

How much mathematics could be associated with the children's visits to London or their walks down to the river? Are these activities exploited sufficiently in terms of mathematical possibilities? Take, for example, the visit to London; what are the possibilities for mathematical activities? First, there could have been a vote on the museum to visit. Each child could have been given a voting paper with the alternative museums. The voting paper could ask the children to rank their preferences; these could then be given in and amalgamated into a wall chart. The totals could be calculated and expressed as a bar chart. Secondly, the children could have calculated how far each museum was from Norwich or how far apart they are in London. Next, how long the journey would take at an average speed of thirty miles an hour. Next, how long they would have at each place if they left Norwich at 8.00am and returned by 4.00pm. Next, the cost of the coach and entry fees for each museum; petrol usage, driver, how many seats, plus cost per person, journey, entrance fee, pocket money. One journey provides extensive possibilities for a variety of mathematical ideas and concepts. The children would see a reason in learning new concepts if there was a need for it, for example, percentages, speed-distance. The Cockcroft Report continues:

> Children cannot be expected to be able to make use of their mathematics in everyday situations unless they have opportunity to experience these situations for themselves.

Do children recognize the mathematics, its application to real life and other areas of the curriculum? I believe that if the occasion arises teachers should leave the text books and involve all the class in mathematics 'projects'.

What should the aims in mathematics be for the low achievers?

Since there are a number of children in each class who are underachieving for their age, should there be a standard policy in the school for teaching mathematics: a set of aims/objectives. In the HMI *Handbook of Suggestions: Mathematics 5 to 11*, they suggest a set of criteria that most children by the age of 8 need to be able to:

(i) add/subtract 1 or 2 to/from other numbers up to 10;
(ii) double numbers up to 10 and halve even numbers up to 20;
(iii) understand and use facts such as $5 + 2 = 7 = 2 + 5$. i.e. the commutative law of addition;
(iv) know all addition and subtraction facts up to 10;
(v) add 10 to numbers 0 to 10 with immediate response;
(vi) by quick recall add 9 to numbers 0 to 10;
(vii) by quick recall know 'near doubles';
(viii) understand and use different addition processes;
(ix) understand place value;
(x) by quick recall recognize repeating patterns of numbers.

The handbook sees the above as 'basic number knowledge which children need before they can benefit from formal practice in written calculations'. By introducing such a policy the children of lower ability are seen to be progressing in mathematical development. This does not imply that lower ability children should be left out of practical projects, class lessons and discussions. Could the use of the Bronto reading books also be beneficial to this group of children?

Suggestions for Future Development of the Middle School's Mathematics Curriculum

The Nuffield mathematics team have recently published series E of Bronto Reading Books, which have been linked to book 3 and book 4. The children's text books are now being published in full colour rather than the basic white, black, red and blue colours used at present; however these are more expensive. The team have also produced a video showing how a group of teachers have implemented the scheme in their own classes.

Computers in the Classroom

The Nuffield mathematics team have also produced a series of micro software which is directly related to the text book activities. In the interviews with teachers and observations made in classrooms it was noted that:

(i)   not all teachers felt confident in the use of computers in their classrooms. Teacher A made the comment:

I haven't had the experience of it.

(ii)   Some teachers were not convinced of its value in the classroom. Teacher B made the comment:

problem I have found with trying to use the computer particularly with the slower ones is that they can't read the instructions on the computer anyway so it doesn't in any sense release me from supervising them.

(iii)   When the teacher wanted to use the computer it was unavailable. Teacher C takes the view that every classroom should have its own:

everytime when I want it always someone else has got it.

In general when the computer is used it is for reinforcement and practice of basic skills, for example, tables, four rules. Teacher F has on occasions used programmes for developing 3D shapes from 2D figures; this was an application of mathematical ideas into craft and design activities. It would be conceivably more applicable if micro software was directly related to the text although this does not imply software for reinforcement activities is inapplicable. The Cockcroft Report believes working with computers aids childrens motivation and concentration. The Report would like to see attention paid to development of software for mathematical activities which:

... will encourage problem solving and logical thinking in a mathematical context.

A Mathematics Day in School

One suggestion which I felt was a very valid and plausible idea was made by teacher F:

> not only for the teachers to share but the children to share, you know sort of once a term have a maths day or something like that ... everybody gets together and we sort of give some topics out.

This idea would enable children to see what their peers are undertaking in their work, to discuss mathematics and see it as an enjoyable activity. Each class could choose a subject/topic to display and the class members could make some workcards, investigations for children in other classes to complete.

Workshop Sessions for Teachers in School

A couple of teachers suggested a workshop session where teachers could get together to discuss ideas, problems, construct workcards, games and investigations etc. Teachers D and E felt this type of session would boost teachers' confidence as well as give new ideas for use in the classroom. Other teachers felt a workshop session would not be very useful in terms of workcards etc. mainly because you never really knew what you would need in a mathematics lesson. If a clear list of available equipment and its application to specific chapters was produced this could be kept in the classroom for quick reference; a form of catalogue for mathematics resources.

General Impressions of the Mathematics Teaching and Curriculum

The Nuffield Mathematics Scheme has provided the school with a basis for increasing the continuity of mathematics taught in the school. The use of the scheme has also increased the amount of practical work and the benefits this provides the children. The choice of the scheme matches closely to the ideas presented in the Cockcroft Report and HMI *Handbook of Suggestions Mathematics 5 to 11*. The scheme has increased the confidence of the staff in their mathematics teaching, through the concise, well structured teacher's handbook. The staff aimed to use a standard pedagogy throughout the school; this has not been achieved in all cases. The use of group teaching has in some classes been developed to a high level; in others the potential is there, and with some time, organization and modification from teachers this could be achieved throughout the school. The teachers feel the scheme is operating quite smoothly and successfully in their classes. The benefits of group teaching are quite noticeable when observing mathematic lessons: increased pupil–teacher contact time; cooperation between children working in groups; increased use of equipment due to better organization; greater amount of mathematical dialogue between pupils and with the teacher; an atmosphere of 'enjoyment and fun' and more effective use of teacher time. The one problem that has been highlighted is that of the low ability children. Provision needs to be improved for these children. The problems that have arisen in the third and fourth year classes is that of changing the scheme: in the fourth year's case, a year before they are to leave. The problems for third and fourth year children are the same, that of having missed work in the lower text books. This will be overcome only when the scheme has run throughout all four years of the school. The general consensus from the children was that Nuffield Mathematics was more enjoyable although sometimes harder to do than previous texts used. The children thought mathematics was fun and enjoyable. Comments from the children included:

First and Second Years

G: Some words are hard.
G: You do all different things.
B: The experiments are hard ... writing um out takes too long.

Third and Fourth Years

G: Sometimes boring, keep doing the same things, measuring, weighing, graphs.
G: Harder, Fletcher was really easy.
G: The harder it is the more you learn.
G: I like doing the sums.
B: Enjoy the things in the book ... games and things.
G: Sometimes you come across things which you aint learnt, and you learn um so you learn more things.
B: It explains it quite well.
G: It shows you different ways of doing things ... confusing at first ... helpful.

My favourite quote came from a girl of 10 years:

This book is more *EDUCATIONAL* because its got harder work in it.

Conclusion

An Adversary's Statement

Innovation in a middle school curriculum is no smooth, cheap, easy transition. The cost of innovation is high in many areas.

Providing each child with a colourful text book at £2; the teacher with a book of ideas and answers at £7; spiritmasters to use as convenient handouts £18.50 per text book; plus reading books at £3.50 per set are just the minimum requirements in this innovation project.

The cost of providing extra resources and equipment to use the scheme ideally and efficiently is an extra cost. Broken 20-metre tapes, wasted graph paper, inaccurate scales, dotty paper photocopied by the ream. The stress of responding to children's equipment desires, and remarks when the teacher's improvization looks nothing like the text books illustration.

What is the cost of advocating that six talented teachers modify/change their style of teaching and classroom organization for mathematics lessons? ... The time? ... Energy? ... Pressure? ... Anxiety of getting it right?

How do the children feel to the change of routine, security, classroom climate and teachers' role?

Is the innovation *really* worth all the trouble?

An Advocate's Statement

Innovation in a middle school curriculum shows concern for improvement in the quality of education. A visitor to the school views an effective and efficient mathematics scheme in action.

The quality of learning is high. Children are enjoying, understanding the mathematical concepts through activity and experimentation in group work.

The teachers have excelled in the numerous hours commitment and effort they have directed in to making innovation in the mathematics curriculum a success.

The pupils are on the way to becoming autonomous learners. The teachers have developed knowledge and professional skills. To question and study one's own teaching method, to allow others to observe one's work and to discuss one's own classroom practice openly are outstanding characteristics of the professional.

Innovation has succeeded. It has benefited the teachers and children and improved the quality of the mathematics taught in the school.

Meeting With Teachers' of the Middle School

This report was presented to the staff at the middle school on Monday 25 March 1985. The staff were unable to read through the whole report in the short period of time prior to the staff meeting.

I opened the meeting by asking if in the teachers' brief perusal of the report, they had come across any points they wished to discuss. The remarks concerned the usefulness and volume of the report. I proceeded to give a brief resumé of each section in the report, illustrating where appropriate.

In the third section (page 178), I brought to the teachers' attention that the Cockcroft Report presumes 'vertical grouping' will increase the diversity of mathematical ability in any one class. The teachers agreed with my observations that vertical grouping had decreased the diversity by increasing the number of children in each ability group: 'viable groups by expanding the number of children' was the comment made by one teacher. The teachers were also encouraged that I estimated that 95 per cent of the children's 'talking' during mathematics lessons was task-orientated, very few children were seen or heard 'chatting' off task.

Moving on to the fourth section, I presented some of the issues that had arisen. The sub-section 'equipment in the classroom' was discussed. I suggested there was a need for constant renewal of exisiting equipment. A variety of small miscellaneous items were required, for example, sawdust, marbles and plasticine. One teacher remarked that when buying equipment from educational suppliers you expect certain qualities of the goods purchased:

> when you order something from an educational resource company, you assume certain things about it and when you order plastic money you assume it's going to have the right pictures on it.

In fact the money was not a good replica of 'real' money; it has the value of the coin rather than the Queen's head printed on it.

The next sub-section presented three different teaching strategies that are used in the school to teach the Nuffield Mathematics scheme. The diversity of the three styles/methods concerned one teacher immensely in relation to the fact that only six months prior to this report, when the scheme was introduced, it was decided by the staff that one method of teaching would be used throughout the school:

> We did decide on a group teaching strategy, and we did decide what we meant by teaching in terms of classroom organization, in terms of teaching style.

Yes, they had decided on the basic strategy, philosophy and qualities of group teaching, but had never come to a consensus as to the 'style' which should be adopted, for example, class topic, or following the sequence of chapters in the book. One teacher remarked:

we never actually agreed whether we were going to teach topics ...
we never did settle that.

I reiterated that every teacher will find a 'style' that is most congenial to their mode of teaching and that is why there is such a diversity in 'style' throughout the school:

every teacher has their own ideas of how it should work.

There is only one out of the six classes that does not use a group teaching method. In this particular class children tended to group themselves. In the other classes group teaching was used in a way that suited the teacher: high/low noise level, free/restricted movement, group/class topic. The teacher adopted the method appropriate to his own needs: security, confidence and preference.

With regard to the 'model' adopted, one teacher stated:

if everybody knows the basic strategy that you are starting off with and everybody then made an effort to keep somewhere near that basic strategy, then you wouldn't get so much diversity.

The staff disagreed that there should be a uniform method throughout the school:

you've got to have your own individual method ... until you work the scheme you don't really know how it's going to work.

The teachers came to an agreement that you cannot expect and would not expect uniformity in the 'style' of teaching, but the underlying principles and philosophy of group teaching should be consistent throughout the school. This reinforces Stenhouse's theory that the classroom is a laboratory and that every teacher will adapt the innovation in accordance with their own classroom practice. I suggested that the teachers took it in turn to visit each others classrooms to observe a mathematics lesson organizaion etc. A suggestion was made to use one teacher's methods as a 'model' for the rest of the staff:

Model to follow, an example we could have actually seen being undertaken in the classroom ... see somebody giving a demonstration lesson of how to organize, how to do the administration and set up groups.

Each individual will then at least have some idea of a method rather than interpreting the model in terms of their own ideas. Some members of staff didn't feel this suggestion would work in terms of applying the same model to all classrooms. The model which the premise of group teaching was made on when the scheme was first introduced is based on a one hour lesson: there should be twenty minute introduction, twenty minute follow up and twenty minute extra practice for each group; this model could work effectively and efficiently in a class which had three groups. However, in the third and fourth year there are four or five groups in each class, which makes the above model difficult to operate. The number of groups may well be reduced once the scheme has run throughout the school; this may reduce the wide ability range that exists at present. With regard to the model, the following comments were made:

> there were specific qualities that we agreed were good and valuable in a group teaching philosophy.

> Concentrating on a small group, therefore teacher contact time with them is greater.

> you don't have to use the model everyday ... but it ensures you have contact with every group on those days.

As the above statements highlight, there was concern that pupil-teacher contact time had not increased during the mathematics lessons. From my observations I suggested that pupil-teacher contact time had increased, except in the class where children are not grouped together. In this class a large amount of the teacher's time is given to the children who have the greatest number of difficulties.

The speed of work varied across the school. This often related to the frequency in which the book was used, whether the chapters were used in sequence and the children's motivation. A teacher made the remark:

> the pace we seem to be going seems totally different.

In the third and fourth year classes, children monitored their progress by the number of pages left in their book. One teacher's solution to this was:

> not to do the chapters in sequence, you know exactly if you plan it out, you can then change the sequence of events and the children don't have the problem of working through the book.

The question: 'would children have continuity moving through the school?' was asked. My reply stressed that children would feel secure moving from class to class: (i) they would keep the same text book; (ii) only one out of the six classes doesn't use a group teaching method; (iii) the philosophy of group mathematics teaching was the same throughout the school: practical work, use of equipment, discussion amongst groups, increased pupil-teacher contact time.

For group teaching to work effectively I emphasized six guidelines:

(i)   the desks have to be organized into groups;
(ii) it is suggested that the teacher moves from group to group, rather than remaining at his desk as this encourages children to seek the teacher's attention by going to him;
(iii) a quantity of extension, reinforcement, practice resources, in the

form of workcards, games and alternative text books should be available in the classroom for all individuals, especially those who finish their work quickly. This enables the teacher to keep the groups together;

(iv) there is no reason why there shouldn't be two groups on the same text book but on different pages if this helps to maintain the groups;

(v)   suitable work for the lower ability to improve basic mathematical knowledge and reading which will eventually enable them to move onto the lower Nuffield Mathematics text book;

(vi) the teacher should make it explicit to the children their role in the group organization. A teacher stated her method:

> my children don't interrupt me if I'm working in a group, they know they don't come any where near me until I've finished but they also know if they can not work out what to do amongst themselves there are things they can go and get on with.

The teachers were very interested in the children's views. I was asked if the children conveyed any feelings of success in using the Nuffield Mathematics Scheme:

> did most of them feel they were actually suceeding?

My response was that although I had not asked the children that specific question, I had received positive views of group teaching and the scheme. Many children didn't enjoy the investigations: this could be due to looking for a 'correct' result or the uncertainty in this type of work. The teachers felt that the children had gained confidence:

> very encouraging that they actually are using the terminology.

I agreed that they actually used mathematical terminology when explaining their work to me. The children who found the activities boring could be recognized as either having grasped the concept quickly or more likely that they have already met work on the same topic previously and therefore presume that they have learnt everything:

> they seem to think that if they've tackled it in the past that's it done and they don't need to reinforce it.

It was quite noticeable that there was a 'split' in the staff concerning the implementation of a 'rigid' model and the restrictions this imposed upon them. There was agreement that the general principles outlined in the school's curriculum document for implementing group teaching were beneficial to the children and teachers. It was made clear that the teachers wished to remain 'individual' in their teaching style/method.

Near the end of the meeting I presented the teachers first with an adversary statement, followed by an advocate's statement. The teachers chuckled to themselves but made no comments on these statements. I believe the statements reflected upon what they had achieved by participating in innovation, against a rather detrimental view of innovation. Many teachers were uncertain of the outcome of my report, since they presumed I would be judgemental of the mathematics teaching. I hope this report reflects the development of the schools mathematics curriculum by addressing theoretical as well as practical issues; illustrating different pedagogy, classroom organization and management; and by presenting suggestions for development of the mathematics scheme.

Appendix 1: Contents of each Nuffield Mathematics Book on Length

Book 3:

Length 1:   Measuring with parts of your body
Estimating before measuring
The bits left over
Towards a standard measure
The metre
The 10-centimetre rod

Length 2:   Drawing lines the correct length
Measuring distances
Using a metre ruler to measure longer distances
Addition of centimetres

Book 4:

Length 1:   Parts of a metre
The snail race
The perimeter
The decimetre strip

Length 2:   Looking at the metre ruler
The metre, decimetre and centimetre
Recording measurements on a decimal abacus
Finding the perimeter
Using a measuring tape

Book 5:

Length 1:   Multiplication of metres and centimetres
Division of metres and centimetres

Length 2:   Measuring in millimetres

   Book 6:

Aids to estimation: Estimating distances outdoors,
                      Pacing distances
                      Conversion graphs

Appendix 2: Resources/Equipment Available in Mathematics Cupboard, Autumn 1984

geoboards (different sizes)
money
centimetre/decimal set
cubes (introduction to volume)
shapes — multicolour/size/thickness
visual fractions apparatus
decimal currency dominoes
fraction dominoes
comparative fraction strips
large dice
cuisenaire rods
large plastic number square
unifix cubes
transparent centimetre grid squares
× ÷ squares
clocks
metal volume equipment
weights
tape measures
metre trundle wheels
abacuses
counters
poleidoblocks (solid shapes: wooden and plastic) workcards to use with them
    e.g., pictures that can be made
height measure
balance beam
balance bucket
scales
metre sticks
shape trays
Dienes blocks
bathroom scales

'winner on points'   (spin, match number on wheel with number on the board
            figure by figure)
flexi build strips (different lengths)
game of 'fraction'
tessellation shapes
small dice and shakers
set squares
blackboard protractor
centimetre measure
magnets
'angle race'   game for advanced geometry eg: use of rotations, protractors,
            angles and degrees
decimal strips
bottle tops
spare text books
Bronto reading books: in the reading room

References

COCKCROFT, W.H. (1983). *Mathematics Counts*, HMSO.
GLENN, J.A. (1977). *Teaching Primary Mathematics: Strategy and Evaluation*, Harper and Row.
HAYLOCK, D. (1984) Unit 280, School of Education, University of East Anglia.
HMI, HMI Series: Matters for discussion: *Mathematics 5–11, A Handbook of Suggestions*, DES/HMSO.
The Middle School Mathematics Curriculum Document, December 1984.
Nuffield Mathematics Scheme 7 to 12, (1984).
STENHOUSE, L. (1975). *An Introduction to Curriculum Research and Development*, Open University/Heinemann.

Bibliography

AHIER, J. and FLUDE, M. (Eds), (1983) *Contemporary Education Policy*, Croom Helm

ALEXANDER, R.J., (1984a) *Primary Teaching*, Holt, Rinehart and Winston

ALEXANDER, R.J., (1984b) 'Innovation and continuity in the initial teacher education curriculum', in ALEXANDER, R.J., CRAFT, M., and LYNCH, J. (Eds), *Change in Teacher Education: Context and Provision since Robbins*, Holt, Rinehart and Winston

ALEXANDER, R.J., CRAFT, M. and LYNCH, J. (Eds), (1984) *Change in Teacher Education: Context and Provision since Robbins*, Holt, Rinehart and Winston

ASHTON, P.M.E., HENDERSON, E.S., MERRITT, J.E., and MORTIMER, D.J., (1983) *Teacher Education in the Classroom: Initial and In-Service*, Croom Helm

BALL, S., (1981) *Beachside Comprehensive*, Cambridge University Press

BECHER, T. and MACLURE, S. (Eds), (1978) *Accountability in Education*, NFER/Nelson

BENNETT, N., (1976) *Teaching Styles and Pupil Progress*, Open Books

BENNETT, N. and DESFORGES, C., (1984) 'Ensuring practical outcomes from educational research' in SHIPMAN, M. (Ed.), *Educational Research: Principles, Policy and Practice*, Falmer Press

BLUMER, H., (1962) 'Society as symbolic interaction' in ROSE, A.M. (Ed.), *Human Behaviour and Social Processes: An Interactionist Approach*, Routledge and Kegan Paul

BLUMER, H., (1969) 'The methodological position of symbolic interactionism' in HAMMERSLEY, M. and WOODS, P. (Eds), (1976) *The Process of Schooling*, Open University Press

BOARD OF EDUCATION, (1944) *Teachers and Youth Leaders* (McNair Report), HMSO

BOGDAN, R. and BIKLEN, S., (1982) *Qualitative Research for Education*, Allyn and Bacon

BOYDELL, D., (1981) 'Classroom organisation 1970–77' in SIMON, B. and WILLCOCKS, J. (Eds), *Research and Practice in Primary Classrooms*, Routledge and Kegan Paul

BROWN, G., (1975) *Microteaching: A Programme of Teaching Skills*, Methuen

BRUNER, J., (1960) *The Process of Education*, Harvard University Press

BURGESS, R.G. (Ed.), (1984) *The Research Process in Educational Settings: Ten Case Studies*, Falmer Press

BURGESS, R.G., (1985a) *Field Methods in the Study of Education*, Falmer Press

BURGESS, R.G. (Ed.), (1985b) *Issues in Educational Research*, Falmer Press

CALLAGHAN, J., (1976) 'Towards a national debate', *Education*, 22 October

CAMPBELL, R.J., (1985) *Developing the Primary School Curriculum*, Holt, Rinehart and Winston

CARR, W. and KEMMIS, S., (1986) *Becoming Critical: Knowing Through Action Research*, Falmer Press

CCCS — CENTRE FOR CONTEMPORARY CULTURAL STUDIES, (1981) *Unpopular Education: Schooling and Social Democracy in England since 1944*, Hutchinson

COHEN, L. and MANION, L., (1981) *Perspectives on Classrooms and Schools*, Holt, Rinehart and Winston

COSTA, A.L., HANSON, R., SILVER, H., and STRONG, R., (1985) 'Building a repertoire of strategies' in COSTA, A.L. (Ed.), *Developing Minds*, Association for Supervision and Curriculum Development

DEPARTMENT OF EDUCATION AND SCIENCE, (1977a) *Education in Schools: A Consultative Document*, HMSO

DEPARTMENT OF EDUCATION AND SCIENCE, (1977b) *Curriculum 11–16*, HMSO

DEPARTMENT OF EDUCATION AND SCIENCE, (1978) *Primary Education in England: A Survey by HMI*, HMSO

DEPARTMENT OF EDUCATION AND SCIENCE, (1979a) *Local Authority Arrangements For The School Curriculum* (Report on Circular 14/77 Review of LEA Arrangements), HMSO

DEPARTMENT OF EDUCATION AND SCIENCE, (1979b) *Aspects of Secondary Education in England — A Survey by HMI*, HMSO

DEPARTMENT OF EDUCATION AND SCIENCE, (1980a) *A Framework for the School Curriculum*, HMSO

DEPARTMENT OF EDUCATION AND SCIENCE, (1980b) *A View of the Curriculum* (HMI Matters for Discussion), HMSO

DEPARTMENT OF EDUCATION AND SCIENCE, (1980c) *PGCE in the Public Sector*, HMSO

DEPARTMENT OF EDUCATION AND SCIENCE, (1981a) *Teacher Training in the Secondary School*, HMSO

DEPARTMENT OF EDUCATION AND SCIENCE, (1981b) *The School Curriculum*, HMSO

DEPARTMENT OF EDUCATION AND SCIENCE, (1981c) *Curriculum 11–16: A Review of Progress*, HMSO

DEPARTMENT OF EDUCATION AND SCIENCE, (1982a) *Teaching in Schools: The Content of Initial Training* (discussion paper given limited circulation), DES

DEPARTMENT OF EDUCATION AND SCIENCE, (1982b) *Education 5–9: An Illustrative Survey by HMI*, HMSO

DEPARTMENT OF EDUCATION AND SCIENCE, (1982c) *The New Teacher in School*, HMSO

DEPARTMENT OF EDUCATION AND SCIENCE, (1982d) *Teacher Training Circular Letter 5/82*, DES

DEPARTMENT OF EDUCATION AND SCIENCE, (1983a) *The Treatment and Assessment of Probationary Teachers: Administrative Memorandum 1/83*, DES

DEPARTMENT OF EDUCATION AND SCIENCE, (1983b) *Teaching Quality*, HMSO

DEPARTMENT OF EDUCATION AND SCIENCE, (1983c) *Teaching in Schools: The Content of Initial Training*, HMSO

DEPARTMENT OF EDUCATION AND SCIENCE, (1983d) *The Work of HM Inspectorate in England and Wales*, HMSO

DEPARTMENT OF EDUCATION AND SCIENCE, (1983e) *9–13 Middle Schools: An Illustrative Survey by HMI*, HMSO

DEPARTMENT OF EDUCATION AND SCIENCE, (1983f) *Initial Teacher Training: Approval of Courses* (Draft Circular) DES

DEPARTMENT OF EDUCATION AND SCIENCE, (1983g) *Curriculum 11–16: Towards A Statement of Entitlement*, HMSO

DEPARTMENT OF EDUCATION AND SCIENCE, (1984a) *Initial Teacher Training: Approval of Courses (Circular 3/84),* DES

DEPARTMENT OF EDUCATION AND SCIENCE, (1984b) *The Organisation and Content of the 5–16 Curriculum,* HMSO

DEPARTMENT OF EDUCATION AND SCIENCE, (1985a) *Better Schools,* HMSO

DEPARTMENT OF EDUCATION AND SCIENCE, (1985b) *General Certificate of Secondary Education — The National Criteria,* HMSO

DEPARTMENT OF EDUCATION AND SCIENCE, (1985c) *The Curriculum from 5–16,* HMSO

DEPARTMENT OF EDUCATION AND SCIENCE, (1985d) *Quality in Schools: Evaluation and Appraisal,* HMSO

DEPARTMENT OF EDUCATION AND SCIENCE, (1985e) *Education 8–12 in Combined and Middle Schools: An HMI Survey,* HMSO

DOYLE, W., (1985) 'Learning to teach: An emerging direction in research on preservice teacher education', *Journal Of Teacher Education,* 36, 1

EBBUTT, D. and ELLIOTT, J. (Eds), (1985) *Issues in Teaching for Understanding,* Longman

ELBAZ, F., (1983) *Teacher Thinking: A Study of Practical Knowledge,* Croom Helm

ELLIOTT, J., (1978) 'How do teachers learn?' in PORTER, J. (Ed.), *The Contribution of Adult Learning Theories to the In-Service Education and Training of Teachers,* OECD

ELLIOTT, J., (1980) 'Implications of classroom research for professional development' in HOYLE, E. and MEGARRY, J. (Eds), *Professional Development of Teachers,* World Year Book of Education, Kogan Page

ELLIOTT, J. and EBBUTT, D., (1985) *Facilitating Educational Action Research in Schools,* Longman

EVANS, N., (1978) *Beginning Teaching in Professional Partnership,* Hodder and Stoughton

FOX, T., (1983) *New Policies Towards Teacher Education: The Redistribution of Educational Worth,* National Institute of Education, Washington DC

GALTON, M., SIMON, B. and CROLL, P., (1980) *Inside the Primary Classroom,* Routledge and Kegan Paul

GINSBURG, M.B., MEYENN, R.J., MILLER, H.D.R., and RANCEFORD-HADLEY, C., (1977) *The Role of the Middle School Teacher,* University of Aston in Birmingham

GLASER, B. and STRAUSS, A., (1967) *The Discovery of Grounded Theory,* Aldine

GOODLAD, J.I., (1984) *A Place Called School,* McGraw-Hill

GOSDEN, P.H.J.H., (1984) 'The role of central government and its agencies 1963–1982' in ALEXANDER, R.J., CRAFT, M. and LYNCH, J., (Eds) *Change in Teacher Education: Context and Provision since Robbins,* Holt, Rinehart and Winston

GRAHAM, D., (1984) 'Will teacher assessment ever get off the ground?', *The Times Educational Supplement,* 28 November

GRAHAM, D., (1985) *Those Having Torches. . . . Teacher Appraisal: A Study,* Suffolk County Council

HAMMERSLEY, M., (1985) *The Ethnography of Schooling,* Nafferton Press

HAMMERSLEY, M. and ATKINSON, P., (1983) *Ethnography — Principles in Practice,* Tavistock

HAMMERSLEY, M. and HARGREAVES, A. (Eds), (1983) *Curriculum Practice: Some Sociological Case Studies,* Falmer Press

HARGREAVES, A. and TICKLE, L. (Eds), (1980) *Middle Schools: Origins, Ideology and Practice,* Harper and Row

HOLT, M. (1982) *Evaluating the Evaluators,* Hodder and Stoughton

HOPKINS, D., (1985) *A Teacher's Guide to Classroom Research,* Open University Press

HOPKINS, D. and REID, K. (Eds), (1985) *Rethinking Teacher Education,* Croom Helm

HOPKINS, D. and WIDEEN, M. (Eds), (1984) *Alternative Perspectives on School Improvement*, Falmer Press

HUSTLER, D., CASSIDY, T., and CUFF, T. (Eds), (1986) *Action Research in Classrooms and Schools*, Allen and Unwin

JENKINS, R.G., (1984) *An Investigation into Some Problems of Practical Teaching within the Initial Teacher Education Course*, Inner London Education Authority

KEMMIS, S. and McTAGGART, R., (1981) *The Action Research Planner*, Deakin University Press

KERRY, T., (1982) *Effective Questioning: A Teaching Skills Workbook*, Macmillan Education

KOGAN, M., (1978) *The Politics of Educational Change*, Fontana

LACEY, C. and LAWTON, D. (Eds), (1981) *Issues in Evaluation and Accountability*, Methuen

LAWTON, D., (1984) *The Tightening Grip: Growth of Central Control of the School Curriculum*, University of London Institute of Education

LYNCH, J., (1979) *The Reform of Teacher Education in the United Kingdom*, Society for Research into Higher Education

MIDDLETON, D., (1981) *Observing Classroom Processes*, Block 3 Course E 364 Curriculum Evaluation and Assessment in Educational Institutions, Open University

MULCAHY, D.G., (1984) 'The idea of teacher effectiveness and its implications for teacher education', first plenary lecture to the ninth annual conference of the Association of Teacher Educators in Europe, Linz, Austria, September

McINTYRE, D., (1980) 'The contribution of research to quality in teacher education' in HOYLE, E. and MEGARRY, J. (Eds), *Professional Development of Teachers*, World Year Book of Education, Kogan Page

NIAS, J., (1980) 'The ideal middle school: Its public image' in HARGREAVES, A. and TICKLE, L. (Eds), *Middle Schools: Origins Ideology and Practice*, Harper and Row

NIXON, J., (1981) *A Teachers' Guide to Action Research: Evaluation, Enquiry and Development in the Classroom*, Grant McIntyre

OPEN UNIVERSITY, (1982) *Curriculum in Action*, Open University Press

PETERSON, P.L., (1979) 'Direct instruction: effective for what and for whom?', *Educational Leadership*, 37

PLOWDEN REPORT (Central Advisory Council for Education) (1967) *Children and Their Primary Schools*, HMSO

RATHS, J. and KATZ, L., (1982) 'The best of intentions for the education of teachers', *Journal of Education of Teachers*, 8, 3

REID, K., (1985) 'Recent research and development in teacher education in England and Wales' in HOPKINS, D. and REID, K. (Eds), *Rethinking Teacher Education*, Croom Helm

ROBBINS REPORT, (1963) *Higher Education*, HMSO

ROWLAND, S., (1984) *The Enquiring Classroom: An Approach to Understanding Children's Learning*, Falmer Press

RUDDUCK, J. (Ed.), (1982) *Teachers in Partnership: Four Studies of In-Service Collaboration*, Longman

RUDDUCK, J. and HOPKINS, D. (Eds), (1985) *Research as a Basis for Teaching*, Heinemann

RUDDUCK, J. and SIGSWORTH, A., (1985) 'Partnership supervision' in HOPKINS, D. and REID, K. (Eds) *Rethinking Teacher Education*, Croom Helm

SALTER, B. and TAPPER, T., (1981) *Education, Politics and The State*, Grant McIntyre

SANGER, J., (1986) *Classrooms In/Formation: An Action Research Approach*, Final report of the 'Teaching, Handling Information and Learning' Project, British Library

SANGER, J. and TICKLE, L., (1987) 'Art for pupils sakes: Deprogramming student teachers', in TICKLE, L. (Ed.) *The Arts in Education: Some Research Studies*, Croom Helm

SCHON, D., (1983) *The Reflective Practitioner*, Temple-Smith

SHARP, R. and GREEN, A., (1975) *Education and Social Control*, Routledge and Kegan Paul

SHOR, I., (1980) *Critical Teaching and Everyday Life*, South End Press

SLATER, F. (Ed.), (1985) *The Quality Controllers: A Critique of the White Paper 'Teaching Quality'*, University of London Institute of Education

SOCKETT, H. (Ed.), (1980) *Accountability in the English Educational System*, Hodder and Stoughton

SOCKETT, H., (1985) 'What is a school of education?', *Cambridge Journal of Education*, 15, 3

SPINDLER, G.D. (Ed.), (1985) *Doing the Ethnography of Schooling: Educational Anthropology in Action*, Holt, Rinehart and Winston

STENHOUSE, L., (1970) *The Humanities Project*, Heinemann

STENHOUSE, L., (1975) *An Introduction to Curriculum Research and Development*, Heinemann

STENHOUSE, L. (Ed.), (1978) *Curriculum Research and Development in Action*, Heinemann

STENHOUSE, L., (1979) 'Research as a basis for teaching', Inaugural lecture, University of East Anglia, 20 February

STENHOUSE, L., (1984) 'Artistry and teaching: The teacher as focus of research and development' in HOPKINS, D. and WIDEEN, M. (Eds) *Alternative Perspectives on School Improvement*, Falmer Press

TAYLOR, W., (1978) *Research and Reform in Teacher Education*, Council of Europe, European Trend Reports on Educational Research, NFER

TAYLOR, W., (1984) 'The national context 1972–82' in ALEXANDER, R.J., CRAFT, M. and LYNCH, J. (Eds) *Change in Teacher Education: Context and Provision since Robbins*, Holt, Rinehart and Winston

WALFORD, G. (Ed.), (1985) *Schooling in Turmoil*, Croom Helm

WALKER, R., (1985a) *Doing Research: A Handbook for Teachers*, Methuen

WALKER, R., (1985b) *Applied Qualitative Research*, Gower

WALLACE, G., (1985) 'Middle schools through the looking glass' in WALFORD, G. (Ed.) *Schooling in Turmoil*, Croom Helm

WALLACE, G. and TICKLE, L., (1983) 'Middle schools: The heart of schools in crisis', *British Journal of Sociology of Education*, 4, 3

WRAGG, E., (1982) *A Review of Research in Teacher Education*, NFER/Nelson

WRAGG, E.C. (Ed.), (1984) *Classroom Teaching Skills*, Croom Helm

YATES, J.W., (1982) 'Student-teaching: Results of a recent survey', *Educational Research*, 24, 3

Index

through self-knowledge, 79, 80
in *Student Attachment to Schools*, 115,
    116, 119, 122, 147–8
teachers and teacher educators, 1, 5,
    12, 51, 114, 122, 124, 130
dialogue, 62, 84
expectations, 60–2
practice, 13, 45, 47, 62, 84
preparation, 1, 29–37
recognition, granting of, 10
relationships, developing, 140, 142
responsibilities, 25, 31, 54, 60, 61, 70,
    111–2, 114, 151
skills, 14, 16, 18, 32, 33, 34
see also excellence; PPP; 'schedule'
professionalism, 5, 6, 18, 31, 70–1, 75
extended, 37–8, 76
teachers', 11, 19, 26
'professionalization' approach, 25
profile, student, 30, 74, 95
progressivism, 19
psychology, 12, 14, 36, 113
pupils, 9, 23, 24, 36, 152
assessment, 20, 22, 25, 31
learning, 20–1, 36, 45, 49, 75
    passive role in, 64, 75
    processes, 55, 61, 74, 120–2, 142,
        175
    responsible for own, 21, 24, 75
low achievers, 21, 31, 190–1
and research, 1, 2, 27, 31, 84
student attachment to schools, benefits
    from, 113, 122

qualifications and staffing, 15–16

records, written, 74
reflective aspects of learning teaching, 32,
    70–1, 76, 77, 80, 82, 114
reform, educational, 1, 3, 11, 12, 24, 28,
    112–3
reports, 30, 77
research, 15, 31, 39–41, 44, 54, 79, 130
action, 5, 40, 46–7, 48, 49, 50, 79
applied, 1, 29, 30, 36, 50, 51
dissemination, 29, 30, 45, 50–1
and practice, 2, 5, 50, 51, 52, 73, 75,
    78, 112
problems, 30, 47

professional development, base for, 50,
    126, 129
and students, 78, 118, 119, 124, 132,
    133, 139–40
on teacher education, 5, 9, 29, 30, 147
teachers in, 42, 43, 54, 53, 75, 76–7,
    80, 82, 114, 122, 151
-based teaching, 42, 46, 47, 49, 142
techniques, 2, 30, 46, 48, 49, 52, 83,
    112, 115, 133, 143
see also partnership
research-based teacher education
see teacher education
researchers, 30, 43, 46, 49, 54, 78, 81
outsider, 39, 40, 48, 83, 115
resources, financial, 2, 9, 10–11, 17, 21,
    22, 145
responsibility in teacher education, 6
see also professional
Robbins Report (1963), 9

'schedule' document, 72, 73–4, 75, 76,
    85–96, 113
school, 30, 32, 35, 62–3
curriculum, 11, 26, 81
practice, 33, 84
    see also teaching practice
reform, 3, 7, 11, 24, 112–3, 151
self-evaluation, 42, 49, 130
schooling, 16, 37, 44–5, 46, 47
reform and improvement, 1, 6, 12, 28,
    53, 82–4
School of Education, University of East
    Anglia, 116, 117, 118, 120, 127, 149
schools, 6, 64, 72
Better Schools (DES, 1985), 4, 7, 8, 9,
    17, 18, 23, 24, 28, 31
control of, 11, 17, 20, 27, 38
research in, 41, 42, 84, 115
    student, 76–7, 119
teacher training institutions:
cooperation, 3, 15, 16, 34, 35, 52
see also school; schooling; *Student
    Attachment to Schools*; teachers;
    teacher training institutions
secondary education, 13, 14, 20–1, 22,
    24
comprehensivization, 19, 38
teachers in THIL project, 49